REASSESSING
U.S. NUCLEAR STRATEGY

REASSESSING
U.S. NUCLEAR STRATEGY

David W. Kearn, Jr.

Rapid Communications in Conflict and Security Series
General Editor: Geoffrey R.H. Burn

CAMBRIA
PRESS

Amherst, New York

Requests for permission should be directed to:
permissions@cambriapress.com, or mailed to:
Cambria Press
University Corporate Centre,
100 Corporate Parkway, Suite 128
Amherst, New York 14226, U.S.A.

Front cover image: Credit: Trident II (D-5) missile underwater launch,
https://commons.wikimedia.org/wiki/File:Trident_II_missile_image.jpg.

Library of Congress Cataloging-in-Publication Data

Names: Kearn, David W., author.

Title: Reassessing U.S. nuclear strategy / David W. Kearn, Jr.

Description: Amherst, New York: Cambria Press, [2019] |
Series: Rapid communications in conflict and security series |
Includes bibliographical references and index. |
Summary: "This book reassesses the nuclear strategy of the United States. Despite the
appearance of continuity in official policy statements, views within the Obama and
Trump administrations and across the larger defense policy community have diverged
on the appropriate role of nuclear weapons in U.S. national security, the optimal
nuclear strategy for advancing U.S. interests, force structure requirements, and critical
related issues. This is an important book for security and strategic studies and should
be of interest to both scholars and practitioners in political science and international
relations, especially in the field of nuclear weapons policy"-- Provided by publisher.

Identifiers: LCCN 2019031668 (print) | LCCN 2019031669 (ebook) |

ISBN 9781621964728 (paperback) |
ISBN 9781604979640 (hardcover) | ISBN 9781621964940 (epub)

Subjects: LCSH: Nuclear weapons--Government policy--United States. |
National security--United States. | Strategy. | United States--Military policy.

Classification: LCC UA23 .K38457 2019 (print) | LCC UA23 (ebook) |
DDC 355.02/170973--dc23

LC record available at https://lccn.loc.gov/2019031668

LC ebook record available at https://lccn.loc.gov/2019031669

For Emma, Owen, Ava, and Cecelia

TABLE OF CONTENTS

List of Tables

ACKNOWLEDGMENTS

Beyond several years of reading and research, this book is the product of many discussions and debates with mentors, colleagues, and friends over the contribution of nuclear weapons to U.S. national security, and I owe a great debt to many wonderful people. I am especially grateful to Liz and Graham Allison and the Frank Stanton Foundation which has underwritten my journey into the world of nuclear weapons. I was extremely fortunate to be selected as a Stanton Nuclear Security Fellow at RAND in Washington, DC during the 2010-11 academic year. Lynn Davis, Paula Thornhill, Sarah Harting and Andy Hoehn (among many others) contributed to an amazing experience. The Stanton Foundation and the Council on Foreign Relations provided an opportunity to return to Washington and serve in the Defense Department as an International Affairs Fellow in Nuclear Security in 2016–2017. Jay Finch, Andrea Yaffe, David Hodson, Margaret Sloan, Wendin Smith, and my colleagues in the Office for Countering Weapons of Mass Destruction created an incredibly stimulating work environment where nuclear proliferation issues were daily business.

St. John's University has provided me with a good home for over a decade and has afforded me the opportunity to explore nuclear weapons issues in my research and teaching. My colleagues in the Department of Government & Politics have always been generous with their support, friendship, and good advice. Fred Cocozzelli, our chair, was kind enough to read a complete draft of the manuscript and provide extensive comments and has been a valued confidant and sounding board. Some of our talented graduate students—Robert Kaminaris, Joe Lunz, and Melissa Robbins— were kind enough to help out their weary professor during the course of revisions, and Keith Preble, a former student now engaged in his own quest for a doctorate, provided excellent feedback and helped me construct the index. The students in my undergraduate class *Nuclear Strategy in a Complex World* also contributed to the project with energetic and insightful debates on many of the issues examined in the book.

The process of writing, revising, and preparing a book manuscript for publication is a daunting undertaking, but the team at Cambria Press was exceptional and a pleasure to work with. Geoffrey Burn was incredibly helpful, responsive, and persistently supportive of the project from the very beginning. Toni Tan, David Armstrong, and the production team were excellent. A special thank you to Allison Van Deventer for her meticulous copyediting of the manuscript, which was greatly improved by the insightful and constructive feedback of the anonymous reviewers.

Finally, I appreciate the love and support I receive from my family. My mom, Maura, and my sisters Kerry and Jessica have always been there for me. I cannot thank them enough.

List of Acronyms

ABM	Antiballistic Missile
ALCM	Air-launched Cruise Missile
ASW	Antisubmarine Warfare
A2/AD	Anti-Access Area Denial
CBRN	Chemical, Biological, Radiological, Nuclear
CCP	Chinese Communist Party
CPGS	Conventional Prompt Global Strike
C4ISR	Command, Control, Communications, Computer Intelligence Surveillance Reconnaissance
DCA	Dual Capable Aircraft
DOD	Department of Defense
DOE	Department of Energy
EMP	Electromagnetic Pulse
GLCM	Ground-launched cruise missile
HDBT	Hard and Deeply Buried Targets
IAD	Integrated Air Defenses
ICAN	International Campaign Against Nuclear Weapons
ICBM	Intercontinental Ballistic Missile
INF	Intermediate Nuclear Forces
IRBM	Intermediate Range Ballistic Missile

JCPOA	Joint Comprehensive Plan of Action
LEP	Life Extension Program
LNO	Limited Nuclear Options
LOW	Launch On Warning
LRSO	Long-range Standoff Munition
LUA	Launch Under Attack
MAD	Mutual Assured Destruction
MIRV	Multiple, Independently targeted reentry vehicle
NDAA	National Defense Authorization Act
NSDM	National Security Decision Memorandum
NC3	Nuclear Command, Control, and Communications
NGO	Nongovernmental Organization
NPR	Nuclear Posture Review
NPT	Nonproliferation Treaty
NSNW	Non-Strategic Nuclear Weapon
PLA	Peoples Liberation Army
PRC	Peoples Republic of China
SAC	Strategic Air Command
SALT	Strategic Arms Limitation Talks
SDI	Strategic Defense Initiative
SIOP	Single Integrated Operational Plan
SICBM	Small Intercontinental Ballistic Missile
SLBM	Submarine-launched ballistic missiles
SLCM	Submarine-launched cruise missile
SORT	Strategic Offensive Reduction Treaty
SSBN	Ballistic Missile Submarine
START	Strategic Arms Reduction Treaty
THAAD	Theater High Altitude Area Defense
TLAM-N	Tomahawk Land Attack Missile-Nuclear
WMD	Weapons of Mass Destruction

INTRODUCTION

The United States is currently in the early stages of modernizing its nuclear enterprise. Under the Obama administration, a program was established to replace all three legs of the strategic triad over the next three decades: long-range bombers, land-based intercontinental ballistic missiles (ICBMs), and nuclear-powered ballistic missile submarines (SSBNs). Nuclear command, control and communications (NC3) systems and the underlying nuclear weapons production infrastructure are also included in the program. To enhance the country's extended deterrence commitments and hedge against technological change, two other programs are slated for acquisition and deployment: an advanced nuclear-armed, air-launched cruise missile (ALCM) called the Long-Range Standoff Ordinance (LRSO) and the B-61 Model 12 nuclear gravity bomb. It is estimated that the full strategic modernization program will cost as much as $1.2 trillion over thirty years.[1]

The Trump administration effectively endorsed the modernization plans in its 2018 Nuclear Posture Review (NPR), while introducing two additional programs—the development of a new nuclear sea-launched cruise missile (SLCM) and the deployment of a single low-yield warhead on a portion of already deployed submarine-launched ballistic missiles

(SLBMs)—to more effectively counter threats from great power competitors in key regions.[2] Given the Trump administration's focus on great power competition and the increased potential for conflict that is reflected in its National Security and National Defense Strategies, these additional programs were not surprising. Nevertheless, following a post-Cold War pattern, there is considerable continuity between the formal, public Obama and Trump approaches to nuclear modernization and nuclear strategy, albeit with differing points of emphasis.[3]

This book reassesses the nuclear strategy of the United States. Considering the recent conclusion of the Trump administration NPR and the ongoing modernization effort initiated by the Obama administration, one may ask why such a reassessment is necessary. The answer is that despite the appearance of continuity in official statements of policy, views within these administrations and across the larger defense policy community have diverged on the appropriate role of nuclear weapons in U.S. national security, the optimal nuclear strategy for advancing U.S. interests, force structure requirements, and critical related issues.[4] Thus, given the changing security environment, as well as potential economic and political constraints, a reconsideration of the U.S. strategy in light of these divergent views is particularly relevant today.

Only nine years ago, the Obama administration released an NPR that expressed its view of the strategic environment and the threats confronting the United States.[5] Treating nuclear terrorism and proliferation as the central threat to U.S. security, and formally embracing the objective of moving the United States (and thus leading the international community) toward nuclear abolition that President Obama had described in his April 2009 Prague speech, this NPR presented a lofty alternative vision for a future in which nuclear weapons play a highly circumscribed role in U.S. national security policy.[6]

In what was widely viewed as a compromise to achieve Senate ratification of the "New START" treaty that he signed with Russian President Dmitri Medvedev in April 2010, President Obama signed off on a modernization of the U.S. arsenal and a major recapitalization of the nuclear weapons infrastructure operated by the U.S. Department of Energy (DOE).[7] It may seem curious that an administration that had espoused the long-term goal of a world without nuclear weapons should have ultimately endorsed a major modernization program. This move, however, reflects a bipartisan consensus on the need to maintain an effective nuclear arsenal.[8] The Obama administration was reportedly willing to support an additional one-third negotiated reduction of deployed warheads with Russia in Obama's second term, and also reportedly considered a formal "No First Use" policy.[9] But as relations with Moscow deteriorated, particularly after Russia's intervention in Ukraine and annexation of Crimea in 2014, these initiatives were tabled.[10]

Thus, the perception of policy continuity surrounding modernization may be in part the result of the general conservatism of the defense community and the national security bureaucracy with regard to nuclear weapons. At the same time, there is greater uncertainty today about the role of nuclear weapons in the security environment and their contribution to U.S. national security than at any time since the early Cold War.[11] Despite a return of great power competition, which has been the focus of the Trump administration and heavily influenced the 2018 NPR, the nature of the nuclear dimension of that competition remains unclear.[12] While experts are alarmed that Russia appears to have increased its reliance on its nuclear arsenal, Moscow's apparent willingness to use nuclear weapons to avoid a catastrophic military reversal against a superior conventional military power has been a concern for over a decade, predating the downturn in relations with the United States and Europe.[13] Typically, the use of nonstrategic nuclear weapons (NSNWs) is envisioned as a way to compel the adversary (ostensibly the United States or NATO) to relent and/or pause operations long enough to allow Russia to salvage its forces or consolidate its gains. This "escalate to de-escalate" doctrine has received a great deal of attention in the Western press. More recently, the Russian president Vladimir Putin made an expansive public presentation of Russia's new strategic weapons, including a new "heavy"

ICBM that may carry as many as ten multiple independently targetable reentry vehicles (MIRVs) and a potential hypersonic glide weapon that seems to be a direct response to U.S. missile defenses.[14] Moreover, Russia's noncompliance with the 1987 Intermediate Nuclear Forces (INF) Treaty, the last remaining Cold War arms control agreement and a cornerstone of security in Europe, recently led the Trump administration to announce its intention to formally withdraw from the Treaty, exacerbating the downturn in relations and threatening to open a new area of competition between Moscow and Washington.[15]

At the same time, experts have expressed concern that China is modernizing its relatively modest nuclear arsenal.[16] Although China's forces remain much smaller than those of the United States and Russia, in the larger context of China's rapid conventional military modernization, which poses significant challenges to the ability of the United States to project power in the Western Pacific, defense analysts in Washington have expressed concern over China's long-term intentions.[17] Given Beijing's recent assertiveness in territorial disputes with its neighbors in the East and South China Seas, the potential for a diplomatic crisis that could escalate to a military conflict between the United States and China has increased, with important implications for both nations' nuclear arsenals.[18] Moreover, the United States currently faces a growing nuclear threat from the North Korean regime, which has made significant process on the development and deployment of a range of operational nuclear delivery systems that threaten regional allies and U.S. forces and could soon threaten the continental United States.[19]

Beyond these geopolitical challenges, supporters of nuclear modernization make the point that nuclear weapons could serve as an important hedge against technological uncertainty. Such uncertainty is generated, for instance, by the emergence of offensive cyber-capabilities that could have weapons of mass destruction (WMD) effects, or what the Trump administration NPR terms "nonnuclear strategic attacks" on the United States.[20] All of these concerns raise an important question: what type of strategic arsenal—in terms of quantitative force levels and types of deployed weapons—is necessary to effectively perform such hedging while also allowing for investment in the research, development, and acquisition of cutting-edge military applications derived from new and emerging technologies? The United States is now at a critical juncture; it must seek to develop an optimal nuclear strategy and force structure that achieve a balance between strategic and conventional forces and balance investments in current versus future capabilities.[21]

After the stresses on manpower and materiel created by almost two decades of low-intensity conflict and stabilization operations in Afghanistan and Iraq, the maintenance of America's formidable conventional military advantage is a central priority for the Pentagon. In an era of renewed great power competition, it is vitally important to maintain extended deterrent commitments supported by robust U.S. forward-deployed conventional military capabilities that can operate in highly contested environments.[22] Nuclear weapons play the important but less pronounced role of insuring against a cataclysmic event. However, given the defense budgeting realities (and larger fiscal pressures in Washington), it seems that a modernization of the strategic triad—as constituted in the program of record in the context of similarly large-scale conventional military procurement and force readiness needs—may be unsustainable over time.[23] In short, although the nuclear modernization program has been authorized and somewhat expanded, the possibility that spending on nuclear modernization might crowd out other Defense Department priorities may force a reassessment of U.S. nuclear strategy, force structure, and related issues.[24]

In addition to geopolitical and technological trends and U.S. budgeting and programming concerns, it is important to consider the global nonproliferation environment. Whereas President Obama's "Prague agenda" stalled in his second term, the international movement toward "global zero" did not dissipate. The Treaty on the Prohibition of Nuclear Weapons, also known as the "Nuclear Ban Treaty," was adopted by a United Nations

Conference in July 2017 and was opened for signatures in September 2017.[25] Led by global civil society groups like the International Campaign to Abolish Nuclear Weapons (ICAN) and state actors like Mexico, Brazil, Ireland, and Austria, the Nuclear Ban Treaty will go into effect once it is ratified by fifty nations.[26] Whereas it will have little material impact on the nuclear weapons states, for the United States it could complicate extended deterrence commitments to allies and partners. A major concern for U.S. defense officials is domestic political support for the treaty in key U.S. allies that are currently under the American "nuclear umbrella." In other words, there is considerable popular support for the abolition of nuclear weapons in many of the allied countries that benefit most directly from U.S. extended deterrent commitments.[27] Over time, Washington's ability to work with its allies and partners will be significantly influenced by its decisions regarding the development and deployment of nuclear weapons, by global perceptions of the relative importance of nuclear weapons in U.S. national security, and by the perceived willingness of the United States to take a leadership role in nonproliferation and strategic arms control initiatives.

These important trends are likely to shape the current debate on the contribution of nuclear weapons to the national security of the United States. Estimating the overall costs of modernizing the strategic arsenal involves not only tallying the costs of specific programs, but also addressing the potential opportunity costs to conventional modernization, force readiness, and research and development priorities. Given the geopolitical challenges presented by Russia and China, as well as by smaller but more aggressive and potentially risk-acceptant regional actors like North Korea and Iran, the United States will face growing demands for a host of conventional military weapons systems and improvements in force readiness. Moreover, given the nature of technological change and the potential impact of offensive cyber and electronic warfare capabilities, the military use of artificial intelligence, and other ongoing technological developments like additive manufacturing and biological and chemical threats, the United States faces long-term security challenges that will demand the use of scarce resources. As noted, a strong, safe, and reliable strategic nuclear deterrent may play a valuable role in hedging against new threats, but difficult choices lie ahead. Finally, given downward nonproliferation pressures toward further reductions in nuclear arsenals, particularly in the domestic political systems of key U.S. allies, the United States' perceived reliance on nuclear weapons to achieve its national security and foreign policy objectives will come under increasing scrutiny.

To outline an optimal nuclear strategy for the United States, this study proposes and assesses three ideal type (or representative) nuclear strategies for the United States, taking the current geopolitical, technological, proliferation, fiscal, and budgetary trends into consideration and building upon the work of both academic scholars and policy analysts.[28] The discussion of these proposed approaches covers the associated force structure and posture and key related issues such as strategic defenses, nonstrategic nuclear weapons, nuclear command, control and communications, and the underlying nuclear weapons enterprise. This study also considers the implications of the three strategies for several important factors, including the deterrence of adversaries, the assurance of allies, strategic stability (including both crisis stability and arms control stability), strategic arms control, and nonproliferation. It also assesses the relevance of the three strategies to the maintenance of robust conventional forces and the ability of the United States to address new threats arising from technological change.

Given the vast number of potential strategies, the development of three distinct ideal types was inevitably a subjective enterprise. One central assumption this study makes is that nuclear weapons will continue to play a role in assuring the security of the United States in the long term, if only for domestic political reasons. In the context of the planned nuclear modernization program, and because perceptions of major threats to the United States' national security interests are widely shared in the defense and foreign policy communities, further progress toward abolition is unlikely to receive broad domestic support in the short term. Thus, this study does not consider the possibility of a dramatic retirement of strategic nuclear forces in favor of a reliance on conventional forces and "virtual deterrents." Instead, the three ideal types examined here are A) *nuclear primacy*, defined by a commitment to fielding extensive offensive counterforce capabilities and the use of strategic defenses, B) *a robust strategic deterrent strategy* with a sufficient level of redundancy and diversification to maintain a basic equivalence vis-à-vis Russia and to confront China and smaller nuclear powers with formidable capabilities, and C) *a minimum or "finite" deterrent strategy*, characterized by significant (and perhaps even unilateral) reductions in the currently planned force levels and an increased reliance on a smaller but secure and responsive nuclear force to guarantee the security of the United States even under difficult international conditions.[29]

APPROACH AND KEY ASSUMPTIONS

This study's method is straightforward. Each strategic approach is presented on its merits, whenever possible using the best cases made by its advocates, and the key implications for U.S. and international security are explained. The study then identifies the key tradeoffs and potential shortcomings of each approach, engaging both the academic and the policy literature and taking into account relevant history from the Cold War and the past two decades of attempts to restructure U.S. nuclear strategy. In doing so, this study makes a serious attempt to underscore areas where the policy and academic communities may speak past each other or portray opposing positions as straw men, without giving adequate consideration to points of potential agreement.[30]

Beyond the central assumption that nuclear weapons are and will remain important for the overall security of the United States, the analysis that follows is based upon several additional assumptions.[31]

The second assumption relates to the objective of deployed U.S. strategic forces. As indicated in the formal articulations of U.S. policy encapsulated in the NPRs of post-Cold War administrations, the primary objective of U.S. strategic weapons is to deter a nuclear attack on the United States or its allies and (under extreme circumstances) to deter other attacks that may be intended to achieve strategic results or threaten the survival of the United States or its allies. In reality, this means deterring a large-scale nuclear strike against the United States by Russia, a smaller nuclear attack by the People's Republic of China, or a limited nuclear strike by North Korea. It also requires the capacity to deter attacks against European and East Asian allies, particularly in times of crisis, in ways that enhance immediate deterrence while also avoiding escalation or the creation of greater instability. Finally, given the nature of technological change and the potential for emerging threats that could have strategic effects on the United States or its allies, the United States should be capable of deterring what the Trump administration's recent NPR terms "non-nuclear strategic attack[s]," as well as future technologically-driven threats. This last point is discussed in great detail in what follows, as are the requisites for effective deterrence based upon the differing approaches and diverse perceptions of adversaries, allies, and U.S. capabilities.[32]

The third assumption is that the United States confronts a complex international security environment.[33] The United States currently finds itself engaged in a renewed great power competition with Russia and China. Nuclear weapons are central to the Russian threat, in large part because of its relative weakness on most other relevant measures of material power. China's strategic deterrent capacity seems to be undergoing qualitative improvements, but its nuclear forces remain limited. However, given China's growing and improving conventional military power, as well as its technological, industrial, economic, and potential power, it may pose a long-term challenge as a rising great power. North Korea presents an increasingly acute threat to the security of the United States and its East Asian allies. In the event of a breakdown of the Joint Comprehensive Plan of Action (JCPOA) after the United States' withdrawal, Iran may move, again, toward a nuclear program. The threat of global terrorism remains, though the potential for catastrophic terrorism involving chemical, biological, nuclear, or radiological (CBRN) weapons has been decreased through significant U.S. and allied effort. Additionally, a catalytic nuclear war between Pakistan and India that would pull in other states remains possible, as does the acquisition of nuclear weapons by non-state terrorist groups should Pakistan's military lose control of its arsenal in the event of civil conflict.

The key insight of this assumption of complexity is that policies that are developed and implemented to address one issue may have significant implications for other issues. This is an important, though perhaps oversold, insight of the Second Nuclear age literature.[34] Though several of these critical security challenges have a nuclear dimension, it is not clear that they all require (or are best addressed) by a nuclear response. But this insight does underscore the importance of key related U.S. capabilities to the country's strategic nuclear policy. A relevant example is provided by U.S. attempts to enhance theater missile defenses to deter regional adversaries and reassure and more effectively defend U.S. allies.[35] The European missile defense deployments undertaken in the Bush and Obama administrations to protect NATO allies against the threat of Iranian IRBMs have proven a significant problem in U.S.-Russia relations. Despite ample evidence to the contrary, Moscow has rejected assurances from Washington and Brussels that the deployed systems are incapable of undermining Russia's strategic deterrent.[36] Similarly, the deployment of the Theater High Altitude Area Defense (THAAD) theater defense system to protect South Korea against North Korea missiles was met with extremely bellicose rhetoric and threats of economic sanctions against Seoul from Beijing, going well beyond typical Chinese official rhetoric.[37] Echoing Moscow's concerns, Beijing viewed THAAD and its advance radar system as posing a threat to China's limited strategic deterrent. In both cases, the logic behind the opposition seems to be that the forward-deployed programs, although they do not constitute direct threats on their own, may serve as key components of larger systems that could, over time, degrade the strategic deterrents of Russia and China.

Although complexity is acknowledged, this study focuses on the United States' nuclear strategy relative to the great power competitors, Russia and China. This choice was made primarily because the challenges of regional nuclear powers are likely to be addressed mainly by conventional military forces. The current and planned nuclear forces, in the absence of highly improbably large-scale reductions, should be sufficient to deter these new regional nuclear powers. However, key related capabilities such as missile defenses and nonstrategic nuclear weapons are considered because of their implications for U.S. nuclear strategy.

The fourth assumption is that, beyond geopolitical threats and challenges, the United States has entered a period of rapid and dynamic technological change that could have important implications for national security for decades to come.[38] The emergence, exploitation, and diffusion of technologies have already improved the capacity of key adversaries to undermine the United States' ability to project conventional military power around the globe. The dynamic is only expected to intensify. Furthermore, although experts are beginning to grasp the potential impacts of offensive cyber-weapons, hypersonic propulsion, advanced electronic warfare, and the military exploitation of space, other areas of scientific and technical inquiry (such as artificial intelligence, additive manufacturing, and gene editing) remain to be understood.[39] Assessing the military implications of technological change is well beyond the scope of this study. What seems clear, however, is that a secure, reliable, and versatile strategic deterrent force would make a vitally important contribution to the national security of the United States by providing a robust hedge against technological surprise and the emergence of new and decisive threats. A necessary caveat is that during previous eras of rapid technological change, many visionary applications of new technologies failed to come to fruition. The maintenance of a robust U.S. strategic deterrent would help to assuage fears of the future and mitigate the risks of technological surprise.[40]

The final assumption of this study pertains to the current state of the deployed U.S. strategic forces, as well as the state of the NC3 systems and the nuclear weapons infrastructure maintained by the DOE, which is essential to the development, production, and sustainment of nuclear weapons. There is little doubt that the United States nuclear enterprise has seriously eroded over the past two decades. The available reporting indicates that the DOE infrastructure is in dire need of recapitalization and refurbishment.[41] The NC3 system also needs a major upgrade. This crisis is arguably made more acute by the technological environment in which the U.S. Strategic Command currently operates. Strategic command, control, communications, computers, intelligence, surveillance, and reconnaissance (C4ISR) are under threat from state and non-state actors with increasingly sophisticated and diffuse offensive cyberwarfare and electronic warfare capabilities, as well as from electromagnetic pulse (EMP) weapons. This threat would seem to demand an immediate and concerted effort to strengthen vitally important networks.[42] Although most strategic platforms, delivery vehicles, and deployed warheads are approaching the end of their service lives or have already undergone various refurbishments or life extension programs (LEPs), and although the need for new forces is evident, a major effort to recapitalize and modernize the U.S. nuclear enterprise should not be solely focused on those new forces. The renovation of the nuclear weapons development complex and the modernization of the NC3 system should be weighed against a plan to build and deploy new weapons programs. Although the present study focuses on alternative nuclear strategies for the United States, the renovation of the DOE Nuclear Weapons Complex and the modernization of the NC3 system should be viewed as a "necessary condition" to be accomplished concurrently with the modernization of the strategic arsenal.

PLAN OF THE BOOK

The plan of the book is as follows. The first chapter develops an analytical framework for assessing nuclear strategies, drawing upon insights and lessons from policy debates of the Cold War period and afterward. Although relying on history is not without risk, and although the United States could certainly confront novel threats—their novelty arising from geopolitical developments, technological trends, or some combination of the two—the U.S. experience with nuclear weapons can provide valuable insight to analysts grappling with important current and future challenges. The first section of the chapter is organized around four major questions that persisted throughout the Cold War concerning the role of nuclear weapons in deterring attacks against the United States and its allies. Soon after the introduction of nuclear weapons, questions emerged about the size of the U.S. nuclear arsenal and the quantitative levels of deployed forces, the perceived flexibility of those forces and the means with which they could be used under crisis or conflict conditions, the underlying political benefits or perceived diplomatic or coercive leverage provided by a robust nuclear arsenal, and the relative utility of strategic arms control and nonproliferation initiatives. These debates then reemerged at key points during the superpower rivalry. In considering the answers to these questions, this book distills key factors and criteria for evaluating whether alternative nuclear strategies serve U.S. security interests. The second section explicitly lays out these factors, which are in turn used to assess the relative strengths and weaknesses of the candidate strategies that are considered in the following chapters. Aside from the numbers and types of strategic weapons, this section considers the missions required of nuclear forces; declaratory policy; the related contributions of strategic defenses and nonstrategic or tactical nuclear weapons; the requirements for nuclear command and control and the nuclear weapons infrastructure; the perceived contributions to the deterrence of adversaries and the assurance of allies; the implications for strategic stability, particularly on arms race dynamics and crisis or first-strike stability; and the potential impact on strategic arms control and nonproliferation. Finally, programmatic costs and potential opportunity costs for conventional forces are considered.

The second chapter examines the current and emerging security environment and characterizes the central challenges and threats to U.S. national security interests that are arising from geopolitical and technological trends. The analysis focuses on instances where U.S. nuclear weapons may play a central role in deterring provocation or aggression and assuring allies. Thus, the chapter considers the implications of the return of great power competition with Russia and China, as well as the threat of new regional nuclear powers like North Korea. It will also discuss the current plans for the modernization of the strategic arsenal.

Chapters 3, 4, and 5 examine the proposed ideal type alternative nuclear strategies, force structures, and related elements. As noted earlier, each chapter presents an alternative strategy on its merits, as they are articulated by key advocates and supporters, before considering its potential weaknesses, tradeoffs, and objections. Chapter 3 assesses what has become known as nuclear primacy, or a concerted effort to achieve marked quantitative and qualitative strategic superiority over current peer rivals and regional powers. With a logical complementary focus on robust strategic defenses and a likely expansion of tactical or theater nuclear weapons systems, such a strategy would seek to confront adversaries with a U.S. offensive capability to successfully compete at any level of violence the adversary might seek to exploit, as well as a formidable damage limitation capability to undermine the adversary's advantages and/or prevent it from achieving its objectives. Perhaps unsurprisingly, it is likely that this strategy would negatively affect strategic stability with peer competitors like Russia and would decrease the likelihood of strategic arms control; it could even undermine the current nonproliferation regime. It would also require significant resources, straining Defense Department budgets and potentially diverting funds away from conventional procurement or readiness priorities.

A robust strategic deterrent strategy is examined in chapter 4. Focusing on the insights of the Cold War strategic competition, this chapter discusses the dangers of attempting to achieve strategic superiority and the value of strategic stability vis-à-vis peer competitors like Russia and eventually China. The presence of mutual vulnerability and the capacity of assured destruction require robust forces and a perceived willingness to use them under certain limited conditions. However, the proponents of this strategy view additional capabilities such as expanded nonstrategic nuclear forces and the expansion of strategic defenses, particularly those that may undermine the perceived retaliatory capabilities of peer competitors, as self-defeating and ultimately of little value in security or budgetary terms. The current nuclear modernization program of record provides a very conservative force structure for a robust deterrent strategy, but certain reductions may make it possible to maintain a balanced ability to field conventional forces and hedge against technological uncertainty in the event of changes in the medium and long terms. One critical challenge seems to be that certain programs that could be excised from current modernization plans could also undermine extended deterrence, thus underscoring the crucial role of allies like NATO and Japan in the development of a coherent U.S. strategy. Strategic arms control and nonproliferation may contribute to enhancing stability and transparency, but any such contributions will be contingent on relations with Russia, China, and other nuclear powers.

Finally, chapter 5 presents a minimal or finite deterrence strategy and strategic force structure. This ideal type builds upon the premise that the mere presence of nuclear weapons, rather than the quantitative force levels or the qualitative diversification of deployed forces, has a highly restraining effect on leaders. Consequently, the United States could deter the use of nuclear weapons against its territory and its allies with a much smaller strategic force than it currently supports. Such an approach would obviously decrease the overall budgetary footprint of strategic modernization, moving away from current plans and thus freeing up significant resources that could be allocated to conventional force modernization, the preparation of deployed conventional forces, and long-term research and development to harness new technologies. It is less clear that the redirection of resources to conventional capabilities would offset the potential problems of extended deterrence, and although concerted U.S. actions to significantly reduce its nuclear forces may reestablish the country's leadership of the global nonproliferation movement, geopolitical dynamics in key regions may create proliferation pressures that even an enhancement of U.S. conventional military commitments would struggle to overcome.

A brief conclusion summarizes the perceived advantages, critical tradeoffs, controversial issues, and major inconsistencies identified in the three ideal types, building upon the foundational discussion provided in chapter 1. Given the difficulties of predicting how geopolitical development, technological change, and defense budgetary contexts may change over time, this analysis is understandably provisional. Although history can provide only analogies and limited insights, however, the American experience with nuclear weapons does offer some useful insight into the development of U.S. nuclear strategy in the short to medium term. In short, some arguments have been made before, and their predictions can be assessed against the empirical record.

Notes

1. *Approaches for Managing the Costs of U.S. Nuclear Forces, 2017–2046* (Washington, Congressional Budget Office, 2017).
2. *Nuclear Posture Review 2018* (Washington, DC: U.S. Department of Defense, 2018).
3. *Summary of the 2018 National Defense Strategy of The United States of America: Sharpening the American Military Competitive Edge* (Washington, DC: U.S. Department of Defense, 2018); *National Security Strategy of the United States of America* (Washington, Office of the White House, 2017).
4. Brad Roberts, *The Case for Nuclear Weapons in the 21st Century* (Stanford: Stanford University Press, 2016): 43-43.
5. *Nuclear Posture Review Report* (Washington, DC: US. Department of Defense, 2010).
6. Barack Obama, "Remarks by President Barack Obama," Hradcany Square, Prague, Czech Republic, April 5, 2009, http://www.whitehouse.gov/the_press_office/Remarks-By-President-Barack-Obama-In-Prague-As-Delivered.
7. Mary Beth Sheridan, "Arms treaty approval a win for Obama, but GOP critics are gaining momentum," *The Washington Post*, December 23, 2010.
8. *American Strategic Posture: The Final Report of the Congressional Commission on US Strategic Posture* (Washington, DC: United States Institute of Peace, 2009), William J. Perry and Brent Scowcroft, *U.S. Nuclear Weapons Policy* (New York: Council on Foreign Relations, 2009).
9. Josh Rogin, "Obama plans major nuclear policy change in his final months," *The Washington Post*, July 10, 2016.
10. Steven Pifer, "Obama's Faltering Nuclear Legacy: The 3 R's," *Washington Quarterly* 38, no. 2 (Summer 2015): 101–118.
11. Tom Saurer, "A Second Nuclear Revolution: From Nuclear Primacy to Post-Existential Deterrence," *Journal of Strategic Studies*, Vol. 32, No. 5 (October 2009): 745-767.
12. Paul Sonne, "Pentagon unveils new nuclear weapons strategy, ending Obama-era push to reduce U.S. arsenal," *The Washington Post*, February 2, 2018.

13. Olga Oliker, *Russia's Nuclear Doctrine: What We Know, What We Don't, and What That Means* (Washington, DC: Center for Strategic and International Studies, 2106).

14. Tom Balmforth, "Days After Helsinki Summit, Russia Shows Off Putin's 'Super Weapons,'" *Reuters,* July 19, 2018, https://www.reuters.com/article/us-russia-usa-arms/days-after-helsinki-summit-russia-shows-off-putins-super-weapons-idUSKBN1K92HP.

15. Anne Gearan and Karen DeYoung, "Trump pulls United States out of Iran nuclear deal, calling the pact 'an embarrassment,'" *The Washington Post*, May 8, 2018.

16. W. J. Hennigan and John Walcott, "The U.S. Expects China Will Quickly Double Its Nuclear Arsenal," *Time*, May 30, 2019, http://time.com/5597955/china-nuclear-weapons-intelligence/.

17. Paul Sonne, "Pentagon takes aim at China and Russia in proposed $750 billion budget," *The Washington Post,* March 12, 2019.

18. Lolita C. Baldor, "Shanahan to call out China over South China Sea," *The Washington Post,* May 31, 2019.

19. Stephen Rademaker, "The North Korean nuclear threat is very real. Time to start treating it that way." *The Washington Post,* May 18, 2017.

20. *Nuclear Posture Review*, 21.

21. Paul Sonne and Shane Harris, "U.S. military edge has eroded to 'a dangerous degree,' study for Congress finds," *The Washington Post,* November 14, 2018.

22. Dan Lamothe, "Mattis unveils new strategy focused on Russia and China, takes Congress to task for budget impasse," *The Washington Post,* January 19, 2018.

23. Dianne Feinstein, "America's nuclear arsenal is unnecessarily and unsustainably large," *The Washington Post*, December 3, 2014.

24. Lara Seligman, "Will Congress Let Trump Build More Nuclear Weapons?" *Foreign Policy*, April 11, 2019, https://foreignpolicy.com/2019/04/11/will-congress-let-trump-expand-americas-nuclear-arsenal/.

25. Nina Tannenwald, "The U.N. just passed a treaty outlawing nuclear weapons. That actually matters," *The Washington Post*, July 17, 2017.

26. On the Nuclear Ban Treaty, see: https://www.un.org/disarmament/wmd/nuclear/tpnw/.

27. Rebecca David Gibbons, "The 2017 Nobel Peace Prize winner wants to ban nuclear weapons. Here's why the U.S. opposed." *The Washington Post*, December 11, 2017.

28. On the use of ideal types and typologies, see: Alexander George and Andrew Bennett, *Case Studies and Theory Development in the Social Sciences* (Cambridge: MIT Press, 2004): 233-263; Kenneth Bailey, *Typologies and Taxonomies: An Introduction to Classification Techniques* (Thousand Oaks: Sage Publications, 1994).

29. Saurer, "A Second Nuclear Revolution."

30. In doing so, this study is influenced by the approach of previous works that include Charles L. Glaser, *Analyzing Strategic Nuclear Policy* (Princeton, NJ: Princeton University Press, 1990); Lynn Eden and Steven E. Miller, *Nuclear Arguments: Understanding the Strategic Nuclear Arms and Arms Control Debates* (Ithaca, NY: Cornell University Press, 1989); Colin Gray, *Nuclear Strategy and Strategic Planning* (Philadelphia, Foreign Policy Research Institute, 1984).

31. For an alternative view, see: John Mueller, "The Essential Irrelevance of Nuclear Weapons: Stability in the Postwar World," *International Security* Vol. 13, No. 2 (Fall 1988), pp. 55–79.

32. On deterrence, see: Patrick M. Morgan, *Deterrence: A Conceptual Analysis* (Beverly Hills: Sage, 1977); Alexander George and Richard Smoke, *Deterrence in American Foreign Policy* (New York: Columbia University Press, 1974).

33. T.V. Paul, *Complex Deterrence: Strategy in the Global Age* (Chicago: University of Chicago Press, 2009).

34. See, for example, Paul Bracken, *The Second Nuclear Age: Strategy, Danger, and the New Power Politics* (New York: St. Martin's Press, 2012); Paul Bracken, "The Second Nuclear Age," *Foreign Affairs* 79, no. 1 (January–February 2000): 146–156; Colin S. Gray, *The Second Nuclear Age* (Boulder, CO: Lynne Reinner Press, 1999); Keith B. Payne, *Deterrence in the Second Nuclear Age* (Lexington: University Press of Kentucky, 1996).

35. Catherine McArdle Kelleher and Peter Dombrowski (eds.), *Regional Missile Defense from a Global Perspective* (Stanford, CA: Stanford University Press, 2015).

36. Andrew E. Kramer, "Russia Call New U.S. Missile Defense System a 'Direct Threat,'" *The New York Times*, May 12, 2016.

37. Adam Taylor, "South Korea and China move to normalize relations after THAAD dispute," *The Washington Post*, October 31, 2017.

38. Michael C. Horowitz, "Coming next in military tech," *Bulletin of the Atomic Scientists* 70, no. 2 (2014): 54-62.

39. See, for example: Pavel Sharikov, "Artificial intelligence, cyberattack, and nuclear weapons—a dangerous combination," *Bulletin of the Atomic*

Scientists 74, no. 6 (2018): 368-373; Christian Davenport, "Why the Pentagon fears the U.S. is losing the hypersonic arms race with Russia and China," *The Washington Post,* June 8, 2018; Matthew Kroenig and Tristan Volpe, "3-D Printing the Bomb? The Nuclear Nonproliferation Challenge," *The Washington Quarterly* 38, no. 3 (Fall 2015): 7-19; Sonia Ben Ouagrham-Gormley and Shannon Fye-Marnien, "The bright side of synthetic biology and Crispr," *Bulletin of the Atomic Scientists* 74, no. 1 (2018): 19-26.

40. John F. Sargent, Jr., *Defense Science and Technology Funding* (Washington, DC; Congressional Research Service, 2018).

41. Amy F. Woolf and James D. Werner, *The U.S. Nuclear Weapons Complex: Overview of Department of Energy Sites* (Washington, DC: Congressional Research Service, 2018); *Independent Review of the Department of Defense Nuclear Enterprise* (Washington, DC: Department of Defense, 2014).

42. Ashton B. Carter, John D. Steinbruner, and Charles A. Zraket (eds.), *Managing Nuclear Operations* (Washington, DC: Brookings Institution Press, 1987); Bruce G. Blair, *Strategic Command and Control: Redefining the Nuclear Threat* (Washington, DC: Brookings Institution Press, 1985).

Reassessing
U.S. Nuclear Strategy

CHAPTER 1

ASSESSING U.S. NUCLEAR STRATEGY

This study builds upon the foundational assumption that nuclear weapons remain directly relevant to United States' security policy. Although the Obama administration formally embraced the goal of a world without nuclear weapons as a long-term objective of U.S. policy, the decision to modernize the strategic triad underscored the unlikelihood that such a goal would be reached anytime soon. According to the Obama Administration 2010 Nuclear Posture Review (NPR), as long as nuclear weapons remain a reality of the international system, the United States will maintain a safe, secure, and effective nuclear arsenal. Thus, the central question of this study is as follows: what nuclear strategy (and related force structure) best advances the United States' vital national security interests in a complex and fluid international security environment? Fortunately, the United States has confronted similar difficult modernization decisions in the past. Although the program of record authorized by Congress under the Obama administration is already in its early stages and has received some modifications from the Trump administration, as articulated in the 2018 NPR, the present moment remains a prudent time to reassess U.S.

nuclear strategy, given the geopolitical, technological, and budgetary uncertainties that define the current environment.

Although the U.S. strategic modernization program is already underway, the political and diplomatic contexts are perhaps more uncertain than at any time since the end of the Cold War. In his excellent survey of the U.S. nuclear doctrine, Scott Sagan delivered a prescient warning: "Despair about maintaining nuclear deterrence in the future must be avoided, however, for it can lead to the false attraction of utopian, unrealizable schemes to eliminate the risk of war."[1] In the nearly three decades since his writing, and particularly after the collapse of the Soviet Union, this "utopian impulse" has only intensified. In June 2017, the Treaty on the Prohibition of Nuclear Weapons was adopted in the United Nations. When fifty nations formally ratify or accede to the Treaty, it will come into force according to international law.[2] Driven largely by civil society groups and nongovernmental organizations with the support of several non-nuclear weapons states, the so-called "Nuclear Ban Treaty" is likely to have little material effect on the behavior of the United States or other nuclear weapons states, but it has created domestic political challenges for several allies and partners of the U.S. with extended deterrent commitments. The Nuclear Ban Treaty has been criticized by nonproliferation and arms control experts who argue that it will actually undermine the Nonproliferation Treaty (NPT), but the civil society movement's primary grievance is the perceived lack of progress on nuclear disarmament by the nuclear weapons states. Then-president Barack Obama's 2008 Prague speech, followed by the signing of the "New START" Treaty with Russia and the articulation of a world without nuclear weapons as a formal goal of U.S. foreign policy, understandably sparked significant interest in the movement toward "global zero."[3] Nonetheless, after seven years and the precipitous erosion of relations between Washington and Moscow, further arms control proved elusive, and the "Prague Agenda" stalled.[4]

As the same, an alternative trend has emerged within the U.S. defense community: an effort to exploit U.S. advantages in the nuclear realm to maximize the value of the U.S. nuclear arsenal for achieving foreign policy goals. With the emergence of regional nuclear powers like North Korea and Iran, which are perceived to be less rational and thus less easily deterred by the large U.S. strategic nuclear arsenal, the search for more tailored and flexible nuclear capabilities has received new attention.[5] Russia's provocative behavior and its perceived willingness to use its stock of nonstrategic nuclear weapons has only reinforced this interest in limited U.S. nuclear options. This interest highlights a second area of discussion and debate among security experts, also foreshadowed by Sagan, about the "usability" of nuclear weapons:

> A perpetual dilemma, which has been called the "usability paradox," exist at the heart of U.S. nuclear weapons policy. The two central objectives of U.S. policy—to deter aggression against the United States and its allies and to prevent accidental war—require the U.S. nuclear forces be usable, but not too usable. For the sake of deterrence, nuclear forces must be "usable enough" to convince the Soviet Union that a potent U.S. nuclear response would actually be forthcoming in the event of a Soviet attack on the United States or its vital interests. To prevent accidental war, however, U.S. weapons must not be "so usable" that they are ever launched through a mechanical error, used by unauthorized or insane military commanders, or operated in such a provocative manner as to cause the Soviet Union to mistakenly "preempt" what it falsely believes is an imminent attack.[6]

Experts have advocated for more "usable" nuclear weapons, which typically involve lower-yield warheads to minimize radioactive fallout and therefore collateral civilian damage. Such weapons would allow the United States to more effectively address military challenges like hard and deeply buried targets (HDBTs), including leadership bunkers and WMD infrastructure, and mobile, relocatable targets such as enemy missile transporter erector launchers. These experts argue that although deterrence remains the objective, to deter certain new actors, the United States requires capabilities different from those that deterred the Soviet Union.[7] Conversely, opponents argue that the use of more and smaller exotic nuclear weapons and the development of operational plans and doctrine to employ them effectively "lowers the threshold to nuclear use" and therefore increases the perceived reliance upon nuclear weapons to maintain the security of the U.S. and its allies.[8] The Trump administration's Nuclear Posture Review largely embraced the Obama administration's plan for modernizing the strategic nuclear triad but supplemented the existing plan with two new programs, a single low-yield warhead variant of the W76-1 warhead for use on the Trident II D5 submarine launched ballistic missile (SLBM) and a new sea-launched nuclear cruise missile, explicitly designed to be more usable in order to provide decision-makers with a wider spectrum of limited, proportional nuclear options and thus enhance deterrence against actors that may threaten limited nuclear use against the United States or its allies.[9]

Thus, while the Obama and Trump administration NPRs reflect a significant degree of continuity relative to the importance of the strategic deterrent, the difference of emphasis reflects a much greater divergence of view in the larger policy community. Despite an appearance of broad consensus, the contradictory pulls of Sagan's utopian impulse and usability paradox are perhaps more prevalent than at any previous time in the nuclear era.[10] Some experts argue for a dramatic reduction in U.S. nuclear forces to best address national security priorities while others disagree and argue that a greater reliance on and expanded U.S. nuclear arsenal provides the best means of keeping America safe. Somewhere in between are those who remain committed to the maintenance of a strong nuclear arsenal and the importance of the strategic deterrent but are skeptical of significant shifts in U.S. policy in either direction. What would the U.S. nuclear arsenal look like if it was constructed by the prescriptions of these different groups of experts? What would be the implications of those alternative nuclear strategies, forces structures and postures, and related issues for U.S. national security?

This study seeks to critically assess these important arguments and answer these questions. In doing so, it also acknowledges a more fundamental intellectual fault line that emerged during the Cold War and the superpower arms race over the role of nuclear weapons: the seemingly intractable divide between much of the academic/scholarly community and the policy/practitioner community.[11] It draws on the literature from both key communities to attempt present the best cases for and the most rigorous assessment of alternative approaches to U.S. nuclear strategy.

The divide between scholars and practitioners of nuclear strategy boils down to two differing views on two fundamental issues: the first is the impact of nuclear weapons on international security and the second is the source of conflict in world politics.

Most of the academic literature on nuclear weapons was significantly influenced by the early civilian nuclear strategists, most notably Bernard Brodie.[12] The implications of the "nuclear revolution" stem from Brodie's assessment that traditional concepts of military strategy had effectively become meaningless with the advent of atomic weapons that deterrence of Soviet (or other adversaries') nuclear weapons was the singular mission of the U.S. nuclear arsenal.[13] Because conflict in the nuclear era would precipitate such devastation upon any state that initiated it, no possible national interests or political objectives could be served by using such force.[14] Moreover because it was impossible to escape the vulnerability that societies now faced, resolve, not capabilities would determine the outcomes of diplomatic crises. The presence of hostages and the irrelevance of defense made deterrence the only viable strategy.[15] The possession of sufficient stocks of nuclear weapons (refined over time to the deployment of secure retaliatory capabilities) would lead to peace among nuclear powers, a decrease in diplomatic crisis, and an acceptance of the status quo. As Robert Jervis claimed, "mutual assured destruction exists as a fact, irrespective of policy. No amount of flexibility, no degree of military superiority at levels less than all-out war, can change the fundamental attribute of the nuclear age."[16] Military experts charged with protecting the nation and, if necessary, utilizing nuclear weapons never accepted this view of the security environment.[17] Moreover, many defense policy experts and civilian advisors were justifiably focused on responding to the growing Soviet threat.[18] Albert Wohlstetter famously depicted a "Delicate Balance of Terror" between the superpowers, something that must be maintained, in part because of the perceived nature of the adversary and in part because of the expected impact of technological change and the challenges of consistently maintaining a favorable balance of forces.[19] More broadly, many of these experts never accepted that nuclear weapons were an "absolute" weapon. A nuclear war between the superpowers could be fought and one side could emerge in a relatively better position than the other.[20] Even if the magnitude of the conflict was on a much greater scale, traditional military strategy had not been made irrelevant simply by crossing the nuclear threshold. This "Clausewitzian" approach—attempting to employ the Prussian strategist's guidance that war should only be waged to achieve political objectives—approach to nuclear conflict was rejected by adherents to the nuclear revolution school, as Hans Morgenthau expressed in his criticism of what he perceived as "the conventionalization of nuclear weapons."[21] Nevertheless, military experts and civilian defense policymakers were tasked to think about the unthinkable and therefore focused much greater attention to the capabilities required to fight and win a nuclear war than their academic counterparts, who focused on the requisites of stable deterrence and the avoidance of such a potentially catastrophic outcome.[22]

The second major point of contention is perhaps more fundamental and relates to the root causes of conflict in the international system. Within the military and policy community, deterrence was vitally important. But here it also maintained a view consistent with conventional military realm. Deterrence demands that one take strong, decisive measures to prevent a bad actor from doing bad things.[23] Failure to do so is to risk further transgressions. In the early Cold War period, this was probably reinforced by the shared experiences of Munich and later Korea among many in senior leadership roles.[24] Even if an adversary is rational, it may also be more risk-acceptant, possess a significantly different value system, and misinterpret good faith gestures.[25] The only real means of communicating resolve to avoid provocation and conflict is through strength and conflict is best be avoided through confronting an adversary with superior forces, while conciliatory policies are inherently risky.[26] Therefore, when confronted by a superpower adversary possessing nuclear weapons, the United States had little choice but to make the sacrifices necessary to field the capabilities necessary to defeat a potentially ideologically driven, risk-acceptant, expansionist Soviet Union in a protracted nuclear war.[27] These capabilities would have provided the United States with clear and unambiguous superiority.[28]

Within the academic community a different view emerged that was also predicated upon traditional concepts of great power politics but that embraced a more tragic view of world politics.[29] States have interests, the most important being their continued survival and security. To best provide for that the security, they may take actions that can lead to conflict with others. But conflict is risky and war is an extremely costly endeavor. There are considerable downsides for overly aggressive policies and statesman that do not understand this are likely to serve their states poorly. Prudent leaders would thus not shy away from the use of force if left with no recourse but were also cognizant of the potentially self-defeating ramifications of overly aggressive behavior and sensitive to the perceptions of other states, whether allies or adversaries.[30] The notion of the security dilemma, where one state's unilateral attempts to improve its own security creates effectively decreases the security of others, thus pressing them to take action to rectify the situation, ultimately making all worse off and heightening the probability of crisis of conflict is a central concept in this literature.[31] In the world of conventional weapons, high levels of uncertainty, the influences of military technology, potential for alliances, and diplomatic intrigue all can exacerbate the plight confronting peaceful states.[32] Conversely in a world of nuclear weapons, and particularly after the achievement of secure retaliatory capabilities, deterrence should be relatively easy.[33]

Differing views on these two primary questions shaped the views of academic experts and military and civilian defense intellectuals throughout the Cold War and can still be seen today.

Although a comprehensive nuclear strategy is more than just an accounting of different types of weapons, the quantity and quality of the deployed systems will necessarily play a major role in determining the missions that can be accomplished. The components, strategic implications, and strengths and weaknesses of three ideal type nuclear postures for the United States are presented in the subsequent chapters. The remainder of this chapter first considers four major arguments (or sets of debates) that shaped U.S. decision making concerning nuclear strategy and forces during the Cold War. The second section addresses the roles of two key related capabilities that significantly influence the effectiveness of a given alternative nuclear strategy: strategic defenses and nonstrategic (or tactical) nuclear weapons. The third section then presents a set of criteria by which each alternative can be assessed, derived from the discussion in this chapter.

THE ROLE OF NUCLEAR WEAPONS: INSIGHTS FROM THE COLD WAR AND BEYOND

There are a number of ways to organize a discussion of the relative merits and drawbacks of alternative U.S. nuclear strategies and the numerous subsidiary and related questions associated with such an endeavor. To provide grounding for this analysis, this chapter revisits four of the major issues that have persistently confronted policymakers, policy experts, and academic specialists since the beginning of the Cold War.[34] The first concerns the nature of U.S. nuclear forces. In short, this issue boils down to the question Alain Enthoven and Wayne Smith sought to answer in their influential work: "How much is enough?" As important staff members in the McNamara Defense Department, they had intimate knowledge of the processes that developed U.S. strategic force level requirements in the 1960s.[35] Their word was certainly not the last, however, and as the Soviet Union approached and achieved strategic parity in the 1970s, defense experts questioned the validity of the proposed requisites for assured destruction that had been considered effective in both deterring the Soviet Union (by confronting Soviet leaders with an unacceptable level of damage if they were successful in launching an attack on the United States) and providing strategic stability and therefore avoiding the downsides of unrestrained arms development.[36] Given the quantitative and qualitative superiority of U.S. strategic forces during the era when these programming decisions were made, outside experts were skeptical that the same requisites or the underlying logic of assured destruction would hold in a new environment in which the Soviets were equal or superior to the United States.[37] Moreover, given the expansions of Soviet strategic forces and the qualitative improvement of those forces throughout the 1970s, even in the context of the Strategic Arms Limitation Talks (SALT) accords, Soviet leaders were perceived as increasingly hostile and as willing to engage in a protracted nuclear war to achieve their political objectives.[38] Embracing a more traditional (Clausewitzian) view of nuclear weapons, these experts questioned their "absolute" nature and implications for international conflict and competition, and argued that nuclear war-fighting capabilities were necessary to effectively deter a more belligerent, risk-acceptant Soviet actor.

This fundamental debate concerning the requisite force levels for effective deterrence leads to a second major issue of contention: the flexibility of deployed U.S. nuclear forces. From the early Kennedy administration's concerns over the perceived rigidity of the Eisenhower administration New Look policy to the development of the Single Integrated Operational Plan (SIOP) and ultimately the doctrine of Flexible Response, several consecutive administrations engaged in a near-constant search for flexibility in the use of U.S. nuclear forces.[39] Limited nuclear options (LNOs) were perceived as necessary to effectively meet the Soviet Union at different levels of conflict, and policymakers feared a situation in which a U.S. president would be forced to choose between doing nothing and launching a massive nuclear strike that would likely result in a similar attack upon the United States. Though various academic and policy studies on limited war in the nuclear age had implied the likelihood that any nuclear use could escalate to a large-scale exchange between the superpowers, there was nonetheless a strong and persistent effort, particularly in the strategic policy community, to tailor nuclear forces (particularly nonstrategic nuclear weapons) to provide the national command authority with the capacity to take limited actions in response to limited Soviet provocations or actions, and thus maintain some measure of escalation control in the event of a conflict or crisis.[40] Some experts argued that a lack of proportional nuclear options and a reliance on (typically larger-yield) central strategic systems would undermine effective deterrence because of a lack of credibility. Conversely, many academics argued that the presence of strategic nuclear weapons would instill restraint and caution in leaders (including Soviet leaders), decreasing the likelihood of crises that involved vital national interests in the first place.[41] Moreover, although such discussions focused on the nature and effects of certain weapons, an important contribution drew attention to the necessity of maintaining a robust and resilient nuclear command, control and communications (NC3) capability, without which attempts to manage lower-level nuclear exchanges or even the early stages of a larger conflict would be futile.

A third debate, which is less explicit in the policy community but has been the topic of considerable empirical analysis in the academic community, is about the political influence of nuclear weapons. Many scholars have taken a relatively sanguine view of nuclear weapons and their influence on international politics, including on the superpower strategic rivalry. In the late 1970s and early 1980s, proponents of the "Nuclear Revolution" theory, who believed that assured destruction (or, perhaps more accurately, assured vulnerability) was a fact of the international system in the nuclear age, argued that deterrence was relatively easy when the vital interests of one of the superpowers were involved.[42] Outside such situations or in the context of a crisis, they asserted, the possession of nuclear weapons had little political value.

Indeed, it was more likely to push leaders toward restraint and willingness to make concessions than to provide coercive leverage or diplomatic benefits.[43] This view was rejected by many policy practitioners and experts, who were much more pessimistic about the intentions and motivations of the Soviet leadership and argued that the scholars' view of the nuclear revolution and its implications for international stability was not universally shared by the Kremlin and other more risk-acceptant leaders.[44] These practitioners and experts held that the capabilities fielded by the United States should be not only quantitatively superior, but also diverse and flexible to provide U.S. leaders with a menu of options from which to choose proportionate and specialized responses to Soviet provocation or aggression. Moreover, they believed that U.S. strategic superiority provided a range of diplomatic and political benefits beyond the direct and extended deterrence missions against the Soviet Union and offered significant leverage in other matters, especially in the effort to dissuade third parties such as China and regional actors from even considering challenging the United States. In this area, the division between policymakers and academic scholars is still notable today.

Finally, the relative contributions of strategic arms control and nonproliferation initiatives to U.S. security constitute a fourth major area of contention among policy experts.[45] In the view of some academic and policy experts, strategic arms control is a complement to U.S. nuclear force structure, posture, or strategy. Even in the context of the superpower competition, cooperative agreements were useful in providing shared expectations and decreasing uncertainty around the quantitative and qualitative aspects of the superpower arms race, as well as avoiding potential accidents or inadvertent conflicts. A logical prerequisite for successful arms control is the capacity to monitor and verify agreement, and the United States has been able to rely on extensive satellite technologies or unilateral national technical means of verification. Skeptics have tended to believe that arms control agreements restrain U.S. capabilities and provide opportunities for the Soviet Union/Russia to exploit advantages that will ultimately place the United States at a disadvantage over time. The debates surrounding the SALT process in the 1970s were particularly intense, though arms control played a major role in creating the conditions that facilitated the conclusion of the Cold War and the transformation of the security environment after the collapse of the Soviet Union. Today, valid questions have been raised about the continued relevance of bilateral arms control between the United States and Russia, considering the expansion of other nuclear programs, though the quantitative differences between the former superpowers and other rising nuclear powers remain significant.

The debate about nonproliferation is similar. Nonproliferation emerged as a major objective of U.S. national security policy at the outset of the nuclear age.[46] Preventing the development of nuclear weapons programs in new states was an important—if often understated—interest of the United States even at the height of the superpower competition. Although the size and shape of the U.S. nuclear arsenal and the specific objectives of U.S. nuclear strategy are not directly related to nonproliferation policy, they necessarily influence the efficacy of U.S. nonproliferation efforts, in large part due to the perception and interpretations of U.S. nuclear forces and declared policy by other actors.

These four major questions allow the development of several criteria for assessing the relative strengths and weaknesses of alternative nuclear strategies for the United States. Beyond specific configurations of planned and deployed strategic forces, the effectiveness and resiliency of NC3 and the alert status of deployed forces, and the state of the nuclear weapons complex, these criteria have several key related components. Specifically, strategic defenses and nonstrategic nuclear weapons are critical to forming a coherent nuclear strategy. These components directly shape a strategy's capacity to address national security challenges, including the execution of various counterforce and countervalue missions, the maintenance of flexibility among U.S. nuclear forces, and the challenge of hedging against geopolitical and technological change. Ultimately, the discussion of these four major debates provides a means to assess alternative strategies in terms of their respective contributions to central deterrence, extended deterrence and the reassurance of allies, strategic stability (including crisis or first-strike and arms race stability), the dissuasion of new adversaries, strategic arms control, and nonproliferation. Lastly, the financial and opportunity costs (in terms of resources that cannot be used for conventional force modernization and military readiness or for research and development of new technologies) are considered.

Force Levels and Structure

Throughout the Cold War, the seemingly straightforward question "How much is enough?" proved surprisingly difficult to answer.[47] After the breakthrough of atomic weapons at the close of World War II, the nuclear weapons program under the Truman administration initially foundered in the postwar period.[48] The Russian explosion of an atomic weapon refocused U.S. efforts, and the outbreak of the Korean War drove a major expansion of the existing stockpile. In 1953, the United States tested a hydrogen bomb, another technological breakthrough that was achieved with remarkably little debate or discussion.[49] By the mid-1950s, the United States possessed an overwhelming nuclear superiority in quantitative terms, based on its formidable long-range bomber force under the Strategic Air Command (SAC). Seeking to maintain control over military budgets and resist domestic political pressures for increased conventional forces, the Eisenhower administration relied heavily on its strategic advantage, initially embracing a policy of massive retaliation in the context of the president's "New Look."[50]

The Soviet launch of Sputnik in August 1957 shocked the United States and signaled a major technological shift: the arrival of the missile age. Now the greatest source of U.S. strategic power projection, the SAC bomber force, was vulnerable to missile attack, which dramatically shortened warning times and heightened crisis instability. Despite the shock of Sputnik and a domestic political debate that focused on the potential of a U.S. "missile gap" in the 1960 presidential election, the United States stayed ahead of the Soviet Union and made progress in the development and deployment of strategic missile programs.[51] The perception of strategic inferiority seems to have been the driving force behind Soviet Premier Nikita Khrushchev's gamble of surreptitiously introducing intermediate-range ballistic missiles into Cuba in 1962. The crisis that erupted when the Kennedy administration learned of the deployment brought the world to the brink of nuclear war.[52] After backing down and acquiescing to the removal of missiles from Cuba (in exchange for a pledge not to invade Cuba and a secret agreement to remove aging, obsolete Jupiter missiles from Turkey), Khrushchev and hardliners led by Leonid Brezhnev (who would soon replace Khrushchev) instituted a large-scale, long-term strategic modernization program that would end Soviet strategic inferiority.[53]

The Kennedy administration, and specifically Secretary of Defense Robert S. McNamara, had a lasting impact on U.S. nuclear weapons policy.[54] Confident in the quantitative advantages of the United States, McNamara initially endorsed a counterforce doctrine, articulated in his "No Cities" speech at the University of Michigan in 1962. As several scholars have discussed, it was the sheer magnitude of U.S. forces, rather than any traditional concept of strategy, that drove the development of targeting packages and planning.[55] However, in the face of extensive pressure by the U.S. Air Force for more intercontinental ballistic missiles (ICBMs) and the likelihood of Congressional support for greater expenditures, McNamara and his advisors developed the concept of assured destruction to establish a ceiling on force levels and avoid what was feared would be an uncontrolled arms buildup.[56] With the somewhat arbitrary number of one thousand Minuteman ICBMs (with fifty-four remaining Titan IIs) and the deployment of new submarine-launched ballistic missiles (SLBMs) aboard nuclear submarines (SSBNs), the United States would be able to address almost any conceivable Soviet buildup.[57] Assured destruction, which was premised upon the capacity to destroy approximately fifty percent of Soviet industry and twenty percent of the Soviet population, would confront Soviet leaders with an unacceptable level of damage that would deter them from contemplating an attack on the United States.[58] Beyond its existing quantitative advantage, a critically important hedge that the McNamara Defense Department viewed as insurance against a greater than expected expansion of Soviet strategic forces was the development of multiple independently targetable reentry vehicle (MIRV) technology, which would soon dramatically increase the number of warheads deployed on the U.S. Minuteman III and Poseidon SLBM forces. Initially devised as a hedge against a Soviet breakthrough in ballistic missile defenses, the deployment of U.S. strategic missile forces with MIRVs was perceived as a decisive advancement of U.S. capabilities that would undermine any advantages the Soviet Union might achieve with a quantitative expansion of its offensive force.[59] At the same time, the concept of the strategic triad of ICBMs, SLBMs, and strategic bombers also became entrenched within much of the defense policy community.[60] In order to achieve necessary levels of penetrability, reliability, and survivability, each leg provided unique attributes: the ICBM force could reliably deliver prompt long range strikes and were virtually guaranteed to successfully hit their targets given the low probability of the deployment of effective strategic defenses by the Soviets; the bomber force was relatively survivable if on alert, was responsive and could control escalation, and with the advent of cruise missiles could still deliver munitions even if penetrability decreased with improvements in air defenses; and finally the submarine force was the highly survivable, given the low likelihood of a breakthrough in Antisubmarine Warfare (ASW) capabilities, and SLBMs, even with less expansive range, could penetrate any defenses.[61] Thus, each component made a vital contribution to an overall robust, versatile, and credible strategic deterrent and recommendations to move away from the triad almost inevitably faced strong criticism.[62]

Within much of the academic community, the achievement of parity created an objective reality of mutual assured destruction (MAD), which appeared to be formalized in SALT and the signing of the Antiballistic Missile (ABM) Treaty and an Interim Agreement on Offensive Weapons in Moscow in 1972.[63] Despite the mutual acceptance of mutual vulnerability that seemed to be endorsed in SALT, the continuing Soviet offensive buildup, and specifically the eventual deployment of MIRVs by the Soviets, sparked concerns about Soviet intentions beyond SALT I and about an emerging threat to the U.S. Minuteman Force.[64] Specifically, Soviet heavy missiles like the SS-9 and the SS-18 were seen, because of their size and throw weight, as capable of destroying a large portion of the land-based leg of the U.S. strategic triad. Although the United States would still have a large percentage of its warheads afloat on MIRVed SLBMs in its SSBN force (as well as a significant portion of the alert bomber force that had not been destroyed on the ground), a U.S. president could have been deterred from launching a primarily countervalue campaign against Soviet cities and industry for fear that Moscow maintained capabilities to respond in kind.[65] This perceived "window of vulnerability" may have been overblown, but because of the inability to effectively address the MIRV and ICBM vulnerability issues and deteriorating diplomatic conditions relating to the Soviet invasion of Afghanistan and support for communist forces in Africa, SALT II was never ratified.[66]

Given the challenging security environment, the United States embarked on a new round of strategic modernization under the administration of President Jimmy Carter, centered on the deployment of the "MX" (Peacekeeper) heavy ICBM (which would carry ten MIRVs and thus provide the United States with a counterforce capability on par with that of the Soviet Union), the B-1 strategic bomber, and the Trident SLBM.[67] Carter initially cancelled the B-1 program. He opted instead to invest in the acquisition of air-launched cruise missiles to be used on newer variants of deployed B-52s, preferring an enhanced standoff capability over the already questionable penetration capacity projected for the B-1.[68] Carter's Defense Department did not abandon the penetrating bomber mission, as plans were authorized for the development of a new and highly advanced penetrating strategic bomber that would use cutting-edge technologies, including stealth capabilities. However, the B-2 did not enter service until after the Soviet Union collapsed. Ronald Reagan, who had campaigned in 1980 on a platform of improving U.S. military capabilities and taking a hard line against the Soviets, took office with a modernization program well underway.[69] He reinstated the B-1 bomber program and supported the deployment of the MX Missile, although given the intense debate that had emerged concerning ICBM vulnerability in the late 1970s, basing for the new missile became a major political controversy. Because of the Peacekeeper's formidable offensive counterforce attributes, it was expected that the Soviets would target it in any first strike on the United States. A variety of options were considered, including mobility, but eventually it was deployed in retrofitted Minuteman silos.[70] As a result of the MX controversy, a small, single warhead ICBM (SICBM), or "Midgetman," was programmed to complement the massive Peacekeeper deployment.

Both programs were curtailed and eventually eliminated with the end of the Cold War, leaving the legacy Minuteman III force as the backbone of the land-based pillar of the strategic triad after the last Peacekeeper was removed from service in 2005.[71] The B-1 was removed from the strategic mission under the START Treaty, and the B-2, which was indeed a technological marvel but was prohibitively costly at approximately $2 billion per unit, was limited to a force of twenty-one aircraft. With a portion of the B-52 fleet, this force serves as the air-breathing leg of the strategic triad. The current sea leg of the triad was similarly developed during this last period of modernization. The fleet of fourteen *Ohio*-class nuclear-powered ballistic missile submarines carrying up to twenty-four Trident D5 SLBMs (each of which can be loaded with up to eight MIRVs) is programmed to be removed from service at the end of the next decade.

It is interesting to note that before the abrupt end of the Cold War, in Moscow's view, the United States had embarked on a program to obtain a formidable and highly threatening counterforce capability. By the late 1980s, this view had led Soviet leaders to perceive the Soviet Union's strategic deterrent as intensely vulnerable.[72] This situation suggests a reversal of roles from the perceived ICBM vulnerability episode and underscores the potential for misperception surrounding the intentions of major modernization programs.

Although numbers alone do not constitute a comprehensive strategy, quantitative force levels played a significant role in determining the approach to targeting and the targets that could be held at risk throughout much of the early Cold War.[73] During the course of the Cold War, the United States implemented elements of the counterforce and assured destruction doctrines. Given the early quantitative superiority of the U.S. Air Force in the 1950s and early 1960s, its planners developed increasingly large target packages, focused on the growing Soviet strategic forces and support infrastructure, to blunt or preempt a potential Soviet nuclear attack on the United States. Assured destruction requirements were developed to place some prudent limits on the potentially open-ended expansion of the strategic arsenal under the Kennedy and Johnson administrations, and the numbers of delivery vehicles eventually plateaued. With the introduction of land-based ICBM forces, the development of SLBMs, and the achievement of MIRV technology, the U.S. and Soviet arsenals expanded significantly throughout the 1960s and into the 1970s.[74] However, even as the prospect of a large-scale exchange remained a central concern, the challenge of maintaining extended deterrence commitments took on greater importance as the Soviet Union approached and achieved strategic parity. This development pushed U.S. defense experts to revisit the question of LNOs that could enhance the credibility of extended deterrence by providing the national command authority with capabilities to respond to Soviet aggression in more proportionate ways without relying on a massive and potentially catastrophic strategic attack.

The Question of Flexibility

Beyond the requisite numerical levels required to maintain a credible deterrent, operational flexibility emerged as a critical issue of nuclear strategy.[75] The development and deployment of a nuclear force that would provide the national command authority with flexible options was a key objective of U.S. nuclear policy for much of the Cold War. Whereas the initial period of U.S. superiority under the Eisenhower Administration used a strategy of massive retaliation predicated on a large-scale strategic bomber attack on the Soviet Union, the credibility of the threat of an "all out" attack on the Soviets decreased over time, particularly as Soviet nuclear capabilities increased and the Soviet intercontinental ballistic missile force emerged as a potent threat to the United States. The initial SIOP, developed in the early 1960s in the McNamara Pentagon, envisioned a large-scale nuclear strike on the Soviet Union. By endorsing a "No Cities" counterforce doctrine, however, it depicted a nuclear conflict with the Soviet Union as essentially similar to conventional warfare.[76] The targets were primarily military in nature. The move toward assured destruction represented an intellectual shift that acknowledged that the destructive power of nuclear weapons, even if used against military targets, would create such societal devastation that the distinction between counterforce (targeting the opponent's military forces and supporting infrastructure) and countervalue (population centers and urban areas) operations would be effectively meaningless. The vulnerability of the Soviet Union and eventually the United States to catastrophic societal damage would deter each country from initiating a conflict, thus introducing some measure of stability into the strategic relationship. As long as the United States maintained the quantitative force levels required to deliver such an attack, even in the event of a successful Soviet first strike that significantly degraded U.S. strategic forces, the Kremlin would be deterred from contemplating such a strategy. Thus, survivable retaliatory capability became the central component of what would become known as mutual assured destruction (MAD).[77]

Many U.S. experts remained uncomfortable with what they saw as a rigid insistence on using the threat of a large-scale nuclear strike as the primary deterrent to Soviet aggression, particularly as the Soviet Union moved toward achieving numerical strategic parity with the United States.[78] When the Kennedy Administration developed a policy of Flexible Response, it was focusing on the difficult challenge of extending its deterrent guarantee to its NATO allies, despite the conventional imbalance in forces between NATO and the Warsaw Pact, as the Soviet capacity to devastate the continental United States grew in the late 1960s and early 1970s.[79] Within the academic community, this challenge spurred interest in the concept of limited war in the nuclear age. The possibility of a first use of tactical nuclear weapons by NATO was seen as a necessary part of deterring what would likely be a large-scale conventional Soviet attack.[80] Tactical nuclear weapons were viewed as a means of controlling escalation to prevent a rapid defeat and signal resolve and willingness to move to higher levels of violence.[81] However, the potential for escalation—whether deliberate or inadvertent—to an exchange of strategic weapons and ultimately a large-scale catastrophic nuclear war between the United States and the Soviet Union undermined the confidence that any conflict in Europe could be kept "limited."[82] Implementing Flexible Response only became more difficult as the Soviet Union achieved strategic parity with the United States, and it became increasingly unlikely that a decision would be made to resort to nuclear weapons when U.S. cities were at risk of destruction.[83]

Experts agree that the SIOP, which was first drafted by the McNamara Defense Department after President John F. Kennedy took office, did indeed allow for a range of limited strikes and sub-packages that could be provided to the president during a crisis.[84] The SIOP was developed in large part because McNamara viewed the previous Eisenhower administration plans as lacking such flexibility. But what was meant by "flexibility?" Jerome Kahan, for example, defined strategic flexibility in the following way:

> Strategic flexibility has many meanings but can be said to encompass those doctrines, plans, and force capabilities that permit strategic armaments to be employed in a variety of ways besides massive strikes against urban areas. This set of employment options runs the gamut from the "surgical" application of one or two weapons against a selected target—whether a single city or nonurban target, such as nuclear storage sites, military bases, or industrial facilities—to heavy counterforce attacks against all of an opponent's deployed delivery systems. The doctrinal justifica-

tions for flexibility are as varied as the options themselves, but in general, two major reasons are given in favor of such strategies—to strengthen deterrence and to limit damage.[85]

The search for Limited Nuclear Options became a key component of what would be called the Schlesinger Doctrine, after Nixon Defense Secretary James Schlesinger.[86] Arguing that the Kennedy-era SIOP was too restrictive and effectively left a president with no choice but to meet Soviet aggression with a massive retaliatory strike, he directed the development of plans that offered the options of proportional and limited strikes. National Security Directive Memorandum (NSDM) 242 captured this mandate. The incoming Carter administration similarly sought to deny the Soviets victory at any level of violence in what would become known as the "Countervailing Strategy," associated with Secretary of Defense Harold Brown.[87] What is important is that neither of these approaches sought more effective ways to carry out a nuclear "war-fighting" strategy. Rather, they reflected the growth and diversification of Soviet nuclear capabilities in the post SALT-I period and the perception that Soviet intentions were increasingly expansionist. The best way of deterring a Soviet Union with these military capabilities and intentions was to develop doctrine and capabilities to prevent it from exploiting its advantages. Presidential Directive 25 (PD-25) encapsulated the countervailing strategy, and many of its insights were subsequently embraced and extended by the Reagan administration.[88]

This discussion not only underscores the difficulties that policymakers grappled with concerning the credibility of an extended deterrence commitment to NATO, but also leads to another important question that was consistently asked of administration officials in the 1970s. To the question of "How much is enough?" these experts introduced a vitally important addendum: "To do what?" A major critique of the development and acceptance of the assured destruction requirement was that it assumed some degree of rationality on the part of the Soviet leadership. Given the persistent Soviet buildup of strategic forces, even after the SALT I accords and throughout the later 1970s (admittedly within the contours of the SALT II agreed force levels), a school of strategic experts argued that the motivations and intentions of the Soviet Union differed significantly from those of the United States.[89] With their own worldview, history, and (most importantly) perception of the impact of nuclear weapons, the Soviet military and political leaders did not see the world or the strategic environment in the same way that U.S. leaders did. Basing their assessments of Soviet intentions on Soviet behavior, including its ongoing strategic buildup, considerable investments in extensive air and civil defenses, and maintenance of a domestic political system based upon rigid and forceful Party control, these experts argued that the United States' policies were ill suited to deter an adversary that it did not understand. For these experts, the question of "What deters?" became the central question.[90] The presumed answer was that assured societal destruction, as terrible as the prospect may have been for American audiences, was not a threat sufficient to deter an adversary that was prepared to prosecute and win a protracted nuclear war.[91]

This approach has important implications for addressing not only the challenge of extended deterrence, but also the more basic matter of general, direct deterrence. In terms of the former, the availability of diverse, flexible limited nuclear options, as well as formidable conventional forces, is essential for maintaining the capacity to prevent escalation from a local conflict to a larger nuclear exchange. With respect to the latter, it would have been folly to accept a rough numerical equality that allowed the Soviets to improve the quality of their forces. Any perceived strategic stability that was achieved in the SALT process placed the United States at a significant disadvantage, as the ICBM vulnerability issue underscored.[92] Rather, an effective deterrent against a risk-acceptant, cost-tolerant adversary like the Soviet Union required both U.S. quantitative superiority and employment policies that held at risk what the Soviet leadership truly valued: its strategic forces, its military infrastructure, the sources of its political control over Russian society, and its leadership.[93] Although many of the experts who developed this view of deterrence found support in the Reagan administration, pressures to move away from a strict reliance on assured destruction influenced the development of LNOs and debates on preferred targeting packages in the Nixon, Ford, and Carter administrations, as noted previously.[94]

The Political Influence of Nuclear Weapons

The nature of the political influence of nuclear weapons has been the subject of academic and policy debate for some time. Advocates of quantitative strategic nuclear superiority, expansive war-fighting capabilities, and highly flexible limited nuclear options often portray nuclear weapons as having important political effects on relations with both nuclear and non-nuclear states.[95] Conversely, skeptics of superiority, particularly those who advocate for a minimal or finite deterrence strategy, argue that the possession of nuclear weapons has very limited political effects. Such weapons may prove useful in preventing crises with other nuclear powers from escalating to nuclear conflicts, but they have little deterrent value beyond the clearly articulated and understood vital national interests of the state and almost no independent compellent value.[96]

Scholars and practitioners may disagree, but the history of the Cold War does not provide support for the argument that nuclear superiority provides significant political benefits.[97] Although nuclear weapons may have deterred an attack on the United States or on close allies like NATO and Japan, there is little empirical evidence for the argument that a larger arsenal translated into enhanced influence over political outcomes.[98] Clearly, context matters. Whereas advocates of superiority argue that it was the favorable strategic balance that drove Khrushchev to acquiesce during the Cuban missile crisis, an equally persuasive case can be made that he reversed the illicit attempt to deploy missiles in Cuba precisely because he understood that President Kennedy (and the American political and military establishment) viewed the situation as engaging vital U.S. national security interests, and thus that there was a real probability of escalation to nuclear conflict. Scholars have also examined the case of the 1973 Middle East Crisis, when the Soviet Union threatened to intervene in the Yom Kippur War to prevent Israel from destroying Egypt's encircled Third Army on the Sinai Peninsula.[99] After public and private recriminations between Washington and Moscow, President Nixon ordered U.S. nuclear forces for DEFCON 3, and a ceasefire was announced between Cairo and Tel Aviv soon afterward. Although some scholars have argued that President Nixon's escalation signaled a willingness to take military action in the event of a Soviet intervention, thus deterring Brezhnev from supporting Egypt, the historical record implies that the Soviets had little intention of intervening in the Arab-Israeli conflict. Any lessons of the 1973 crisis are less than apparent. Moreover, following the signing of the 1972 SALT I accords in Moscow, the Soviet Union had achieved numerical parity with the United States in strategic forces and, perhaps just as importantly, had recently concluded a diplomatic arrangement with its adversary that underscored its position as a superpower and cemented its image as an equal peer of the United States. In short, achieving parity does not seem to have made the Soviet Union more aggressive in challenging the United States in areas of perceived vital interests, like Europe or East Asia. As one important scholarly analysis of the role of nuclear weapons during the Cold War explains:

> Our analysis suggests that the balance went through three distinct phases. The first, 1948 to 1960, was a period of mounting American advantage. The second, 1961 to 1968, was characterized by a pronounced but declining American advantage. The third, 1968 to 1985, was an era of strategic parity. There is no positive correlation between shifts in Soviet assertiveness and shifts in the strategic balance. Soviet challenges were most pronounced in the late 1940s and early 1950s in central Europe and Korea and again in the late 1950s and early 1960s in Berlin and Cuba. A third, lesser period of assertiveness occurred from 1979 to 1982 in Africa and Afghanistan. The first and second peaks occurred at a time when the United States has unquestioned nuclear superiority. The third peak coincides with the period of strategic parity, before the years of the putative American "window of vulnerability."[100]

Nevertheless, the expansion of Soviet activity in the late 1970s, and specifically its intervention in Afghanistan and its support for insurgencies in Africa, has been by viewed by some experts as driven by a renewed confidence provided by a favorable "correlation of forces" vis-à-vis the United States and its allies. Thanks to the belief that U.S. power had declined in the wake of the Vietnam War, pressure mounted at the end of the 1970s for a renewed effort to address the perceived strategic advantages of the Soviet Union, undermining the conclusion of the SALT II Treaty and precipitating a buildup of strategic and conventional forces under the Carter and Reagan administrations. During this period, the Soviet deployment of the formidable SS-20 intermediate-range ballistic missile system created a crisis within NATO, leading to the Carter administration's "Dual Track Decision." This decision deployed two new systems to Europe, the Pershing II IRBM and the ground-launched cruise missile (GLCM), which were viewed as reestablishing the "Euro-strategic balance."[101] The hardline approach of the early Reagan administration, combined with the "Euromissile Crisis" and events of 1983 that included the accidental shooting down of Korean Airline Flight 007 by a Soviet fighter and the Soviet response to NATO's Able Archer Exercise, marked a dangerous nadir in U.S.-Soviet relations and stoked fears of a nuclear war.[102] At any rate, the political influence of nuclear weapons, beyond their ability to deter provocation and military aggression, remains a subject of significant debate.

The Contribution of Strategic Arms Control and Nonproliferation

Strategic arms control is widely viewed as an important complement to U.S. nuclear strategy. Although debates over the value and utility of strategic arms control agreements were frequent during the Cold War, cooperative agreements were useful in establishing shared expectations and decreasing uncertainty around the quantitative and qualitative aspects of the superpower arms race.[103] Given the nature of the superpower rivalry, it is perhaps unsurprising that a prerequisite for successful arms control was the presence of an effective capacity to monitor and verify agreements. Starting in the late 1960s, the United States was able to rely on extensive satellite technologies or unilateral national technical means of verification to assure Soviet compliance with arms control treaties.[104] Similarly, nonproliferation has been a major objective of U.S. national security policy for decades.

Strategic Arms Control

In the aftermath of the Cuban Missile Crisis, the United States and the Soviet Union implemented several important confidence-building measures, including the "hotline" agreement to link the two capitals in times of crisis. Washington and Moscow also concluded the Partial Test Ban Treaty in 1963. The process of reaching the first major strategic arms control agreement, SALT, spanned over fifteen years and resulted in two arms control treaties, SALT I and SALT II, although the latter was never ratified. The process was characterized by arduous negotiations between the United States and the Soviet Union over the qualities and quantities of their respective nuclear (strategic) arsenals. While the negotiations were initiated by the Johnson Administration, President Richard M. Nixon signed the SALT I accords with Soviet Premier Leonid Brezhnev in May 1972.[105] The centerpiece of the SALT I accords was the Anti-Ballistic Missile Treaty, in which the United States and the Soviet Union agreed to permanent, strict limitations on missile defense programs.[106] In addition, the superpowers concluded an Interim Agreement on Strategic Offensive Arms, in which the Soviet Union and the United States agreed to ceilings on offensive ballistic missile systems. The Nixon administration presented the accords as a major diplomatic achievement, and they did seem to provide two clear benefits. First, in first limiting and eventually proscribing national missile defense systems, the ABM Treaty allowed both superpowers to relax their efforts to achieve a breakthrough in strategic defenses and thus avoid a new and potentially destabilizing round of the arms race. Second, the limitations on offensive weapons seemed to acknowledge the importance of a relatively stable strategic balance, in which both countries could maintain a guaranteed second strike and thus an assured destruction capability in the face of a first strike.

In retrospect, the major failure of the SALT I accords was the inability of the superpowers to cooperatively address the challenge of MIRV technology.[107] This was in large part due to the U.S. refusal to broach or discuss MIRV restrictions. Initially developed by the United States as the most effective means of overcoming any future Soviet strategic defenses, MIRVs rapidly increased the number of deployed warheads in the U.S. arsenal. Developed in extreme secrecy and forcefully defended by military leaders as the Johnson administration laid the groundwork for the SALT negotiations, MIRV technology was essentially "off the table" in the view of the United States. A vague MIRV limitation was broached during the SALT negotiations in Geneva in 1970, but it was not treated seriously, and it seemed clear that the Soviets would not sign an agreement that prevented them from developing and deploying what was seen as a decisive weapon that would permit both a breakthrough in Soviet defenses and quantitative expansions of Soviet forces.

However, by the time President Nixon signed the SALT I accords, it appeared that the strategic balance had begun to shift in Moscow's favor. Soviet modernization had resulted in an expansion of land-based ICBMs and SLBMs. Part of the diplomatic victory of SALT for Nixon and Kissinger was constraining the expansion of Soviet strategic programs and maintaining a balance that fit with the notion of "sufficiency" advocated by Nixon. As discussed earlier, the (predictable) Soviet testing and planned deployment of MIRVs threatened the perceived balance and sparked an intense debate about the state of the U.S. deterrent in the mid- and late 1970s. To illustrate, so-called "heavy" Soviet missiles like the SS-9 and its successor the SS-18, which could carry higher numbers of MIRVs, were seen as a threat to the land-based leg of the United States strategic triad. Soon there were fears that a well-coordinated, disarming strike could knock out a significant portion of U.S. ICBMs, leaving Washington with the unenviable option using less-precise SLBMs to launch retaliatory strikes against Soviet cities, even if U.S. cities had not yet been hit. Under these conditions, would an American president be "self-deterred" from launching a second strike? Such worst-case scenarios populated the domestic debates within the United States as President Gerald Ford and Secretary Kissinger attempted to achieve a viable SALT II Treaty.[108]

Though it was never ratified by the United States Senate, SALT II, which was based on the Vladivostok Agreement signed by President Ford and Secretary Brezhnev in 1974, was effectively observed by both superpowers into the 1980s.[109] Focusing on the MIRV issue, as well as several other contentious holdovers from the SALT I negotiations like FBS and cruise missiles, SALT II is perhaps best known for introducing "counting rules" and ceilings and sub-ceilings for various offensive systems. The lack of stricter limitations was due in part to the difficulties inherent in monitoring any MIRV limitation with confidence. Moreover, the perceived qualitative challenge of the Soviets' "heavy" missiles made it necessary to allow the U.S. to modernize its ICBM force. SALT II, therefore, was essentially a coordination mechanism rather than an agreement that meaningfully limited or reduced the superpowers' arsenals. Frustration with this outcome contributed to President Carter's dramatic and ultimately futile offer of "deep cuts" in a revised SALT II, but given the deteriorating relationship between the U.S. and the Soviet Union, Moscow had little appetite for such an agreement.[110] It is unsurprising that the momentum behind arms control negotiations disappeared as relations between Washington and Moscow deteriorated in the late 1970s and early 1980s. Nevertheless, the Reagan administration maintained a dual track of negotiations with the Soviets, and although there was little progress during the course of President Reagan's first term, his efforts proved momentous in his second term after Secretary General Mikhail Gorbachev took power in the Soviet Union.

Though it pertained to theater nuclear weapons rather than strategic armaments, the Intermediate Nuclear Forces (INF) Treaty was a major control success. After years of negotiations, on December 8, 1987, President Reagan and Soviet General Secretary Gorbachev signed the INF Treaty in Washington, DC.[111] The treaty—formally the Treaty on the Elimination of Intermediate-Range and Shorter-Range Missiles—represented a major diplomatic achievement and signified the beginning of a transformation in the relationship between the United States and the Soviet Union and in the European security environment. Under the requirements of the treaty, an entire class of weapons was to be eliminated from the arsenals of both superpowers, marking the first time an arms control agreement actually removed weapons systems rather than instituting numerical limits. Intermediate-range (1,000–5,500 km) and shorter-range (500–1,000 km) missiles—both nuclear and conventionally armed—were both covered under the treaty obligations, leading to the destruction of 2,692 missiles, with their launchers, equipment, and support and basing facilities. Two formidable opposing medium-range ballistic missile systems, the U.S. Pershing II and the Soviet SS-20 as well as U.S. GLCMs were removed from the European theater and scrapped, setting the stage for an end to the Cold War in Europe.

To bolster U.S. national technical means of verification, a comprehensive Elimination Protocol established specific procedures for destruction so that the reconstitution of these missile forces would be effectively impossible. A production and test flight ban also prevented the development of new forces to replace those destroyed. To implement the treaty, the superpowers agreed to an extensive program of on-site inspections and the establishment of a Special Verification Commission to resolve any compliance problems. Thus, the treaty was both straightforward and comprehensive. It essentially codified a bargain of "global double-zero," which had been under consideration for years, eliminating the potential problem of mobile systems located in the eastern Soviet Union and in the United States that could be quickly reintroduced and also avoiding monitoring and verification problems by banning both nuclear and conventional systems of proscribed ranges.

The United States and Soviet Union also signed the Strategic Arms Reduction Treaty, START 1, in July 31, 1991.[112] President George H. W. Bush and Secretary Gorbachev agreed to large cuts in deployed warheads and delivery vehicles, including ICBMs and strategic bombers. The superpowers agreed to a limit of 6,000 deployed warheads, with sublimits on so-called heavy missiles and mobile ICBMs to address the perceived problem of MIRVs and the verification challenges of mobile missiles, and a total of 1,600 deployed strategic nuclear delivery vehicles. Further reductions proved more difficult to achieve, largely because Russia experienced difficulties in the 1990s. A follow-on agreement, START II, was signed in 1992 but never went into force.[113]

In Moscow in May 2002, the George W. Bush administration signed the Strategic Offensive Reduction Treaty (SORT), which further reduced the deployed warheads to a range of 1,700–2,200 but placed no specific limitation on the mix of delivery vehicles.[114] Signaling a new relationship with Russia, the Bush Administration argued that the more formal, structured Cold War agreements with extensive counting rules were unnecessary in the new security environment. Perhaps more importantly, the Bush administration decided to unilaterally withdraw from the 1972 ABM Treaty because of its perceived constraints on the development and deployment of U.S. national missile defenses.[115] Although Russia had attempted to keep the United States in the treaty, negotiations on mutually acceptable amendments failed.

Most recently, the so-called New START Treaty, signed by President Barack Obama and Russian President Dmitri Medvedev on April 8, 2010, in Prague, replaced both the START I treaty, which expired in December 2009, and the SORT Treaty.[116] The New START Treaty entered into force on February 5, 2011, after ratification by the United States Senate in 2010 and the Russian Duma in January 2011. Under New START, both states agreed to limits of 1,550 deployed warheads on 800 ICBMs, SLBMs, and heavy bombers.

As the record reflects, strategic arms control has played a significant role in contributing to U.S. national security since the middle of the Cold War and was vitally important in managing the most dangerous aspect of the superpower rivalry as the Cold War ended. The nuclear arsenals of the United States and the Russian Federation are far smaller than their Cold War predecessors. Nonetheless, pressures for further reductions persist. The New START Treaty remains in effect until 2021. It is unclear whether the Trump administration intends to extend the Treaty or work toward a follow-on agreement. The current strategic nuclear modernization plan of record is based upon the New START limitations, though various factors bode ill for cooperation: the United States' concern over the perceived violations of the INF Treaty and perception that Russia is increasingly willing to brandish and rely on its nuclear weapons, Russia's concerns about U.S. theater and national missile defense programs and strategic modernization, and the generally poor state of U.S.-Russia relations.

Nonproliferation

Even before the United States detonated the first atomic bomb, policymakers grappled with the prospect that nuclear weapons could spread to other states. There was overwhelming consensus within the scientific community and eventually across the political and military leadership of the Roosevelt and Truman administrations that the atomic bomb represented a truly revolutionary weapon system, fundamentally different from even the most powerful conventional weapons.[117] Perhaps more importantly, these leaders came to understand that nuclear weapons in the hands of other states would represent a catastrophic threat to the United States. Despite the traditional view of America as protected by large oceans, these leaders saw that the country's large, densely populated urban centers would be particularly vulnerable to devastation by nuclear weapons in a future war. This thinking drove policy decisions in the immediate postwar period and in the negotiations over the fledgling United Nations.[118]

However, two very different and seemingly paradoxical policies emerged from this consensus on the nature of nuclear weapons and their potential future proliferation. The first, driven by the scientific and (later) the diplomatic communities, envisioned a robust international system of monitoring and verification that could support the development of peaceful civilian uses of atomic energy and also the complete, foolproof prevention of the development of nuclear weapons, under the auspices of the United Nations.[119] The approach was premised on a clear understanding that the peaceful use of atomic energy could have great benefits and an acknowledgment that the diffusion of nuclear technology and know-how could not be blocked or effectively restrained. Thus, the optimal approach was the construction of a regime that could manage and control the diffusion of technological knowledge and support the peaceful research and exploitation of atomic energy, in return for a concrete guarantee that states would forego the opportunity to build atomic weapons and accept the intrusive safeguards and surveillance mechanisms that would be necessary to monitor that guarantee. The ideas developed by leading technical and diplomatic minds in the Truman administration were captured in the Acheson-Lilienthal Plan, which was revised and eventually presented as "the Baruch Plan" in the negotiations on the development of the United Nations Atomic Energy Commission in New York in 1946.[120]

The stark alternative, advocated by military and some defense leaders, was to launch a campaign to prevent the Soviet Union from achieving nuclear weapons and thus remove the unacceptable threat that Soviet nuclear weapons would pose to the survival of the United States.[121] Support for this policy grew within the Truman administration as the Soviet Union's intentions seemed to become more aggressive and its policies more provocative, with a consequent deterioration in Washington-Moscow relations in 1946 and 1947. Ultimately, the military option was dismissed from serious consideration because of moral reservations expressed by Truman's senior advisors and material constraints on the U.S. capacity to execute an effective preventive campaign against the

Soviet Union. Among Truman's defense and military advisors, however, the hardline approach was often supported alongside the seemingly contradictory impulse toward cooperation in the United Nations.[122]

Driven by the acute threat of nuclear proliferation, these contradictory policy impulses shaped the U.S. approach to the challenge of nuclear proliferation and have consistently influenced the development of national security policy throughout the administrations of both parties since Truman's advisors first grappled with this critical challenge in the mid-1940s.[123] These conflicting policy impulses have manifested in different ways. U.S. administrations have seriously considered the use of preventive military force to destroy nuclear programs while at the same time offering the prospect of cooperation. Perhaps most importantly, despite the superpower rivalry, Washington was willing to work with Moscow, its existential adversary, to prevent the spread of nuclear weapons to other countries at the height of the Cold War.[124] The United States also been has been willing to bully and threaten allies to prevent proliferation. All of these seemingly incoherent policies were driven by two simple fears: that the United States was uniquely vulnerable to nuclear weapons, and that the spread of nuclear weapons was antithetical to U.S. national security interests. The centerpiece of U.S. nonproliferation efforts was the successful negotiation of the NPT, which was signed by the United States and the Soviet Union in July 1968. It entered into force in March 1970. The subsequent development of the Nuclear Suppliers Group and the Zangger Committee and the establishment of Nuclear Weapons Free Zones further limited the spread of nuclear weapons.[125]

It is difficult to argue that the Nonproliferation Regime has been anything but a major success. In March 1963, President John F. Kennedy feared that as many as twenty-five states would possess nuclear weapons by the 1980s. Nonetheless, only four states (India, Pakistan, North Korea, and Israel) beyond the five nuclear weapons states that make up the Permanent Five of the United Nations Security Council have acquired nuclear weapons—a fact that is evidence of this success. Moreover, the strength of the Nonproliferation Regime over time is reflected in the reversal of the South African nuclear weapons program, the successful negotiation of the Lisbon Protocol, the removal of nuclear weapons from the former Soviet states of Ukraine, Belarus, and Kazakhstan, the accession of states like Argentina and Brazil to the NPT, and the barriers that have confounded proliferators like Iraq, Libya, and Iran. This is not to say that the NPT has been an unqualified success. The uncovering of the AQ Khan network, the discovery of Iraq's progress toward a nuclear capability in the aftermath of the 1991 Gulf War, and the existence of a substantial number of latent nuclear powers in possession of civilian nuclear and industrial capabilities that would allow for "crash programs" in relatively short periods are reminders that challenges persist.

In the wake of President Obama's embrace of a world without nuclear weapons in his Prague speech, the subsequent New START Treaty, and the Nuclear Security Conference initiatives, many global civil society organizations viewed the goal of "global zero" as achievable. Notably, President Obama did not envision the abolition of nuclear weapons "in his lifetime," and he committed to the modernization of the U.S. nuclear arsenal to obtain the ratification of New START. His administration, however, was keenly attuned to the threat of nuclear terrorism, as evidenced by the 2010 NPR. It also emphasized Negative Security Assurances for states that met their NPT obligations and expressed support for the CTBT. Multilateral nonproliferation diplomacy won a significant though temporary victory when the Obama administration, the so-called P-5+1 (the United Nations Security Council members and the European Union), and Tehran concluded the Joint Comprehensive Plan of Action (JCPOA) to eliminate the most troubling components of Iran's nuclear program and impose a robust verification and compliance regime on its civilian program.[126]

The international security environment has deteriorated since that point, however, and the relative salience of Russian, Chinese, and even North Korean nuclear weapons has increased in U.S. national security. The early optimism of the Obama administration's "Prague Agenda" dissipated, and efforts to re-engage Moscow stalled, even as unilateral efforts like ratifying the CTBT and embracing a No First Use Doctrine were deemed politically infeasible.[127] More recently, the Trump administration's NPR has explicitly supported a more central role for nuclear weapons and a potential expansion of capabilities in response to the embrace of more competitive strategies by both Russia and China. It has also decertified the JCPOA with Iran and downgraded the United States' nonproliferation commitments.

These apparent setbacks, along with the United States' and Russia's failures to make progress toward nuclear disarmament as mandated in Article VI of the NPT, have led civil society organizations and a coalition of non-nuclear weapons states (NNWS) to press for negotiation on a multilateral treaty to ban nuclear weapons. Transnational nongovernmental organizations (NGOs) like the International Campaign to Abolish Nuclear Weapons (ICAN) and states including Mexico, Ireland, Brazil, and Austria succeeded in passing the Treaty on the Prohibition of Nuclear Weapons in July 2017.[128] No nuclear weapons states took part in the negotiations, and none of the United States' extended deterrent partners participated, with the exception of the Netherlands. Although the "Ban Treaty" has not received the necessary state signatures to enter into force, and although the nuclear weapons states will not be bound by it when it does, it enjoys significant popular support in many of the allied states under the U.S. nuclear umbrella. In light of the movement toward removing U.S. nonstrategic nuclear weapons in several key NATO allies in recent years, this treaty may pose a growing challenge to alliance management.

These four critical questions, which have shaped debates on the role of nuclear weapons since the early Cold War, provide a number of important criteria with which to assess nuclear strategies for the United States in this era of geopolitical and technological change. Before discussing these criteria, the discussion will briefly turn to two key capabilities related to the strategic nuclear arsenal that were debated during the Cold War and have assumed greater salience in the post-Cold War environment.

KEY RELATED CAPABILITIES

Strategic Defenses

Antiballistic missile defense systems have been viewed as a potentially decisive application almost from the time offensive missiles emerged as a central application of the post-World War II strategic environment.[129] The United States began experimenting with ABM technology in the mid-1950s, with little success. The Soviet Union also invested in the development of strategic defenses and appeared to be making progress. The Tallinn line system, which was viewed as either a primitive ABM system or a more advanced air defense network, caused deep concern within the United States defense establishment, and ultimately served as a major driver of what would become the American MIRV program.

The United States delayed the deployment of ABM technology precisely because of the relative surplus of security provided by the offensive superiority of the Kennedy strategic buildup. The difficulties inherent in the development of an effective area defense capability were understood early, and initial concerns about the potential impact of an effective Soviet ABM system influenced U.S. planners to focus on penetration aids in future offensive systems to overcome or overwhelm any strategic defenses that could be deployed. The technology essential to ballistic missile technology seemed to favor the offensive.

By 1967, pressure had mounted within the Johnson defense department, particularly among the uniform military leadership, to deploy a system, even if it was limited in scope. Secretary McNamara, along with the civilian leadership of the Department of Defense (DOD) and the majority of the scientific advisors in the Johnson administration, felt that the deployment of ABM would not improve the United States' position and would only undermine the system of assured destruction and stable deterrence between the superpowers. When, in September 1967, Secretary McNamara announced the administration's decision to deploy the Sentinel ABM system, it was presented as a "thin" system, focused on countering the emerging Chinese threat, the problem of accidental launches, and possible blackmail attempts.[130]

After assessing the state of U.S. force posture and readiness at the outset of the administration, the Nixon administration opted to transform the thin, Chinese-focused Sentinel ABM program into Safeguard. Although the ABM deployment was limited, military planners viewed the fundamental mission of Safeguard as maintaining the credibility of the U.S. deterrent posture by protecting the land-based ICBM component of the strategic triad against Soviet attack.[131] However, with the signing of the SALT I Treaty in Moscow on May 21, 1972, and specifically the ABM Treaty, the superpowers agreed to forego a race for strategic defenses. Together with the subsequent 1974 agreement to limit each nation to one rather than two ABM sites, this treaty removed an important category of competition from the arms race.

In the late 1970s, as the Soviet Union appeared to continue building and qualitatively improving its offensive forces in the context of the ongoing SALT II negotiations, the issue of U.S. ballistic missile defenses remerged. Strategic defenses returned to the center of the national security stage in March 1983, when President Reagan gave a speech outlining a grandiose vision of a shield against ICBMs that would protect the United States and render Soviet missiles useless.[132] Based upon a large, complex constellation of space-based assets that could identify, track, and ultimately destroy ICBMs in the upper atmosphere, the Strategic Defense Initiative (SDI), or "Star Wars," fundamentally changed the debate over ballistic missile defenses in the United States. Although it is not clear that either President Reagan or his advisors viewed the large-scale area defense as feasible anytime soon, SDI was viewed as an important step forward by advocates of war-fighting strategies.[133] A true damage limitation capability is impossible to achieve with offensive forces alone;

at least some capacity to intercept the residual forces of an adversary after the majority of its arsenal has been destroyed is essential. Although little real progress was made on the program, and strategic arms control agreements with Moscow soon took priority, the announcement of the SDI program altered the contours of the domestic political discussion on missile defenses. Support for missile defense took hold within much of the Republican Party establishment, and although the salience of missile defense declined in the immediate aftermath of the collapse of the Soviet Union, support for missile defenses to address the emerging challenge of missile proliferation and WMD grew in the 1990s.[134] It was thus unsurprising that the George W. Bush administration decided to unilaterally withdraw from the 1972 ABM treaty. Although the public messaging surrounding the decision was focused on assuaging Russians' fears about the relevance of their strategic deterrent, the subsequent deployment of interceptors in Fort Greely, Alaska and Fort Vandenberg, California, as well as large radar and support structures, underscored a renewed U.S. interest in ABM defense. Moscow and Beijing (among others) now view the U.S. vision of "layered, multi-tiered, missile defenses" as a growing reality, considering the United States' large-scale investments in theater missile defenses in the shape of Aegis-capable Destroyers and Cruisers, primarily devoted to the defense of fleets and aircraft carriers; its Theater High Altitude Area Defense (THAAD) forward deployed in the Republic of Korea; and the deployment of a NATO Phased Adaptive Approach in Eastern Europe to address the growing threat of Iranian IRBMs.[135] Today, the question of whether strategic defenses truly remain limited to addressing specific threats such as North Korea or Iran is particularly pressing. In the debate on the modernization of offensive strategic forces, advocates of more expansive strategic defenses argue that they would rely upon space-based assets that could address larger threats like China and perhaps even Russia. Ultimately, policymakers must consider whether costly investments in strategic defenses improve the security of the United States, perhaps providing some measure of damage limitation against smaller nuclear powers, or whether the attempt to achieve effective ballistic missile defense undermines the deterrent of major nuclear powers, driving them to rectify perceived vulnerabilities, and taking action that leaves the United States worse off.[136] This vitally important question should be considered closely alongside alternative nuclear strategies and force structures.

Nonstrategic Nuclear Weapons

As discussed earlier, during the Cold War, the United States deployed a variety of tactical or "battlefield" nuclear weapons to Europe.[137] Precisely because of the perceived imbalance of conventional forces in favor of the Warsaw pact, it was important to prepare for a first use of tactical nuclear weapons by NATO to prevent a catastrophic defeat and maintain some measure of control over the conflict without being forced to resort to a strategic attack on the Soviet Union, which would likely escalate to a large-scale exchange. Tactical nuclear weapons were also viewed as a means of linking the U.S. strategic deterrent to NATO's defense. The possibility of a graduated response was never viewed favorably by the European allies, as it would likely have meant fighting a nuclear conflict in Europe. More basically, there was a debate about whether tactical nuclear weapons were useful in deterring provocation in the first place.[138] The mere presence of tactical weapons meant that any provocation would almost certainly escalate, thus providing a highly credible deterrent. The number and kind of deployed weapons, therefore, mattered less than the mere fact of their deployment. Conversely, skeptics worried that the Soviet Union was much more willing and able than the U.S. to fight a nuclear war (or a largely conventional conflict with tactical nuclear weapons), and thus they viewed the expansion and enhancement of U.S. and NATO conventional military forces as the most effective means of deterrence.[139] Although the Cold War ended without a conflict in Europe, the investment in enhancing U.S. conventional military capabilities led to several innovations, such as precision-guided munitions, that provided the foundation for American conventional dominance in the subsequent two decades.[140]

Many of the deployed tactical nuclear weapons were removed imme-
diately after the conclusion of the Cold War and scrapped under the
Presidential Nuclear Initiatives under President George H.W. Bush.[141]
Today, the United States maintains approximately 150 B61 gravity bombs
for use with dual-capable strike aircraft at six bases in Europe. NATO has
consistently reaffirmed its commitment to nuclear weapons, particularly
in light of Russian aggression in Georgia and Ukraine. However, within
many Western European polities, there is strong support for the removal
of nuclear weapons. The B61-12 gravity bomb, which is programmed to
be deployed to Europe with new fifth-generation strike aircraft like the
U.S. F-35A Joint Strike Fighter, has emerged as a controversial capability,
given its estimated costs and the relatively limited role of tactical nuclear
weapons in U.S. policy. Its development has progressed, however, and its
eventual deployment has been accepted by the NATO allies. This is an
important related issue for U.S. nuclear strategy and will be considered
in the assessment of the proposed alternatives.

Criteria for Assessing Alternative Nuclear Strategies

Revisiting the critical debates concerning the role of nuclear weapons
in the Cold War and post-Cold War environments makes it possible to
distill a set of criteria and key issues with which to assess alternative
nuclear strategies and force structures.

Force Structure and Force Employment

The quantitative force levels of the U.S. strategic arsenal will necessarily
play a significant role in the contribution of nuclear weapons to U.S.
national security strategy. The size and diversification of U.S. strategic
forces will largely determine the kinds of missions that can be accomplished and the employment policy that will be available to U.S. leaders.
As discussed previously, each leg of the strategic triad provides a specific
capability, and together they form a complementary hedge against a

failure of one leg to achieve its primary mission.[142] As the most survivable leg, the SSBN force and its MIRVed SLBM inventory provide a virtually invulnerable retaliatory capacity. The strategic bomber force enhances immediate deterrence in the event of a crisis, signaling American resolve in a graduated and controlled way, without introducing first-strike dynamics that could undermine stability. The land-based ICBM force confers the ability to strike promptly anywhere around the globe, and it confronts an adversary with a target that must be addressed in any large-scale conflict (the so-called warhead sponge function). Depending on the quantitative levels of each component, the United States may be capable of devising and implementing several strategies. At the very least, the current triad, or even a proportionally reduced triad, would be capable of executing an assured retaliation mission. Although the United States has consistently refused to embrace a countervalue mission that would deliberately target civilian population areas, even a reduced force would be capable of inflicting unacceptable societal damage on an adversary. The number of warheads dedicated to the SSBN force is sufficient to devastate even larger peer competitors. The current force structure is also likely to be sufficient to effectively execute a counterforce mission against its competitors. As some experts have argued, given the quantitative imbalance of forces vis-à-vis China, the United States may currently possess the capacity to disarm Beijing, severely degrading its deterrent forces in a disarming first strike. Russia presents a more difficult challenge, given the number of mobile missile systems that would be targeted. Importantly, the current level of forces also seems to be sufficient to hedge against a breakout by either Russia or China for the foreseeable future. Whether these missions would remain achievable in the context of a significant further reduction of quantitative levels or a shift away from the strategic triad is an important question that is considered in the following chapters.

For more ambitious offensive counterforce missions that would likely be incorporated within a damage-limitation or war-fighting strategy, quantitative increases may be necessary, but two related capabilities are also likely to play a critical role: the effectiveness and capacity of strategic defenses and the availability of a relatively large and diverse stock of nonstrategic nuclear weapons.

In addition to quantity and quality of deployed nuclear forces, two key elements of U.S. strategic capabilities are often overlooked in discussions about nuclear modernization: the effectiveness, resilience, and reliability of U.S. NC3 networks, as well as critical infrastructure like early warning and alert systems, and the underlying nuclear weapons development complex that is managed primarily by the U.S. DOE. Both of these vital national assets have eroded due to neglect and lack of resources since the end of the Cold War, and as mentioned in the introduction, both should be considered fundamental priorities moving forward, perhaps even more pressing than the development, acquisition, and deployment of offensive strategic forces.

Finally, the declaratory policy associated with a given alternative strategy plays an important role in shaping the expectations and views of adversaries, allies, and other states. Although formal declaratory policy and employment policy (targeting) have diverged at times in the history of the United States' strategic policy, declaratory policy is often viewed as an important signal of U.S. intentions.

Deterrence of Adversaries and Reassurance of Allies

As the previous discussion of strategic debates indicates, the question of "what deters" was central to views of the efficacy and sufficiency of planned and deployed U.S. strategic nuclear forces (and of strategic defenses and tactical and theater nuclear weapons) throughout the Cold War.[143] Unsurprisingly, this debate did not end with the collapse of the Soviet Union. The role of nuclear weapons in the deterrence of new threats to U.S. national security and the security of its allies remains a hotly contested issue. At the same time, as the famous Healey theorem shows, devising the necessary types of forces and diplomatic and political commitments to effectively assure allies was exceedingly difficult during the Cold War and remains so today. With the return of great power competition, key allies in Europe and East Asia rely on the United States for security against threats from revisionist Russia and China, respectively. The emergence of new regional nuclear powers like North Korea and Iran also creates deterrence and reassurance challenges for the United States.[144] In the face of more risk-acceptant and less rational leaders, debates over the nature of the deployed capabilities that are necessary to address them have become increasingly prominent. Predicated on differing views of the difficulty of deterring actors, experts and policymakers have offered alternative means of dealing with these regional nuclear powers. The underlying challenge of achieving a balance between effective deterrence and reassurance of allies also invites consideration of the effect of deployed systems on strategic stability and the perceived value of such stability.

Strategic Stability

During the Cold War superpower relationship, leaders in Washington and (to some extent) Moscow developed the concept of strategic stability. New arms programs and negotiated arms control agreements are evaluated for their effect on the relationship between the two superpowers and whether such action as the deployment of new weapons would create incentives for the adversary to consider launching a first strike.[145] There have been frequent disagreements about the importance and desirability of strategic stability as a goal or objective of U.S. policy. Typically, academic experts and arms control advocates, who generally view the world in terms of security dilemmas or spiral models, view with disfavor the acquisition of new weapons that could instill fear in peer competitors and drive them to acquire similar or better systems.[146] The logic is that unilateral efforts to achieve superiority are not only futile, but also dangerous for America's security. Moreover, other states may perceive U.S. efforts as hostile and selfish, leading them to embrace more competitive policies that, again, make the United States worse off.

To be precise, there are typically two distinct concepts that contribute to what may be considered "strategic stability." These concepts are *crisis* (or first strike) stability and *arms race* stability.[147] The former concept relates to the impact of a weapons system or the deployment of troops or materiel on the existing security environment, which accounts for both the number of forces or relevant actors and the prevailing trends in military technology. In short, the effect of a given weapons system on crisis stability boils down to whether it makes the political-military leadership on either side (or both sides) more likely to launch a preventive or preemptive first strike in the event of a diplomatic crisis. Certain weapons, due to their unique characteristics, may be especially useful in a first strike, or conversely may be more vulnerable to actions by an adversary, creating a "use them or lose them" pressure on leaders. The balance has shifted over time, but typically systems that are perceived as both valuable and vulnerable, particularly in the early phases of a military campaign, are seen as "destabilizing." They are thus opposed by a segment of experts because their mere presence may increase the likelihood of a conflict if a serious crisis erupts. In recent years, forward-deployed systems that could be targeted in the early stages of a conflict are typically viewed as destabilizing.[148]

In contrast, systems that are perceived as survivable (whether because they can be deployed in hardened bunker facilities or because they are mobile or otherwise hidden) are viewed as contributing to stability. These systems could ostensibly survive a first strike and remain viable.[149] Thus, decision-makers would have little pressure to use them in the event of an escalation of tensions in a diplomatic crisis or even during a perceived attack.

Arms race stability is reduced when the introduction of a new weapon into an adversarial relationship would push the adversary to seek to acquire that system in similar or greater numbers.[150] Conversely, the presence of arms race stability implies that neither side has an incentive to acquire new weapons. Whereas the model of an action-reaction dynamic captures a theoretical arms race, the reality of the Cold War often indicated an arms race dynamic in which the Soviets and then the Americans overreacted to the programs of their opponent.[151] Whether or not there was a real "missile gap" in late 1950s, the unambiguous buildup of the United States in the early 1960s expanded U.S. superiority, which led to a concerted Soviet buildup from the mid-1960s to the mid-1970s. The qualitative improvement of Soviet forces with the achievement of MIRV technology sparked intense fears within the U.S. defense community, as evidenced by the ICBM vulnerability episode, leading to the United States' second major buildup in the late 1970s and 1980s. This buildup in turn led to the fielding of advanced weapons (MX, Trident, B-2) that were far ahead of what the Soviets had built, thus undermining the confidence of Soviet military leaders and stoking fears of a U.S. first-strike capability in the mid-1980s.

Strategic Arms Control and Nonproliferation

As noted earlier, strategic arms control played an important complementary role in U.S. national security throughout the Cold War and was vitally important in bringing about its conclusion. At the same time, arms control has certain limitations and is predicated on the relations between the parties. The United States and Russia are currently observing the limitations of the New START Treaty, which restricts the number of deployed warheads to 1550, a major reduction from the Cold War peak. However, as discussed previously, the movement toward further mutual reductions that was being considered by the Obama administration stalled, as relations with Moscow declined during Obama's second term. The Trump administration has already announced its plan to formally withdraw from the INF Treaty in response to persistent Russian violations and a refusal by Moscow to return to compliance. The Trump administration will have to decide whether it will agree to negotiate a follow-on agreement to New START or perhaps extend the treaty before its expiration in 2021. It can be extended for an additional five years with the agreement of both parties.[152]

Choices related to the nature of strategic force levels may facilitate or hinder future arms control agreements. Whether such agreements should be a priority for the United States remains an open question, and given the current relations with Russia, it is not clear that further cooperation can be achieved. Moreover, with the expansion of other nuclear weapons programs, the country faces the larger question of whether bilateral strategic arms control remains a useful tool of U.S. foreign and security policy. A shift toward multilateral strategic arms control may be logical, but it would also be extremely difficult and complex, given the diversity of interests, capabilities, and geopolitical positions of the erstwhile participants.

In assessing U.S. nuclear strategy, and particularly the implications of choices concerning force structure and declaratory policy, the impact on American nonproliferation goals should be considered. Different experts value a robust nonproliferation regime differently. Some policymakers and experts view the NPT as a success, having limited the spread of new programs, while others have less concern for the health of the regime and would prefer a more unilateral and forceful emphasis on counterproliferation. To some extent, these divergences over policy occur because of differing perceptions of the efficacy and appropriateness of multilateral versus unilateral action in the international realm. Underlying this divergence, however, is a shared belief that the proliferation of nuclear weapons constitutes an existential threat to the United States. Therefore, with regard to the modernization of U.S. nuclear weapons, several important questions arise. What effect does modernization have on international audiences and their views on the U.S. commitment to Article VI of the NPT? Similarly, what are the respective roles of U.S. nuclear weapons, as formally stated in U.S. declaratory policy? Do these roles limit or expand the perceived utility of (or reliance upon) nuclear weapons in U.S. national security?

Program Costs

Although military capabilities should ideally be fielded to achieve vital national security objectives irrespective of cost, the current nuclear modernization program of record, currently estimated to cost approximately $1.2 trillion over the next thirty years, has already faced financial pressure.[153] The Trump administration was successful in passing a defense budget, the 2016 National Defense Authorization Act (NDAA), which alleviated the enforced cuts to defense spending that had been planned under the Budget Control Act, otherwise known as "sequestration." Without further legislation, however, those automatic cuts are due to return in 2020. There is consensus that nuclear modernization is an important defense priority, but many key conventional procurement programs are also underway, and the Joint Chiefs of Staff have expressed serious concern about readiness levels after two decades of conflict in Afghanistan and Iraq. Thus, the nuclear modernization program is viewed by some as likely to crowd out other defense spending priorities, and the issue is likely to continue to be a source of contention in the future.[154]

This chapter has presented four major debates that shaped the development of U.S. strategic nuclear forces during the Cold War. Considering these important questions and the different approaches of policymakers, experts, and scholars provides a basis for developing a set of criteria for assessing alternative nuclear strategies and force structures for the United States in the current era of geopolitical and technological uncertainty. Before assessing these strategies, the next chapter will briefly consider the security environment confronting the United States and the key issues that leaders must address to formulate an optimal nuclear strategy.

NOTES

1. Scott D. Sagan, *Moving Targets: Nuclear Strategy and National Security* (Princeton, NJ: Princeton University Press, 1989), 4.
2. On the status of the Treaty, see https://www.un.org/disarmament/wmd/nuclear/tpnw/.
3. Ivo Daalder and Jan Lodal, "The Logic of Zero: Toward a World Without Nuclear Weapons," *Foreign Affairs* 87, no. 6 (November/December 2008): 80-95; Charles D. Ferguson, "The Long Road to Zero: Overcoming Obstacles to a Nuclear-Free World," *Foreign Affairs* 89, no. 1 (January/February 2010): 86-94.
4. Steven Pifer, "Obama's Faltering Nuclear Legacy: The 3 R's," *Washington Quarterly* 38, no. 2 (Summer 2015): 101–118; C. Raja Mohan, "Prague as the Nonproliferation Pivot," *The Washington Quarterly* 36, no. 2 (Summer 2013): 109-122.
5. Elbridge Colby, *Prevailing in Limited Wars* (Washington, DC: Center for a New American Security, 2016); Jeffrey A. Larsen and Kerry M. Kartchner (eds.), *On Limited Nuclear War in the 21st Century* (Stanford, CA: Stanford University Press, 2014).
6. Sagan, *Moving Targets*, 4–5.
7. Keith B. Payne, "The Nuclear Posture Review: Setting the Record Straight," *Washington Quarterly* 28, no. 3 (Summer 2005): 135–151.
8. Madelyn Creedon, "A Question of Dollars and Sense: Assessing the 2018 Nuclear Posture Review," *Arms Control Today* (March 2018).
9. *Nuclear Posture Review 2018* (Washington: Department of Defense, 2018): 34.
10. Robert Jervis termed the contrary impulses attempts to "escape" mutually assured destruction in *The Illogic of American Nuclear Strategy* (Ithaca: Cornell University Press, 1984): 47-56.
11. There is no neat dividing line here. Within the policy community there are also significant differences. For discussions, see: Michael Krepon, *Strategic Stalemate: Nuclear Weapons and Arms Control in American Politics* (New York: Palgrave Macmillan, 1986); Graham T. Allison, Albert Carnesale, and Joseph S. Nye (eds.) *Hawks, Doves, & Owls: An Agenda for Avoiding Nuclear War* (New York: W. W. Norton & Company, 1985): 206-222;

12. Bernard Brodie, *The Absolute Weapon: Atomic Power and World Order* (New York: Harcourt Brace, 1946); *Strategy in the Missile Age* (Princeton: Princeton University Press, 1959); "The Anatomy of Deterrence," *World Politics*, 11, no. 2 (January 1959): 173-191.

13. Robert L. Jervis, *The Meaning of the Nuclear Revolution: Statecraft and the Prospect of Armageddon* (Ithaca: Cornell University Press, 1989); Michael Mandelbaum, *The Nuclear Revolution: International Politics Before and After Hiroshima* (Cambridge: Cambridge University Press, 1980);

14. Bernard Brodie, "The Development of Nuclear Strategy," *International Security* 2, no. 4 (Spring 1978): 65-82, 2.

15. Thomas Schelling, *Arms and Influence* (New Haven: Yale University Press, 1966).

16. Jervis, *The Illogic of American Nuclear Strategy*, 146. Elsewhere e describes MAD "as a fact, not a policy" in *The Meaning of the Nuclear Revolution*, 74-106. Charles Glaser embraces a similar view of MAD as a "state of affairs" in *Analyzing Strategic Nuclear Policy* (Princeton: Princeton University Press, 1990): 281.

17. Because the Manhattan Project was such a tightly guarded secret, most senior military leaders were unaware of the program and little time and effort had been devoted to the potential implications of atomic weapons. One significant exceptions is: "'Foreign Policy Aspects of United States Development of Atomic Energy,' Memorandum by the Commanding General, Manhattan Engineer District (Groves), 2 January 1946,"*Foreign Relations of the United States* (Washington, DC: U.S. Government Printing Office, 1972): 1204-1207. In the early Cold War period, doctrine and targeting was driven by the rapidly increasing size of the arsenal. See: Richard K. Betts, "A Nuclear Golden Age? The Balance Before Parity," *International Security*, Vol. 11. No 3 (Winter 1986-1987): 3-32.

18. Fred Kaplan, *The Wizards of Armageddon* (New York: Simon & Schuster, 1984).

19. Albert Wohlstetter, "The Delicate Balance of Terror," Foreign Affairs 37, no. 2 (January 1959): 211-234.

20. Herman Kahn, *On Thermonuclear War* (Princeton: Princeton University Press, 1961).

21. Hans J. Morgenthau, "The Fallacy of Thinking Conventionally about Nuclear Weapons," David Carlton and Carlo Schaerf (eds.), *Arms Control and Technological Innovation* (New York: Halsted Press, 1976): 255-264.

22. Herman Kahn, *Thinking About the Unthinkable* (New York: Horizon Press, 1962).

23. John J. Mearsheimer, Conventional Deterrence (Ithaca:: Cornell University Press, 1983); Patrick M. Morgan, *Deterrence: A Conceptual Analysis* (Beverly Hills: Sage, 1977).

24. Kenneth N. Waltz, "Nuclear Myths and Political Realities," *American Political Science* Review 84, no. 3 (September 1990): 731-745.

25. Richard Pipes, "Why the Soviet Union Thinks It Can Fight and Win a Nuclear War," *Commentary* Vol. 64, no 1 (July 1977): 21-34.

26. Colin S. Gray, "War-Fighting for Deterrence," *Journal of Strategic Studies* 7, no. 1 (March 1984): 5-28

27. Colin S. Gray and Keith Payne, "Victory Is Possible," *Foreign Policy* 39 (Summer 1980), 14-27.

28. Colin S. Gray and Jeffrey C. Barlow, "Inexcusable Restraint: The Decline of American Military Power in the 1970s," *International Security* 10: 2 (Fall 1985), 27-69.

29. The "realist" school emerged after the Second World War. See, for example: Hans J. Morgenthau, *Politics Among Nations: The Struggle for Power and Peace* (Boston: McGraw-Hill, 1993); Edward Hallett Carr, The Twenty Years' Crisis: *An Introduction to the Study of International Relations* (New York: Harper & Row, 1964); Reinhold Niebuhr, *The Nature and Destiny of Man* (New York: Charles Scribner's Sons: 1949).

30. Robert Jervis, *Perception and Misperception in International Politics* (Princeton: Princeton University Press, 1976): 58-113.

31. Robert Jervis, "Cooperation under the Security Dilemma," *World Politics* 30, no. 2 (January 1978): 167-214; Charles L. Glaser, "The Security Dilemma Revisited," *World Politics* 50, no. 1 (October 1997), 171-201.

32. Stephen Van Evera, *Causes of War: Power and the Roots of Conflict* (Ithaca: Cornell University Press, 1999).

33. Jervis, *The Meaning of the Nuclear Revolution*, 29-38.

34. Gregg Herken, *Counsels of War* (New York: Alfred A. Knopf, 1985); Janne Nolan, *Guardians of the Arsenal: The Politics of Nuclear Weapons* (New York: HarperCollins, 1991).

35. Alain C. Enthoven and K. Wayne Smith, *How Much Is Enough? Shaping the Defense Program 1961–1969* (Santa Monica, CA: RAND Corporation, 2005).

36. Robert S. McNamara, *The Essence of Security* (New York: Harper and Row, 1969).

37. Robert Jervis, "Why Nuclear Superiority Doesn't Matter," *Political Science Quarterly* 94, no. 4 (Winter 1979–1980): 617–633.

38. Colin S. Gray, "Nuclear Strategy: The Case for a Theory of Victory," *International Security* 4, no. 1 (Summer 1979): 54–87.
39. Lawrence Freedman, *The Evolution of Nuclear Strategy*, 3rd ed. (New York: Palgrave MacMillan, 2003).
40. Henry A. Kissinger, *Nuclear Weapons and Foreign Policy* (New York: W. W. Norton & Company, 1969); Robert E. Osgood, *Limited War: The Challenge to American Strategy* (Chicago: University of Chicago Press, 1957); Robert E. Osgood, *Limited War Revisited* (Boulder, CO: Westview Press, 1979).
41. Jervis, *The Meaning of the Nuclear Revolution*, 23-38.
42. Robert Jervis, "Mutual Assured Destruction," *Foreign Policy* no. 133 (November/December 2002): 40–42; Robert Jervis, "The Madness beyond MAD-Current American Nuclear Strategy," *PS* (Winter 1984): 33–40.
43. Richard Ned Lebow and Janice Gross Stein, "Deterrence and the Cold War," *Political Science Quarterly* 110, no. 2 (Summer 1995): 157–181.
44. Colin S. Gray and Keith Payne, "Victory Is Possible," *Foreign Policy* 39 (Summer 1980): 14–27.
45. Alexander L. George, Philip J. Farley and Alexander Dallin (eds.) *U.S.-Soviet Security Cooperation: Achievements Failures Lessons* (Stanford: Stanford University Press, 1988); Albert Carnesale and Richard N. Haass (eds.), *Superpower Arms Control: Setting the Record Straight* (Cambridge: Ballinger Publishing Company, 1987).
46. Francis J. Gavin, "Strategies of Inhibition: U.S. Grand Strategy, the Nuclear Revolution and Nonproliferation," *International Security* 40, no. 1 (Summer 2015): 9–46.
47. This section is based on Lawrence Freedman, *The Evolution of Nuclear Strategy*; Desmond Ball and Jeffrey Richelson (eds.), *Strategic Nuclear Targeting* (Ithaca, NY: Cornell University Press, 1986); Aaron L. Friedberg, "The Evolution of U.S. Strategic Doctrine, 1945–1950," in Samuel P. Huntington (ed.), *The Strategic Imperative: New Policies for American Security* (Cambridge: Ballinger, 1982), 53-100.
48. Melvyn P. Leffler, *A Preponderance of Power: National Security, the Truman Administration, and the Cold War* (Stanford, CA: Stanford University Press, 1992).
49. Richard Rhodes, *Dark Sun: The Making of the Hydrogen Bomb* (New York: Touchstone, 1996).
50. John Lewis Gaddis, *Strategies of Containment: A Critical Appraisal of American National Security Policy During the Cold War* (Oxford: Oxford University Press, 2005).

51. Desmond Ball, *Politics and Force Levels: The Strategic Missile Program of the Kennedy Administration* (Berkeley: University of California Press, 1980).
52. Bruce J. Allyn, James G. Blight, and David A. Welch, "Essence of Revision: Moscow, Havana, and the Cuban Missile Crisis," *International Security* 14, no. 3 (Winter 1989–1990): 136–172.
53. David Holloway, *The Soviet Union and the Arms Race* (New Haven, CT: Yale University Press, 1983).
54. Herken, *Counsels of War*, 172-173; Nolan, *Guardians of the Arsenal*, 34-88.
55. Desmond Ball, "The Development of the SIOP, 1960–1983," in *Strategic Nuclear Targeting*, ed. Desmond Ball and Jeffrey Richelson (Ithaca, NY: Cornell University Press, 1986), 57–83.
56. Jerome H. Kahan, *Security in the Nuclear Age: Developing U.S. Strategic Arms Policy* (Washington, DC: Brookings Institution Press, 1975).
57. Ball, *Politics and Force Levels*, 50.
58. Enthoven and Smith, *How Much Is Enough?*, 165–196.
59. Ted Greenwood, *Making the MIRV: A Study in Defense Decisionmaking* (Lanham, MD: University Press of America, 1988); Ronald L. Tammen, *MIRV and the Arms Race: An Interpretation of Defense Strategy* (New York: Praeger Publishers, 1973).
60. Herken, Counsels of War, 202.
61. Kahan, Security in the Nuclear Age, 200-216.
62. Ibid., 219-223.
63. John Newhouse, *Cold Dawn: The Story of SALT* (New York: Holt, Rinehart and Winston, 1973); Fen Olser Hampson, "SALT I: Interim Agreement and ABM Treaty," in *Superpower Arms Control: Setting the Record Straight*, ed. Albert Carnesale and Richard N. Haass (Cambridge: Ballinger Publishing Company, 1987).
64. Nolan, *Guardians of the Arsenal*, 89-139.
65. Paul H. Nitze, "Deterring Our Deterrent," *Foreign Policy* 25 (Winter 1976–1977): 195–210.
66. Roger P. Labrie, ed., *SALT Handbook: Key Documents and Issues 1972–1979* (Washington, DC: American Enterprise Institute, 1980).
67. Brian Auten, *Carter's Conversion: The Hardening of American Defense Policy* (Columbia: University of Missouri Press, 2009).
68. Alton H. Quanbeck and Archie L. Wood, *Modernizing the Strategic Bomber Force: Why and How* (Washington, DC: Brookings Institution, 1976); John F. McCarthy, Jr., "The Case for the B-1 Bomber," *International Security* 1, no. 2 (Fall 1976): 78–97; Archie L. Wood, "Modernizing the

Strategic Bomber Force Without Really Trying—A Case Against the B-1," *International Security* 1, no. 2 (Fall 1976): 98–116.

69. Raymond L. Garthoff, *Détente to Confontation: American-Soviet Relations from Nixon to Reagan* (Washington, DC: Brookings Institution Press).

70. Lauren H. Holland and Robert A. Hoover, *The MX Decision: A New Direction in U.S. Weapons Procurement Policy?* (Boulder, CO: Westview Press, 1985).

71. Jan Lodal, "SICBM Yes, HML No," *International Security* 12, no. 2 (Fall 1987): 182–186.

72. Steven J. Zaloga, *The Kremlin's Nuclear Sword: The Rise and Fall of Russia's Strategic Nuclear Forces: 1948–2000* (Washington, DC: Smithsonian Books, 2002).

73. Richard K. Betters, "A Nuclear Golden Age? The Balance Before Parity," *International Security* 11, no. 3 (Winter 1986-1987): 3- 32; David Alan Rosenberg, "The Origins of Overkill: Nuclear Weapons and American Strategy, 1945-1960," *International Security* 7, no.4 (Spring 1983): 3-71.

74. Herken, *Counsels of War*, 200-2.

75. Much of this section is derived from discussion in Ball and Richelson, *Strategic Nuclear Targeting*; and Friedberg, "The Evolution of U.S. Strategic Doctrine, 1945–1950."

76. Scott D. Sagan, "SIOP-62: The Nuclear War Plan Briefing to President Kennedy," *International Security* 12, no. 1 (Summer 1987): 22–40.

77. Donald Brennan, "Strategic Alternatives: I," *The New York Times*, May 24, 1971.

78. Herken, *Counsels of War*, 266-269.

79. Lawrence Freedman, *Kennedy's Wars: Berlin, Cuba, Laos, and Vietnam* (Oxford: Oxford University Press, 200); Gaddis, *Strategies of Containment*, 197–234.

80. Kissinger, *Nuclear Weapons and Foreign Policy*; Osgood, *Limited War*; Osgood, *Limited War Revisited.*

81. Herman Kahn, *On Escalation: Metaphors and Scenarios* (Baltimore: Penguin Books, 1968).

82. Desmond Ball, "Control of Theater Nuclear War," *British Journal of Political Science* 19, no. 3 (July 1989): 302-327.

83. Wofgang K. H. Panofsky, "The Mutual Hostage Relationship Between American and the United States," *Foreign Affairs* 52:1 (October 1973): 109-118.

84. Herken, *Counsels of War*, 266-8.

85. Kahan, *Security in the Nuclear Age*, 223-224.

86. Terry Terriff, *The Nixon Administration and the Making of U.S. Nuclear Strategy* (Ithaca, NY: Cornell University Press, 1995).

87. Walter Slocombe, "The Countervailing Strategy," *International Security* 5, no. 4 (Spring 1981): 18-27.

88. Desmond Ball and Robert C. Toth, "Revising the SIOP: Taking War-Fighting to Dangerous Extremes," *International Security* 14, no. 4 (Spring 1990): 65-92.

89. Richard Pipes, "Why the Soviet Union Thinks It Can Fight and Win a Nuclear War," *Commentary* 64, no. 1 (July 1977): 21-34.

90. Spurgeon M. Keeny, Jr. and Wolfgang K. H. Panofsky, "Nuclear Weapons in the 1980s: MAD vs. NUTS," *Foreign Affairs* 60, no. 2 (Winter 1981-82) 287-304; Barry E. Carter, "The Strategic Debate in the United States," *Proceedings of the Academy of Political Science* 33, no. 1 (1978): 15-29; Bernard Brodie, "The Development of Nuclear Strategy," *International Security* 2:4 (Spring 1978).65-83; Ted Greenwood and Michael Nacht, "The New Nuclear Debate: Sense of Nonsense," *Foreign Affairs* 52, no. 4 (July 1974): 761-780.

91. Colin Gray, *Nuclear Strategy and Nuclear Style* (Lanham, MD: Hamilton Press, 1986).

92. Colin S. Gray, "The Strategic Forces Triad: The End of the Road?" *Foreign Affairs* 56, no. 4 (July 1978): 771–789.

93. Colin S. Gray, "War-Fighting for Deterrence," *Journal of Strategic Studies* 7 (March 1984): 5-28.

94. Lynn Etheridge Davis, *Limited Nuclear Options: Deterrence and the New American Doctrine*, Adelphi Paper 16, no. 121 (London: IISS, 1975/76).

95. Colin S. Gray and Jeffrey C. Barlow, "Inexcusable Restraint: The Decline of American Military Power in the 1970s," *International Security* 10, no. 2 (Fall 1985): 27–69.

96. Robert Art, "To What Ends Military Power?" *International Security* 4, no. 4 (Spring 1980): 3–35.

97. For recent analysis see Todd S. Sechser and Matthew Fuhrmann, *Nuclear Weapons and Coercive Diplomacy* (Oxford: Oxford University Press, 2017) and Matthew Kroenig, *The Logic of American Nuclear Strategy: Why Strategic Superiority Matters* (Oxford: Oxford University Press, 2018).

98. Richard Betts, *Nuclear Blackmail and Nuclear Balance* (Washington, DC: Brookings Institution, 1987).

99. Barry Blechman and Douglas Hart, "The Political Utility of Nuclear Weapons," *International Security* 7, no. 2 (Summer 1982): 132-156.

100. Lebow and Stein, "Deterrence and the Cold War," 173.

101. Garthoff, *Détente and Confrontaton*, 849–870.

102. Mark Ambinder, *The Brink: President Reagan and the Nuclear War Scare of 1983* (New York: Simon & Schuster, 2018).

103. Thomas C. Schelling and Morton H. Halperin, *Strategy and Arms Control* (Mansfield Center CT: Martino Publishing, 2014); James H. Lebovic, *Flawed Logics: Strategic Nuclear Arms Control from Truman to Obama* (Baltimore: Johns Hopkins University Press, 2013); George Bunn, *Arms Control by Committee: Managing Negotiations with the Russians* (Stanford, CA: Stanford University Press, 1992).

104. David W. Kearn, Jr., *Great Power Security Cooperation: Arms Control and the Challenge of Technological Change* (Lanham, MD: Lexington Books, 2015).

105. Newhouse, *Cold Dawn.*

106. Condoleezza Rice, "SALT and the Search for a Security Regime," in Alexander George, Philip J, Farley, and Alexander Dallin (eds.), *U.S.-Soviet Security Cooperation*, 293-306; Fen Osler Hampson, "SALT I: Interim Agreement and ABM Treaty," in Albert Carnesale and Richard N. Haass (eds.), *Superpower Arms Control*, 65-105.

107. Kearn, *Great Power Security Cooperation*, 157-201.

108. Labrie, *SALT Handbook.*

109. Stephen J. Flanagan, "SALT II," in Carnesale and Haass, *Superpower Arms Control*, 105-139.

110. Strobe Talbott, *Endgame: The Inside Story of SALT II* (New York: Harper & Row, 1979); Garthoff, *Détente and Confrontation*, 801–827.

111. Maynard W. Glitman, *The Last Battle of the Cold War: An Inside Account of Negotiating the Intermediate Range Nuclear Forces Treaty* (New York: Palgrave Macmillan, 2006); George L. Rueckert, *Global Double Zero: The INF Treaty from Its Origins to Implementation* (Westport, CT: Greenwood Press, 1993).

112. Kerry M. Kartchner, *Negotiating START: Strategic Arms Reduction Talks and the Quest for Strategic Stability* (New York: Transaction Publishers, 1991).

113. Strobe Talbot, "Why START Stopped," *Foreign Affairs* 67, no. 1 (Fall 1988): 49-69.

114. Amy F. Woolf, *Nuclear Arms Control: The Strategic Offensive Reductions Treaty* (Washington, DC: Congressional Research Service, 2011).

115. Stephen J. Hadley, "A Call to Deploy," *The Washington Quarterly* 23, no. 3 (Summer 2000): 95–108.

116. Rose E. Gottemoeller, "The Development and Ratification of New START," in *Challenges in U.S. National Security Policy: A Festschrift Featuring Edward L. (Ted) Warner*, ed. David Ochmanek and Michael Sulmeyer (Santa Monica, CA: RAND Corporation, 2014): 169–174.

117. Robert Jungk, *Brighter Than a Thousand Suns: A Personal History of the Atomic Scientists* (New York: Harcourt Brace, 1958); Richard Rhodes, *The Making of the Atomic Bomb* (New York: Simon & Schuster, 1986).

118. Kearn, *Great Power Security Cooperation*, 125-156.

119. Richard G. Hewlett, Oscar E. Anderson, Jr. *The New World, 1939–1946: A History of the United States Atomic Energy Commission Volume 1* (University Park: The Pennsylvania State University Press, 1962).

120. David W. Kearn, Jr., "The Baruch Plan and the Quest for Atomic Disarmament," *Diplomacy & Statecraft* 21 (2010): 41–67.

121. Russell D. Buhite and W. Christopher Hamel, "War for Peace: The Question of an American Preventive War against the Soviet Union 1945–1955," *Diplomatic History* 14, no. 3 (1990): 367–384.

122. Joseph I. Lieberman, *The Scorpion And The Tarantula: The Struggle To Control Atomic Weapons, 1945-1949* (Boston: Houghton Mifflin, 1970).

123. Gregg Herken, *The Winning Weapon: The Atomic Bomb in the Cold War, 1945-1950* (New York: Alfred A. Knopf, 1981).

124. Joseph Nye, "The Superpowers and the Non-Proliferation Treaty," in *Superpower Arms Control: Setting the Record Straight*, ed. Albert Carnesale and Richard N. Haass (Cambridge: Ballinger Publishing Company, 1987), 165-190.

125. Thomas C. Reed and Danny B. Stillman, *The Nuclear Express: A Political History of the Bomb and Its Proliferation* (Minneapolis: Zenith Press, 2009).

126. Paul K. Kerr and Kenneth Katzman, *Iran Nuclear Agreement and U.S. Exit* (Washington, DC: Congressional Research Service, 2018).

127. Pifer, "Obama's Faltering Nuclear Legacy."

128. Paul Meyer and Tom Sauer, "The Nuclear Ban Treaty: A Sign of Global Impatience," *Survival* 60, no. 2 (April–May 2018): 61–72.

129. Ashton B. Carter and David N. Schwartz, eds., *Ballistic Missile Defense* (Washington, DC: The Brookings Institution, 1984); Ernest J. Yanarella, *The Missile Defense Controversy: Strategy, Technology, and Politics, 1955–1972* (Lexington: The University Press of Kentucky, 1977).

130. Morton H. Halperin, "The Decision to Deploy the ABM: Bureaucratic and Domestic Politics in the Johnson Administration," *World Politics* 25, no. 1 (1972): 62–95.

131. Lynn Etheridge Davis and Warner R. Schilling, "All You Ever Wanted to Know about MIRV and ICBM Calculations But Were Not Cleared to Ask," *Journal of Conflict Resolution* 17, no. 2 (June 1973): 207–242.

132. Francis Fitzgerald, *Way Out There in The Blue: Reagan, Star Wars, and the End of the Cold War* (New York: Touchstone, 2000).

133. Keith B. Payne, *Strategic Defense: "Star Wars" In Perspective* (Lanham: Hamilton Press, 1986); Colin Gray, "Strategic Defense, Deterrence, and the Prospect for Peace," *Ethics* 95, no. 3 (April 1985): 659–672.

134. Nancy W. Gallagher, "Congress and Missile Defense," in *Regional Missile Defense from a Global Perspective*, ed. Catherine McArdle Kelleher and Peter Dombrowski (Stanford, CA: Stanford University Press, 2015), 84-106.

135. James M. Acton, "U.S. National Missile Defense Policy," in Kelleher and Dombrowski, *Regional Missile Defense from a Global Perspective*, 33-47.

136. Charles L. Glaser and Steve Fetter, "National Missile Defense and the Future of U.S. Nuclear Weapons Policy," *International Security* 26, no. 1 (Summer 2001): 40-92; Charles L. Glaser, "Why Even Good Defense May Be Bad," *International Security* 9, no. 2 (Fall 1984): 92-123.

137. William R. Van Cleave and S.T. Cohen, *Tactical Nuclear Weapons: An Examination of the Issues* (London: Macdonald and Jane's, 1978); Fran Barnaby and S. T. Cohen (eds.), *Tactical Nuclear Weapons: European Perspectives* (London: Taylor and Francis, 1987).

138. Philip W. Dyer, "Will Tactical Nuclear Weapons Ever Be Used?" *Political Science Quarterly* 88, no. 2 (June 1973): 213-229.

139. Philip W. Dyer, "Tactical Nuclear Weapons and Deterrence in Europe," *Political Science* Quarterly 92, no. 2 (Summer 1977): 245-257.

140. Elliott Cohen, "A Revolution in Warfare," *Foreign Affairs* 75, no. 2 (March/April 1996): 37–54.

141. Susan J. Koch, *The Presidential Nuclear Initiatives of 1991–1992* (Washington, DC: National Defense University Press, 2012).

142. Amy F. Woolf, *U.S. Strategic Forces: Background, Developments, and Issues* (Washington, DC: Congressional Research Service, 2017).

143. Paul Huth, *Extended Deterrence and the Prevention of War* (New Haven, CT: Yale University Press, 1988); Alexander George and Richard Smoke, *Deterrence in American Foreign Policy* (New York: Columbia University Press, 1974).

144. Forest E. Morgan et al., *Confronting Emergent Nuclear-Armed Regional Adversaries* (Santa Monica, CA: RAND Corporation, 2015); David Ochmanek and Lowell H. Schwartz, *The Challenge of Nuclear-Armed*

Regional Adversaries (Santa Monica, CA: RAND Corporation, 2008); Dean Wilkening and Kenneth Watman, *Nuclear Deterrence in a Regional Context* (Santa Monica, CA: RAND Corporation, 1995);

145. Brad Roberts, "Strategic Stability Under Obama and Trump," *Survival* 59, no. 4 (August–September 2017): 47–74; Dean A. Wilkening, "Strategic Stability Between the United States and Russia," in Ochmanek and Sulmeyer, *Challenges in U.S. National Security Policy: A Festschrift Featuring Edward L. (Ted) Warner*, 123–141; Elbridge A. Colby and Michael S. Gerson (eds.), *Strategic Stability: Contending Interpretations* (Carlisle: U.S. Army War College Press, 2013).

146. Attempts to achieve superiority, whether quantitative or qualitative is likely to be self-defeating. See Jervis, *The Illogic of American Nuclear Strategy*, 164; Charles L. Glaser, *Analyzing Strategic Nuclear Policy* (Princeton: Princeton University Press, 1990): 136, 210-211.

147. Kurt Gottfried and Bruce G. Blair (eds.), *Crisis Stability and Nuclear War* (Oxford: Oxford University Press, 1988).

148. Glaser, *Analyzing Strategic Nuclear Policy*, 157 -8.

149. Jervis, *The Illogic of American Nuclear Strategy*, 168.

150. Robert Jervis, "Arms Control, Stability, and Causes of War," *Political Science Quarterly* 108, no. 2 (Summer 1993): 239–253.

151. Herbert York, *Race to Oblivion: A Participant's View of the Arms Race* (New York: Clarion, 1970); Colin Gray, "The Urge to Compete: Rationales for Arms Racing," *World Politics* 26, no. 2 (January 1974): 207-233 and Gray, "The Arms Race Phenomenon," *World Politics* 24, no. 1 (October 1971): 39-79.

152. Amy F. Woolf, *The New START Treaty: Central Limits and Key Provisions* (Washington, DC: Congressional Research Service, 2018).

153. *Approaches for Managing the Costs of U.S. Nuclear Forces, 2017–2046* (Washington, Congressional Budget Office, 2017); Todd Harrison and Evan Braden Montgomery, *The Cost of U.S. Nuclear Forces: From BCA to Bow Wave and Beyond* (Washington, DC: Center for Strategic and Budgetary Assessments, 2015); Jon B. Wolfsthal, Jeffrey Lewis, and Marc Quint, *The Trillion Dollar Triad: US Strategic Nuclear Modernization Over the Next Thirty Years* (Monterey, CA: James Martin Center for Nonproliferation Studies, 2014).

154. David Ochmanek, *U.S. Military Capabilities and Forces for a Dangerous World* (Santa Monica, CA: RAND Corporation, 2017).

CHAPTER 2

ASSESSING THE CURRENT SECURITY ENVIRONMENT

The current security environment presents a number of important challenges for the United States. As recent Trump administration policy documents have underscored, a return of great power competition, spurred by the aggressive, revisionist policy of Russia under President Vladimir Putin and the continuing rise of China, is posing a potent challenge to the United States' global leadership and the security of its key allies.[1] Russia has a considerable nuclear stockpile (currently undergoing a sustained program of modernization); an apparent willingness to use irregular and conventional military force against its neighbors, as exhibited in Georgia and Ukraine; and a stated policy of counterbalancing U.S. power around the globe, as evidenced by its intervention in Syria. It has therefore emerged from the domestic turbulence of the first decade of the post-Cold War world to directly challenge American interests and reintroduce security fears in Europe.[2]

Similarly, although China's foreign policy for much of the past two decades had focused on assuaging the fears of its smaller neighbors in East Asia, Beijing has shifted to a much more assertive posture since 2010 and seems increasingly willing and able to confront the United States and its allies in the Western Pacific.[3] Given the deep interdependence of the world's two largest economies, the United States' relationship with China is much more complicated and complex than its relationship with Moscow. However, China's rapid and extensive conventional military modernization, its willingness to energetically defend its own interests in regions like the East and South China Seas, and the persistent issue of the status of Taiwan make it possible that the United States and China could find themselves in a diplomatic crisis or even a military conflict in the near future, even if neither state seeks a direct confrontation.[4] Moreover, Beijing has engaged in a modernization of its nuclear forces, although this modernization is less pronounced than its conventional military buildup. Although the Chinese nuclear arsenal remains relatively small compared to the deployed forces of the United States and Russia, it is reportedly undergoing a program of qualitative improvements to enhance survivability.[5] This program seems primarily aimed at maintaining China's traditional assured retaliation posture, which is predicated on possessing a moderate but effective and reliable strategic force that guarantees extensive damage in response to an attack on China. In the context of an intensifying rivalry with the United States, however, these growing capabilities have sparked significant concern.[6]

A more acute threat to U.S. national security interests is presented by the North Korean nuclear program.[7] Despite the recent diplomatic breakthrough involving a rapprochement with South Korea and meetings between Kim Jong-un and President Trump in Singapore and Hanoi, the North Korean nuclear program has made significant progress in the past three years.[8] It now directly threatens U.S. allies in East Asia and potentially the United States homeland.[9] Similarly, while Iran constitutes a potential longer-term nuclear threat to regional allies of the United States and perhaps NATO, it is not evident that the latent Iranian nuclear capability should be a direct influence on U.S. nuclear strategy. A combination of conventional weapons, bolstered by forward deployed theater missile defenses, close coordination with allies and partners, and diplomatic pressure should provide measures to dissuade, deter and, if necessary, address further development of Tehran's nuclear ambitions.[10] Concerns about the proliferation implications of an Iranian nuclear breakout are more relevant to larger U.S. bilateral and multilateral nonproliferation initiatives.[11] The nuclear rivalry on the Subcontinent is also more directly relevant to U.S. diplomatic and nonproliferation objectives than to the construction of U.S. nuclear strategy, force structure or posture.[12] While some experts have conjured very troubling but relatively improbable scenarios in which a future Pakistan-India conflict turned nuclear, and drew in the United States and China, it is difficult to distill and practical implications for U.S. nuclear force planning.[13] The recent 2019 crisis originating in Kashmir and shifting to Pakistani territory and the shooting down of two Indian fighter jets seems to underscore the restraining impact of nuclear weapons as initial conventional escalation quickly shifted to a search for diplomatic resolution.[14]

Finally, beyond these geopolitical challenges, the current security environment is marked by rapid technological change, most notably involving the increasing prevalence of cyber warfare and the emergence of hypersonic weapons. These current and growing challenges have sparked concern about the sustainability of the U.S. deterrent. However, the potential military applications of emerging technologies such as additive manufacturing, gene editing, and artificial intelligence may have significant implications for U.S. and international security in the longer term. The United States must consider these implications while addressing the current security challenges. The United States' strategic arsenal is viewed as a formidable hedge against technological surprise, but given scarce resources, it is also imperative that the United States maintain its own technological edge to address these new threats.

This chapter assesses the current strategic environment, focusing on Russia and China and the implications of their policies and behavior for U.S. nuclear strategy. These two competitors present distinct challenges that have different implications for U.S. nuclear policy. It also considers the challenge of regional nuclear actors like North Korea that present direct threats to U.S. allies and increasingly threaten the United States. Finally, to provide context for the discussion of alternative nuclear strategies in subsequent chapters, it addresses threats emerging from technological change that may influence the effectiveness of U.S. strategic forces in the long term.

RUSSIA: INCREASING STRATEGIC CAPABILITIES, REVISIONIST INTENTIONS

U.S.-Russia relations have steadily eroded since the mid-2000s. While the initial period of post-Cold War relations was positive but increasingly turbulent, as Russia's domestic political and economic systems struggled to adapt to the post-Soviet world, President Vladimir Putin seemed to become increasingly concerned about U.S. hegemony, and particularly its commitment to a "freedom" agenda under President Bush.[15] NATO expansion had already gone beyond what Putin and hardliners viewed as appropriate. To these Russian leaders, NATO expansion signaled the United States' willingness to exploit Russian weakness. In response, a key tenet of Russian policy became the reassertion of its interests within its traditional sphere of influence, its "near abroad." Moreover, Putin seemed to hold the larger objective of balancing the U.S. leadership of the global system, as his 2007 speech at the Munich Security Conference indicated:

> I consider that the unipolar model is not only unacceptable but also impossible in today's world. And this is not only because if there was individual leadership in today's—and precisely in today's—world, then the military, political and economic resources would not suffice. What is even more important is that the model itself is flawed because at its basis there is and can be no moral foundations for modern civilization.[16]

In his second tenure as Russian president, Putin has proven to be a highly opportunistic, risk-acceptant, and cost-acceptant actor who may indeed have revisionist preferences in his dealings with the international system.[17] He has based his foreign policy (and his domestic political appeal) on opposing the perceived hegemony of the United States and, where possible, undermining its unipolar positon in the international system. Exploiting an opportunity created by the Maidan Revolution in Kiev, he intervened directly with military force to seize territory in Ukraine and formally annexed the region of Crimea.[18] More recently, in March 2018 Putin brandished several new nuclear systems including a strategic boost-glide hypersonic system (*Avangard*), a high-speed, long-range nuclear torpedo (*Poseidon*), and an intercontinental-range nuclear cruise missile (*Burevestnik*) that seemed to surpass the ongoing strategic modernization program in an outlandish public presentation clearly intended for foreign audiences (including the United States) as well as his domestic political base.[19] These actions build upon almost a decade of growing concern on the part of Western defense analysts that Russian military doctrine permits the use of nonstrategic nuclear weapons to end a conventional conflict on Russian terms. The prospect of an increased reliance upon and qualitative improvement of Russian nuclear forces under the command of a risk-acceptant, highly opportunistic leader who has exhibited willingness to use military force against his neighbors (and violence against domestic political opponents) is troubling and objectively increases the threat Russia poses to Europe and the United States.[20] At the same time, it is important to note that the threat posed by an opportunistic leader whose first priority is to maintain political control in the face of domestic opposition is quite different from the threat presented by hardened Soviet leaders who were driven by revolutionary ideology and were ready and willing to fight a protracted nuclear war.

The perception of Russia's reliance on its nuclear forces predates the precipitous decline in its relationship with the United States.[21] Moscow first announced the revision of its formal commitment to no first use of nuclear weapons in 2004, and the published Military Doctrine embraced a policy of escalation to limited nuclear use in the face of an imminent defeat by a technologically superior adversary, which was interpreted to refer to the United States and NATO. Several subsequent versions of Russia's strategic doctrine have maintained an emphasis on the use of nuclear weapons against an adversary in certain scenarios, though perhaps not as provocatively as in 2004. Moreover, Western defense experts have noted the practice of "nuclear use" in several of Russia's major annual war games over the past decade.[22] This has led to a view among some experts that Russian planners have adopted an "escalate to de-escalate" policy that would envision the limited use of nuclear weapons to force the adversary to halt operations, thus salvaging Russian conventional forces, deterring further escalation against Russian targets, and forcing the adversary into a cessation of hostilities on Russian terms.[23] Other Russia experts are less alarmed by what seems to be a Russian reliance on nuclear weapons and note that there has been no visible "lowering of the nuclear threshold" in more recent publications of the strategic doctrine. They acknowledge that if Moscow perceived its forces to be losing badly in a conventional conflict and believed a threat against Russian territory to be imminent, the use of nuclear weapons would not seem farfetched, and it would be escalatory.[24] This view is different, however, from the assumption that Moscow would contemplate first use to consolidate gains or "freeze" a conflict to its advantage.[25]

To support its military doctrine, Russia maintains a significant arsenal (approximately 1,800) of nonstrategic nuclear weapons that provide a formidable capacity for tactical or operational missions. Moscow has also invested significant resources in modernizing its strategic forces.[26] Silo-based and road-mobile versions of the single warhead SS-27 have been deployed in recent years, replacing older Soviet-era intercontinental ballistic missiles (ICBMs). Two programs are currently under development: the SS-X-28 (Yars-M) Mobile Missile is believed to carry four multiple independently targetable reentry vehicle (MIRVs), and the SS-X-29 (Sarmat or "Son of Satan") heavy missile, reportedly capable of carrying ten MIRVs, was advertised by President Putin as a direct response to U.S. investments in strategic missile defense systems.[27] Strategic modernization has long been a component of Russian national security policy to compensate for the severe erosion of Russian conventional power since the end of the Cold War. Thus, whereas Putin's rhetoric and Russia's increasingly belligerent behavior toward its neighbors have been (correctly) interpreted as indicating a more aggressive Russian foreign policy, Russia's nuclear modernization may not be directly linked to a more competitive strategy. Nuclear force modernization has been a fairly constant Russian objective since the mid-2000s. The development and deployment of a ground-launched cruise missile, the 9M729 (NATO designation: SSC-8), with capabilities proscribed under the 1987 Intermediate Nuclear Forces (INF) Treaty, has created a great deal of controversy and mutual recriminations, with Moscow arguing that missile defense interceptors deployed in Poland could constitute an offensive strike capability against Russian territory.[28] Rejecting this position, the Obama administration attempted to quietly bring Moscow back into compliance, with little success. The Trump administration announced its plans to formally withdraw from the treaty in February 2019, and the issue remains contentious.[29] It is worth noting, however, that Moscow has reportedly met its obligations under New START and has offered to extend the treaty.[30]

Although Russia's behavior, rhetoric, and nuclear capabilities make it easy to embrace worst-case thinking, it is also significant that its recent modernization efforts have been carried out within the context of limitations agreed upon under the New START Treaty.[31] Moreover, reluctance on Moscow's part to engage in arms control efforts beyond New START have been influenced by U.S. policy decisions. Russia's strategic force modernization efforts were planned over a decade ago, and it seems clear that the U.S. insistence on unilaterally withdrawing from the Antiballistic Missile (ABM) Treaty in 2002 and the subsequent deployment of theater ballistic missile defense systems in Eastern Europe, as well as discussions of the U.S.'s development of conventional long-range or prompt global strike forces (CPGS), have influenced Russian choices on strategic force modernization.[32]

Although Russia's nuclear arsenal has persistently threatened the United States homeland with a devastating, massive nuclear strike since the early Cold War, the more realistic threat from Russia is the initiation or exploitation of a conflict in Eastern Europe that escalates to nuclear use, precipitating a nuclear response. With its aggression in Ukraine, annexation of Crimea, and use of force in support of anti-Georgian separatists in the provinces of South Ossetia and Abkhazia in August 2008, Russia has established a record of using military force to advance its interests (or what are claimed to be the interests of ethnic Russians or pro-Russian sympathizers) in its traditional "near abroad." Neither Ukraine nor Georgia is a NATO member, but the possibility of future NATO membership for both countries reportedly sparked significant opposition in Moscow.[33] Given the nature of these interventions, experts have expressed concern that Moscow may attempt to follow a similar script in one of the Baltic States. Latvia, Lithuania, and Estonia are relatively new members of NATO; they are small states that directly border Russian territory, contain ethnic Russian minorities, and confront a significant local imbalance in conventional forces vis-à-vis Russia. For all of these reasons, they are difficult to defend.[34] Although the United States and NATO have developed several initiatives to enhance capabilities that could be rapidly deployed to the region in the event of a crisis, it remains doubtful whether Russia could be deterred from exploiting an opportunity, perhaps involving a pretext of protecting ethnic Russians within these nations, to initiate military operations, initially using irregular forces and eventually mounting a large conventional offensive. Studies of this scenario have focused on developing adequate and effective Alliance responses, given the local conventional balance of forces, the geographic realities, and the deployment of advanced integrated air defenses, which together provide Russia with a significant "home field advantage" that may challenge the capacity of the United States and NATO forces to project power into the region.[35] An additional and vitally important question is whether Russia would use nuclear weapons (likely one of its many and diverse nonstrategic nuclear weapons) to seize an advantage early in a conflict or only to prevent a catastrophic conventional defeat, after a successful NATO counteroffensive campaign. How would U.S. and NATO leaders respond to the limited use of nuclear weapons for battlefield or operation effects under these circumstances?[36]

In conclusion, Russia presents a dual threat to the United States that is not wholly different from that of the Soviet Union, although it is on a smaller scale. First, the modernization of Russian strategic forces presents the low-probability but potentially catastrophic threat of a large-scale nuclear attack on the U.S. homeland. With even a portion of the 1,550 deployed warheads it is allowed under the New START Treaty, Moscow possesses the capacity to destroy the United States as a functioning society. This constitutes a formidable deterrent capability, and given underlying conflicts of interest about political developments in Eastern Europe and around the globe, it is clear that Moscow views this deterrent as vital to its national security and central to its status as a great power. It is unsurprising that U.S. investments in limited strategic and theater ballistic missile defense systems that could eventually contribute to a larger multilayered system have precipitated a renewed emphasis on strategic modernization. U.S. offensive modernization programs are also likely to further shape Russian perceptions of U.S. intentions. A key short-term issue will be the future of New START.

Second, Russia confronts the United States with a difficult extended deterrent challenge. Given the local conventional superiority of Russian forces in the Baltic Region and the geographic proximity of any NATO operations to Russian territory in the event of a crisis, significant and rapid escalation is a possibility. Given Russia's perceived willingness to introduce nuclear weapons at some point in a conventional conflict, such a situation is fraught with the risk of miscalculation and escalation. In rough terms, it represents a reverse of the military situation in Central Europe during the Cold War, when it was the United States and NATO that were prepared to use tactical nuclear weapons to prevent a catastrophic defeat at the hands of conventional Red Army forces. However, the current scenario of a Baltic conflict is challenging precisely because of the potential for NATO forces to strike targets on Russian territory. In suppressing integrated air defense (IAD) systems and disrupting early warning and operational command and control, the United States and its allies risk destroying targets that Moscow may interpret as practice for a larger attack against critical Russia targets. Beyond a strictly military defeat on Baltic soil, which could trigger a limited nuclear use to create a pause and de-escalate the conflict, attacks on targets in Russia may create severe pressures for Moscow to escalate beyond the theater of operations, perhaps even to the strategic level against Europe or the United States.

In reassessing U.S. nuclear strategy and the requisite strategic forces in a changing security environment, both of these threats should be considered. With regard to the first, it is clear that it is necessary to maintain strategic retaliatory forces at a level sufficient to deter an attack on the United States by Russia. Determining that level may be a matter of debate. In considering the extended deterrent threat, a larger question should be considered: what are the optimal means to address the potential for the Russian introduction of tactical nuclear weapons and to devise operations that minimize the risk of inadvertent escalation? For example, it is possible that tailored, limited nuclear options would provide a useful alternative to conventional forces.[37]

PEOPLE'S REPUBLIC OF CHINA (PRC): AN INTENSIFYING SECURITY DILEMMA

During the past two decades, China has undertaken a rapid and expansive conventional military modernization program that has followed the larger trend of China's rise to the status of great power.[38] Through much of the first decade of this century, China's foreign policy focused primarily on assuaging the fears and concerns of its smaller regional neighbors and building relations across the globe.[39] More recently, this approach has been focused on President Xi Jinping's "Belt and Road" initiative that links China's growing economy to markets all over the world.[40] However, since 2010, China's policy on regional issues has shifted to a much more aggressive or "assertive" posture in which Beijing is increasingly willing to defend its interests in regional disputes over territorial sovereignty.[41] High-profile political clashes with Japan over the Senkaku/Diaoyu Islands in the East China Sea and programs to develop artificial islands in disputed regions of the South China and claim them as sovereign Chinese territory are clear examples.[42] The deployment of military capabilities on these manmade islands has only increased regional concerns surrounding China's long-term intentions and created potential flashpoints for crisis with the harassment of U.S. naval operations in the disputed areas.[43] More recently, President Xi expressed a hardline formal position toward Taipei's leadership, explicitly threatening the use of force to resolve the question of Taiwan's status.[44]

Experts have noted that Chinese modernization efforts initially focused on deterring the United States from repeating its actions during the 1996 Taiwan Straits Crisis.[45] Among other efforts, China invested in the quantitative expansion and qualitative improvement of its conventional military forces, including conventional short- and medium-range missiles, fighter and strike aircraft, and surface and subsurface warfare vessels.[46] Experts argue that with this concerted effort to improve its conventional forces, the PRC now confronts the United States with a formidable Anti-Access/Area Denial (A2/AD) capability that threatens to impose serious costs on U.S. military operations in maritime areas or airspace near Chinese territory.[47] This "contested zone" has expanded from the area around Taiwan to the East and South China Seas. U.S. naval and air forces operating within the region are now at significant risk, whether they are forward-based on allied territory or afloat at sea.[48]

At the strategic level, China's relatively modest deterrent has led some experts to question whether the United States could exploit its current superiority in strategic forces to make a disarming first strike possible.[49] Recent efforts by China to modernize its arsenal and increase the survivability of its deployed forces make this option much less attractive.[50] But despite these efforts to safeguard the PRC's nuclear forces, there are pathways by which a diplomatic crisis that precipitates a military conflict between the United States and China could lead to a nuclear exchange.[51]

China maintains a formal No First Use policy with regard to its strategic arsenal, but experts are less than confident that this policy will remain viable in the face of U.S. modernization efforts.[52] It has reportedly already been under stress in light of what Beijing perceives as U.S. efforts to develop extensive strategic defenses and conventional prompt global strike capabilities. Beijing seems concerned that the United States may seek to degrade its strategic deterrent capability and thus leave China vulnerable to nuclear coercion or blackmail.[53]

This belief among Chinese leaders is critically important precisely because current U.S. operational planning for a military conflict with China, most notably for a large-scale conventional conflict in the Taiwan Straits, seems predicated on strikes against targets on the Chinese mainland. Moreover, many of the potential responses to the current challenge of China's A2-AD capability, such as the deployment of new conventional IRBMs and/or the implementation of a version of the U.S. military's AirSea Battle Concept, explicitly target mobile missiles, command and control, and other elements of China's military infrastructure.[54] These plans may also entail a "blinding" or "dazzling" campaign that attacks Chinese strategic command, control, communications, computers, intelligence, surveillance, and reconnaissance (C4ISR) assets and thus erodes situational awareness and early warning, which may be interpreted as preparation for an attack on the strategic deterrent or the regime leadership. These factors create a significant possibility of inadvertent escalation.[55]

Chinese military leaders have focused on pushing U.S. forces away from their immediate littorals to prevent strikes against the mainland and complicating efforts to support Taiwan in the event of a conflict. The People's Liberation Army (PLA) has made significant progress in achieving these objectives, from developing the capability to hold short-range strike aircraft deployed at forward bases in the region at risk in the early stages of a conflict to developing and deploying capabilities to prevent U.S. Navy carrier strike groups, the most visible symbol of U.S. military power, from operating with impunity in the Western Pacific.[56] If the United States plans to deny China a sanctuary from which to execute military operations and is therefore prepared to target forces on the Chinese mainland early in a conflict, the potential for both concerted and inadvertent escalation increases. Two distinct pathways to escalation seem plausible.

First, in the event of a military conflict arising from a crisis over Taiwan or another flashpoint in the region, Chinese forces may launch a coordinated operation against U.S. forces that are forward deployed in the region. In such a case, the American military response will likely involve attacking military targets on China's mainland. However, as U.S. forces degrade China's military forces, particularly its mobile missile forces and command and control nodes, Chinese leaders may believe either that their central deterrent capabilities are under threat or that a decisive military failure will result in the permanent loss of Taiwan. In either case, there may be strong incentives for the Chinese leaders to threaten nuclear escalation to avoid losing their deterrent and/or being forced to accept an "unacceptable" post-conflict settlement that would undermine the legitimacy and viability of the regime. Beijing may therefore seek to "de-escalate" the conflict, halt any advances by United States and allied forces, and minimize its losses.[57]

Second, in a scenario in which U.S. and allied forces conduct a counter-offensive against targets on the Chinese mainland, it is not clear that operational control of Chinese strategic forces would remain exclusively in the hands of the Chinese Communist Party (CCP) leadership in Beijing. Organizational analyses of the PLA are unclear about the control or devolution of decision-making under conflict conditions. However, the risk that a commander would take the initiative to launch a nuclear missile in the event of a perceived decapitation of the regime leadership or the disruption of effective control over nuclear forces is significant. In an intense fog of war, exacerbated by cyberattacks and electronic warfare operations intended to "blind" or "dazzle" Chinese command and control elements with the objective of delinking of combatant commanders from the central political leadership, these risks and dangers would only increase. Although the nuclear-armed deterrent component of the Chinese missile force (the PLA Rocket Forces) is geographically separate from the conventional missile forces that would likely be engaged in a military conflict, the degradation of Chinese C4ISR capabilities and the potential erosion or loss of operational control of its nuclear deterrent forces should be primary concerns of U.S. planners.[58]

As this discussion indicates, the most relevant scenario for a nuclear exchange with China is one in which a conventional military conflict escalates to a threshold where Beijing perceives the survival of the CCP to be at stake and interprets the war aims of the United States and its allies as regime change or an alteration of the status of Taiwan. Given prevailing understandings of Chinese strategic thought, such a scenario seems relatively improbable. However, it also seems clear that even among experts on China's military strategy and doctrine, the potential for misperceptions and miscalculation, particularly under crisis or conflict conditions, is significant and warrants further study.

NORTH KOREA

Prior to the thawing of diplomatic relations with South Korea, the historic meeting between President Trump and Kim Jong-un in Singapore in June 2018, and the somewhat disappointing follow-up meeting in Hanoi in February 2019, the expansive schedule of missile and nuclear tests in 2016 and 2017 seemed to indicate a fundamental strategic shift toward the achievement of an operational strategic nuclear force.[59] With a significant stock of intermediate-range ballistic missiles capable of hitting targets within the region (including U.S. bases on Okinawa, Japan, and Guam) and existing short-range rocket and artillery forces capable of holding Seoul and U.S. forces in Korea at risk, Kim possesses a formidable range of capabilities to deter an attack on his regime.[60]

One key unanswered question is whether North Korea has successfully completed the critical task of miniaturizing nuclear warheads for its growing missile force. If it has crossed this key technical threshold, North Korea possesses the capabilities to implement an "asymmetric escalation" strategy, as the scholar Vipin Narang has termed it.[61] Pyongyang would consider the use of nuclear weapons in a diplomatic crisis or in the early stages of a conventional military conflict to prevent escalation by the United States and its allies, or later in a conflict to avoid catastrophic military defeat and to ensure the survival of the Kim regime. If limited nuclear strikes failed to achieve their objectives, North Korea could threaten to attack regional targets in East Asia, thus expanding the geographic scope of the conflict, degrading the capacity of the United States and its allies to launch offensive conventional operations against the North, and raising the expected costs of the conflict with the objective of coercing its adversaries to cease operations. Maintaining its limited ICBM forces in reserve, the Kim regime would hold targets in the United States at risk to deter attempts at regime change and maintain its hold on power.[62]

The achievement of a relatively diverse operational nuclear missile force constitutes a deterrent (or compellent) capability that exceeds the early nuclear aspirations of Kim's father, Kim Jong-il, who seemed to view the possession of an active nuclear program and a relatively primitive missile program as both a sufficient deterrent and a source of leverage for extracting concessions from the international community.[63] Under Kim Jong-un's direction, the functional nuclear arsenal has improved in both qualitative and quantitative terms. This improvement has significantly increased the nature of the threat to the United States, its deployed forces, and its allies in East Asia. It also greatly increases the likely severity of a conflict on the Korean Peninsula. North Korea persists in presenting an acute military threat to Seoul and to U.S. military forces and civilians in South Korea.[64]

North Korea is estimated to possess thousands of long-range conventional artillery pieces, and rocket launchers are deployed by North Korea along the demilitarized zone with ranges that allow them to target Seoul. North Korea has also deployed a significant number of short-range missiles that could be equipped with rudimentary nuclear warheads. Most experts agree, moreover, that North Korea possesses one of the world's largest chemical weapons programs and likely has a significant biological weapons program.[65]

This situation has confounded U.S. policy over the past twenty years and makes almost any preventive attack on North Korea unthinkable, whether such an attack would be a limited operation narrowly focused on neutralizing the nuclear weapons program or a larger-scale campaign aimed at removing the Kim regime. In the former case, escalation dynamics could easily result in a conflagration that spiraled out of control, whereas in the latter, the Kim regime would have little reason to exercise restraint.

The threat to the United States is real and growing, and given Kim's past behavior, it is not inconceivable that he may engage in risky behavior with the mistaken notion that his new strategic capabilities will deter his adversaries from effectively responding. An unprovoked attack on the United States still seems improbable, precisely because of the unambiguous capacity of the U.S. to annihilate his nation and end the Kim family dynasty. Nonetheless, provocative rhetoric and actions by Kim toward South Korea or Japan may increase tensions in the region to the point of precipitating a diplomatic crisis.

The central mission of the U.S. strategic arsenal is deterrence: it guarantees to even a risk-acceptant leader like Kim Jong-un that he, his family, his regime, and his society will be destroyed if he attacks the United States. There is considerable uncertainty, however, about what types of nuclear forces are required to deter new regional nuclear powers like North Korea beyond assured destruction. Whereas some experts argue that conventional forces expanded missile defenses and the threat of retaliation with strategic nuclear weapons would be sufficient (and preferable) to address a North Korean threat, others advocate for the use of tailored, limited nuclear options, particularly if nuclear weapons or other WMD have been used by the Kim regime.[66]

TECHNOLOGICAL CHANGE

The international system is undergoing a period of particularly rapid technological change.[67] Although the longer-term military and security implications of such change may be difficult to discern, particularly with regard to cutting-edge technologies, it is possible to assess the threats emanating from more mature technologies that have been adopted by civilian and private actors and have quickly diffused throughout the global system. The most pressing challenge is arguably that of cyber warfare.[68] Given the dependence of governmental systems (both military and civilian), critical infrastructure, and private actors (including economic, financial, and industrial organizations) on integrated networked computer systems and access to increasingly rapid flows of information, the prospect that an adversary might use offensive cyber weapons to destroy or degrade these essential networks with strategic-level "real world" effects has emerged as an acute threat to U.S. national security interests.[69] If an adversary used cyber weapons to shut down major components of the U.S. power grid, create a meltdown at a civilian nuclear power plant, or disrupt the U.S. financial markets or banking system, the United States could suffer significant economic losses or even civilian casualties.[70]

At a military operational level, cyber warfare, electronic warfare, and antisatellite weaponry have been viewed as important means to blunt or offset the traditional U.S. advantage in conventional military power and the formidable offensive capabilities derived from advanced, highly integrated, and networked C4ISR capabilities. Particularly in the context of high-end conventional operations against great power competitors like Russia and China, these capabilities to degrade or disrupt U.S.

information technology networks and thus undermine power projection are seen as a central challenge in what the U.S. military has termed "Multi-Domain Battle."[71] The military challenges that arise from the exploitation of maturing technologies may be less relevant than others to the U.S. strategic mission, but they do highlight the stresses on the U.S. defense budget and the need for conventional force investments to maintain traditional advantages in technology and innovation.

The military exploitation of hypersonic propulsion has emerged as a potentially important new area of competitive armament among the leading military powers.[72] Russia, for instance, recently showcased a new cruise missile that reportedly uses hypersonic technology to travel intercontinental distances while allowing for retargeting and greater accuracy than traditional ballistic missiles.[73] The United States and China are experimenting on hypersonic munitions, and some advocates have argued that such weapons may prove valuable for a CPGS mission or the suppression of an adversary's air defense and early warning network. [74] At this point, hypersonic munitions seem to be a potentially useful niche capability, likely limited in number, given the projected costs in the short term. However, with both Russia and China apparently focused on exploiting the technology for military purposes, the United States will face pressure to follow suit.

Longer-term threats arising from the exploitation of artificial intelligence, additive manufacturing, and genetic editing are more difficult to envision in concrete ways. Certainly, the ability to develop new and highly contagious diseases could produce devastating biological weapons with strategic-level effects. This has been one of the central fears associated with the diffusion of gene editing technology in recent years. Some experts believe that the use of artificial intelligence has the capacity to erode nuclear deterrence or create the conditions for a nuclear war. It is beyond the scope of this book to assess the credibility of these threats, and an important caveat from previous eras of rapid technological innovation is that many military applications of new technologies ultimately prove impractical or unattainable. Nonetheless, given the strategic-level damage that could be inflicted on the United States by adversaries wielding new technologies, the U.S. nuclear deterrent should continue to provide a hedge against such attacks. The United States must also, however, continue to invest prudently in basic research, science and technology, and innovation to maintain its technological edge.

Beyond deterring direct nuclear threats to the United States and its allies, the U.S. strategic arsenal should provide a strong hedge against technological change, particularly if the exploitation of that change provides adversaries with new capabilities that may have strategic-level effects. However, the nature and size of the arsenal necessary to provide such a hedge, at a time when the United States must also maintain significant commitments in scientific and technical research to meet these technological challenges, deserves close consideration.[75]

CURRENT AND PLANNED U.S. NUCLEAR FORCES

The United States faces a complex security environment in both geopolitical and technological terms. The existing triad provides important complementary and redundant capabilities that complicate an adversary's calculations and thus contribute to a strong deterrent to unwanted action against the United States and its allies.[76] The land-based intercontinental ballistic missiles (ICBM) force, currently made up of 400 single-warhead Minuteman III intercontinental ballistic missiles, provides the national command authority with the capacity to strike promptly anywhere in the world. Given the technical difficulties associated with the development and fielding of effective ballistic missile defenses, the Minuteman force is virtually guaranteed to penetrate the airspace of any adversary and deliver a relatively high-yield W87 warhead to critical targets. Despite concerns that emerged at the height of the Cold War, the survivability of the land-based leg of the strategic triad is also relatively robust. An additional role of the ICBM force is to force an adversary to use a large proportion of its own arsenal to attack the 450 silos dispersed across the northern states. This depiction of the ICBM force as a "warhead sponge" seems counterintuitive but serves to complicate the war plans of adversaries as well as confront them with the daunting prospect of targeting the center of the continental United States, thus contributing to stability.[77]

The ballistic missile submarine (SSBN) force is currently made up of fourteen *Ohio* class submarines, which in turn carry was designed to carry twenty-four Trident D5 submarine-launched ballistic missiles (SLBMs), each of could carry a maximum of eight multiple independently targetable reentry vehicle (MIRVs). Under New START launcher limits, the number of tubes have been reduced to twenty on each boat and each Trident typically carries 4-5 warheads.[78] Thus, an overwhelming proportion of the United States arsenal is at sea at any given time. The SSBN force is typically viewed as the most survivable leg of the strategic triad, given the challenges of anti-submarine warfare, though some experts have questioned the difficulty of the challenge and argue that new technologies may provide a breakthrough in antisubmarine warfare (ASW) capabilities.[79] Nonetheless, with at least six of these submarines on patrol in each ocean at any given time (the two others are in overhaul), they provide an objectively formidable deterrent capability. Finally, the strategic bomber force, currently made up of a portion of the aging B-52 force armed with nuclear air-launched cruise missiles (ALCMs), and several of the nineteen deployed B-2 Spirit stealth bombers provide a mix of standoff and penetrating delivery capabilities, respectively. The bomber force is viewed as the most useful for crisis management and signaling to adversaries.[80] The bombers can be deployed to friendly bases under crisis conditions, thus threatening escalation if an adversary presses forward with unwanted action, but can also be recalled, thus providing extensive control for policymakers under crisis or conflict conditions. Because bombers take time to arrive on target and even stealth bombers can be detected by advanced strategic command, control, communications, computers, intelligence, surveillance, and reconnaissance (C4ISR) assets and integrated air defense (IAD) systems, they do not provide a credible first-strike capability, and so are seen as contributing to stability even under crisis conditions.[81]

Under the current modernization program of record, all three legs of the strategic triad will be modernized. The Ground Based Strategic Deterrent (GBSD) program will replace the Minuteman III, reportedly maintaining the major attributes of the current ICBM and its support infrastructure, including the existing silos. The Minuteman III force was designed to carry three warheads, but since the end of the Cold War, the deployed force has carried only one. Some experts have argued that as a hedge against deteriorating geopolitical or security conditions or rapid technological change, the new missile should be capable of carrying additional warheads if necessary.[82] The Air Force currently plans to procure 642 missiles, which will provide 400 operational weapons deployed in refurbished silos, with additional capacity for testing and spares. The launch centers and associate command and control infrastructure are also scheduled for major upgrades.[83]

The submarine force, which will be approaching 40 years of service, will be phased out starting at the end of the 2020s. To replace the Ohio-class, the current plan is for the procurement of twelve new *Columbia* class boats, which are currently under development and will be phased in over time starting in the early 2030s because of delays. The Columbia class is designed to 16 tubes, and likely carry 5 or 6 warheads per Trident SLBM and its eventual successor. Because of the timing of the replacement program, it is likely that for most of the decade of the 2030s, the SSBN force will consist of ten boats, which has led some to questions whether the full program of twelve boats in necessary to fulfill the sea-based deterrent mission. In addition, because the costs of the program have raised concerns about the Navy's ability to achieve other shipbuilding objectives during this time, the reduction of the planned program to ten or eight vessels is possible.[84]

Finally, the B-21 Raider long-range strategic bomber is programmed to replace the B-52H bombers dedicated to the nuclear mission and eventually the B-2 force. With a planned program of 80–100 units, the B-21 will also provide conventional long-range bombing capabilities, replacing conventional B-52s and B-1Bs. It is not clear what portion of the new bomber fleet will be devoted to the nuclear mission. Because the first B-21 is not expected to enter service until at least 2028, two additional programs are supposed to prevent a gap in capabilities from emerging.

The B61 Mod 12 will consolidate several of the older variants of the B61 gravity bomb into a single, more accurate variable-yield munition that will be carried on the B-2 (and eventually the B-21 when it enter service) and the F-35A, to be forward deployed in Europe as NATO's primary nuclear deterrent. Given its perceived suitability for tactical and theater missions, advocates argue that it will enhance the credibility of the U.S. extended deterrence (and reassure NATO allies) in the face of Russia's large stocks of nonstrategic nuclear weapons.[85] The B61-12 program has proven controversial because of its costs and the perception that it constitutes a "new" weapons program, reversing a pledge by the Obama administration to avoid new systems in favor of replacing aging systems. The second program, the Long-Range Standoff Ordinance (LRSO), will replace the air-launched cruise missile (ALCM) and provide the B-52H with formidable standoff capabilities before the B-21 enters service. A purchase of approximately 1,000 LRSOs is planned, and they are also programmed for use with the B-21.[86] This plan has sparked opposition from arms control advocates and budget hawks because of the seeming redundancy of a highly effective standoff munition deployed with a cutting-edge penetrating bomber. Supporters of both programs argue that the LRSO will provide a necessary hedge against significant improvements in IADs and an erosion of the B-21's capacity to penetrate and operate effectively in highly contested environments.

In October 2017, the Congressional Budget Office released an estimate of the ongoing nuclear modernization program and concluded that the thirty years costs (2017 to 2046) would reach approximately $1.2 Trillion.[87] The modernization of the strategic triad, including the research and development and procurement costs of three major programs, would total $777 billion, while tactical nuclear delivery systems and weapons would cost $25 billion, upgrades to the nuclear command, control, communications (NC3) and early warning systems would cost $184 billion, and investments in renovating the nuclear weapons laboratories and infrastructure would cost $261 billion. This is a significant allocation of scare defense resources and is likely to receive continuing scrutiny in light of alternative conventional procurement and readiness needs, not to mention rapidly increasing U.S. government debt.

The 2018 Trump administration Nuclear Posture Review (NPR) called two for two additional programs beyond the existing modernization plan.[88] The first is the deployment of a single low-yield variant of a W-76 warhead on a portion of deployed SLBM inventory. The second is the development and deployment of new nuclear sea-launched cruise missile (SLCM). Both programs would provide the United States with the ability to credibly threaten limited, gradual nuclear responses thereby enhancing extended deterrence against a range of adversaries. It is unclear what the scope and associated costs of the program will be, and given potential Congressional opposition, their future is uncertain.[89]

While the modernization of U.S. strategic delivery vehicles is a central challenge, the nuclear weapons complex is also grappling with maintaining and managing the nuclear stockpile. Under the Obama administration, the Department of Energy (DOE) and the National Nuclear Security Administration (NNSA) developed and initiated a program to consolidate warheads for strategic delivery vehicles in order to maximize reliability, stockpile efficiency and cost effectiveness.[90] Interoperable Warhead (IW) Version1, which was intended to consolidate and refurbish the Minuteman W78 warhead and the Trident D5 W88 warhead into a single version that could be deployed on both the Minuteman III and Trident replacements. The W87 warhead for the Minuteman III would be replaced by the IW-2, while the W76 warhead for the Trident would be replaced by the IW-3. As noted, the B61-12 program is consolidating

several older variants of the B61 bomb into a single variable-yield munition and it was also programmed to replace the B83 bomb, which would
be retired in 2030. The W80-1 warhead, deployed on ALCMs would likely
require an additional replacement for use with the LRSO. This had been
called the "3 + 2" plan. However, because of budgetary issues as well as
concerns over respective warhead life extension plans (LEP) among the
services, it seems that the IW-1 program has encountered difficulty and
the future of the larger endeavor of warhead consolidation according
to the "3 + 2" is in doubt.[91] This was evidenced by the NNSA's recent
reporting and the recent move to restart a replacement program for
the W78.[92] As noted previously, the sufficient resourcing of the nuclear
weapons complex will be an important component of maintaining a
robust credible s nuclear deterrent, but like modernizing the strategic
triad, this will be a challenge for policymakers in light of other defense
and non-defense budgetary priorities.

The next three chapters describe the major components, explain the
underlying logics and assumptions, and critically assess the ability of three
alternative nuclear strategies to address the current security environment
and position the United States to achieve its national security objectives
in the future.

Notes

1. *Summary of the 2018 National Defense Strategy of The United States of America: Sharpening the American Military Competitive Edge* (Washington: U.S. Department of Defense, 2018).

2. Timothy Frye, "Putin touts Russia as a great power. But he had made it a weak one." *The Washington Post,* June 6, 2019.

3. Aaron L. Friedberg, "The Sources of Chinese Conduct: Explaining Beijing's Assertiveness," *The Washington Quarterly* 37, no. 4 (Winter 2015): 133-150; Alastair Iain Johnston, "How New is China's New Assertiveness? *International Security* 37, no.4 (Spring 2013): 7-48.

4. *Annual Report to Congress: Military and Security Developments Involving the People's Republic of China* (Washington, DC: Department of Defense, 2019).

5. Hans M. Kristensen and Robert Norris, "Nuclear Notebook: Chinese Nuclear Forces, 2018," *Bulletin of the Atomic Scientists* 74, no. 4 (2018): 289-295.

6. Caitlin Talmadge, "Beijing's Nuclear Option: Why a U.S.-Chinese War Could Spiral Out of Control," *Foreign Affairs* 97, no. 6 (November/December 2018): 44-51.

7. Adam Taylor and Tim Meko, "What made North Korea's weapons programs so much scarier in 2017," *The Washington Post,* December 21, 2017.

8. Karen DeYoung and John Wagner, "Trump Kim declare summit a big success, but they diverge on the details," *The Washington Post,* June 13, 2018.

9. Dan Lamothe, "U.S. missile defense and its spotty history have a new challenge in North Korean ICBMs," *The Washington Post,* July 5, 2017.

10. Lynn Davis, Jeffrey Martini, Alireza Nader, Dalia Dassa Kaye, James T. Quinlivan, and Paul Steinberg, *Iran's Nuclear Future: Critical U.S. Policy Choices* (Santa Monica: RAND Corporation, 2011).

11. Tamer El-Ghobashy, Michael Birnbaum and Carol Morello, "Iran announces it will stop complying with parts of landmark nuclear deal," *The Washington Post,* May 8, 2019; Gerry Shih, "4 months after Trump abandons nuclear deal, Iran says it's ready to enrich uranium faster than ever," *The Washington Post,* September 12, 2018; Anne Gearan and Karen DeYoung, "Trump pulls United States out of Iran nuclear deal, calling the pact 'an embarrassment,'" *The Washington Post,* May 8, 2018.

12. Debalina Ghoshal, "India's Recessed Deterrence Posture: Prospects and Implications," *The Washington Quarterly* 39, no. 1 (Spring 2016): 159-170; Devin T. Hagerty, "India's Evolving Nuclear Posture," *The Nonproliferation Review* 21, nos. 3-4 (2014): 295-315; David J. Karl, "Pakistan's Evolving Nuclear Weapons Posture," *The Nonproliferation Review* 21, nos. 3-4 (2014): 317-336.

13. Paul Bracken, *The Second Nuclear Age: Strategy, Danger, and the New Power Politics* (New York: Times Books, 2012): 162-188.

14. Niha Mashh, "India and Pakistan hold talks after nearly going to war," *The Washington Post*, March 14, 2019; Joanna Slater, "India strikes Pakistan in severe escalation of tensions between nuclear rivals," *The Washington Post*, February 26, 2019; Joanna Slater, Shaiq Hussain and Niha Masih, "Pakistan says it will release captured Indian pilot as 'peace gesture," *The Washington Post*, February 28, 2019; Joanna Slater and Pamela Constable, "Pakistan captures Indian pilot after shooting down aircraft, escalating hostilities," *The Washington Post*, February 27, 2019; Joanna Slater, "India strikes Pakistan in severe escalation of tensions between nuclear rivals," *The Washington Post*, February 26, 2019.

15. Allen C. Lynch, *Vladimir Putin and Russian Statecraft* (Washington, DC: Potomac Books, 2011).

16. "Putin's Prepared Remarks and 43rd Munich Conference on Security Policy," *Washington Post*, February 12, 2007, http://www.washingtonpost.com/wp-dyn/content/article/2007/02/12/AR2007021200555.html.

17. Olga Oliker et al., "Russian Foreign Policy in Historical and Current Context," *RAND Perspective*, 2015.

18. Steven Lee Myers and Ellen Barry, "Putin Reclaims Crimea for Russia and Bitterly Denounces the West," *The New York Times*, March 18, 2014.

19. Alexey Arbatov, "Mad Momentum Redux? The Rise and Fall of Nuclear Arms Control," *Survival* 61, no. 3 (June-July 2019): 7-38; Hans Kristensen and Matt Korda, "Nuclear Notebook: Russian nuclear forces, 2019) *Bulletin of the Atomic* Scientists 75, no. 2 (2019): 73-84.

20. Scott Boston and Dara Massicot, "The Russian Way of Warfare: A Primer," *RAND Perspective*, 2017.

21. James T. Quinlivan and Olga Oliker, *Nuclear Deterrrence in Europe: Russian Approaches to a New Environment and Implications for the United States* (Santa Monica, CA: RAND Corporation, 2011).

22. Kristensen and Korda, "Nuclear Notebook: Russian nuclear forces, 2019," 5-6.

23. Nikolai N. Sokov, "Why Russia Calls a Limited Nuclear Strike De-escalation," *Bulletin of the Atomic Scientists*, March 13, 2014, https://thebulletin.org/2014/03/why-russia-calls-a-limited-nuclear-strike-de-escalation/.

24. Katarzyna Zysk, "Nonstrategic nuclear weapons in Russia's evolving military doctrine," *Bulletin of the Atomic* Scientists 73, no. 5 (2017): 322-327.

25. Bruno Tertrais, "Russia's Nuclear Policy: Worry for the Wrong Reasons," *Survival* 60, no. 2 (April-Ma5.y 2018): 33-44; Olga Oliker, *Russia's Nuclear Doctrine: What We Know, What We Don't, and What That Means* (Washington, DC: Center for Strategic and International Studies, 2016); Kristensen and Korda, "Nuclear Notebook: Russian Nuclear Forces, 2019,"

26. Hans M. Kristensen and Robert S. Norris, "Nuclear Notebook: Russian Nuclear Forces, 2018," *Bulletin of the Atomic Scientists* 74, no. 3 (2018): 185–195.

27. Kristin Ven Bruusgaard, "Russian Strategic Deterrence," Survival 58, no. 4 (August-September 2016): 7-26.

28. Michael Fitzsimmons, "Russian Strategy and the End of the INF Treaty," *Survival* 60, no. 6 (December-January 2016): 119-36.

29. Anne Gearan, Paul Sonne, and Carol Morello, "U.S. to Withdraw from Nuclear Arms Control Treaty with Russia, Raising Fears of a New Arms Race," *The Washington Post,* February 1, 2019.

30. Arbatov, "Mad Momentum Redux?" 9.

31. Alexey Arbatov, *Gambit or Endgame? The New State of Arms Control* (Washington, DC: Carnegie Endowment for International Peace, 2011).

32. Terence Neilan, "Bush Pulls Out of ABM Treaty; Putin Calls Move a Mistake," *The New York Times*, December 13, 2001.

33. Andrew Osborn, "Russian PM Warns NATO Admission for Georgia Could Trigger 'Terrible Conflict,'" *Reuters*, August 6, 2018, https://www.reuters.com/article/us-russia-nato-georgia/russian-pm-warns-nato-admission-of-georgia-could-trigger-terrible-conflict-idUSKBN1KR1UQ.

34. David. A. Shlapak and Michael W. Johnson, *Reinforcing Deterrence on NATO's Eastern Flank: Wargaming the Defense of the Baltics* (Santa Monica, CA: RAND Corporation, 2016).

35. Scott Boston et al., *Assessing the Conventional Force Imbalance in Europe: Implications for Countering Russian Local Superiority* (Santa Monica, CA: RAND Corporation, 2018).

36. Matthew Kroenig, "Facing Reality: Getting NATO Ready for a New Cold War," *Survival* 57, no. 1 (February-March 2015): 49-70.

37. Matthew Kroenig, *A Strategy for Deterring Russian Nuclear De-Escalation Strikes* (Washington, DC: The Atlantic Council, 2018).

38. Eric Heginbotham et al., *The U.S.-China Military Scorecard: Forces, Geography and the Evolving Balance of Power 1996–2017* (Santa Monica, CA: RAND Corporation, 2015).

39. Joshua Kurlantzick, *Charm Offensive: How China's Soft Power is Transforming the World* (New Haven: Yale University Press, 2007); Evan S. Medeiros et al., *Pacific Currents: The Responses of U.S. Allies and Security Partners in East Asia to China's Rise* (Santa Monica: RAND Corporation, 2008).

40. Keith Bradsher, "China Proceeds With Belt and Road Push, but Does It More Quietly," *The New York Times*, January 22, 2019.

41. Aaron L. Friedberg, "The Sources of Chinese Conduct: Explaining Beijing's Assertiveness," Alastair Iain Johnston, "How New and Assertive is China's New Assertiveness?"

42. Martin Fackler,"China and Japan Say They Hold Talks Over Island Dispute," *The New York Times*, October 12, 2012.

43. Hannah Beech, "China's Sea Control Is a Done Deal, 'Short of War With the U.S.,'" *The New York Times*, September 20, 2018

44. John Pomfret, "China's Xi Jinping is growing impatient with Taiwan, adding to tensions with U.S.," *The Washington Post*, February 18, 2019; Chris Buckley and Chris Horton, "Xi Jinping Warns Taiwan That Unifications Is the Goal and Force Is an Option," *The New York Times*, January 1, 2019.

45. Robert S. Ross, "The 1995-1996 Taiwan Strait Confrontation: Coercion, Credibiliy, and the Use of Force," *International Security* 20, no. 2 (Fall 2000): 87-123.

46. Robert S. Ross, "Navigating the Taiwan Strait: Deterrence, Escalation Dominance, and U.S.-China Relations," *International Security* 27, no. 2 (Fall 2002): 48-85.

47. Roger Cliff et al., *Entering the Dragon's Lair: Chinese Antiaccess Strategies and Their Implications for the United States* (Santa Monica, CA: RAND Corporation, 2007).

48. David A. Shlapak et al., *A Question of Balance: Political Context and Military Aspects of the China-Taiwan Dispute* (Santa Monica, C: RAND Corporation, 2009); David A. Shlapak, David T. Orletsky, and Barry Wilson, *Dire Strait? Military Aspects of the China-Taiwan Confrontation and Options for U.S. Policy* (Santa Monica, CA: RAND Corporation: 2000).

49. Keir A. Lieber and Daryl G. Press, "The Rise of U.S. Nuclear Primacy," *Foreign Affairs* 85, no. 2 (March/April 2006): 42–54; Keir A. Lieber and Daryl G. Press, "The End of MAD? The Nuclear Dimension of U.S. Primacy," *International Security* 30, no. 4 (Spring 2006): 7–44.

50. Michael S. Chase and Arthur Chan, "China's Evolving Strategic Deterrence Concepts and Capabilities," *Washington Quarterly* 39, no. 1 (Spring 2016): 117–136; Hans M. Kristensen and Robert Norris, "Nuclear Notebook: Chinese nuclear forces, 2018," *Bulletin of the Atomic* Scientists 74, no. 4 (2018): 289-295.

51. Caitlin Talmadge, "Would China Go Nuclear?: Assessing the Risk of Chinese Escalation in a Conventional War with the United States," *International Security* Vol . 41, No. 4 (Spring 2017), pp. 93-132.

52. M. Taylor Fravel and Evan Medeiros, "China's Search for Assured Retaliation: Explaining the Evolution of China's Nuclear Strategy," *International Security* 35, no. 2 (Fall 2010): 48-87; Jeffrey Lewis, *The Minimum Means of Reprisal: China's Search for Security in the Nuclear Age* (Cambridge: MIT Press, 2007).

53. Fiona S. Cunnignham and M. Taylor Fravel, "Assuring Assured Retaliation: China's Nuclear Posture and U.S.-China Strategic Stability," *International Security* 40, no. 2 (Fall 2015): 7-50.

54. Andrew Krepinevich, *Why Airsea Battle?* (Washington, DC: Center for Strategic and Budgetary Assessments, 2010); Jan Van Tol, Mark Gunziger, Andrew Krepinevich, and Jim Thomas, *Airsea Battle: A Point of Departure Operational Concept* (Washington, DC: Center for Strategic and Budgetary Assessments).

55. David W. Kearn, Jr., "Air-Sea Battle and China's Anti-Access Area Denial Challenge," *Orbis* (Winter 2014): 132-146; Talmadge, "Would China Go Nuclear?" 62-64.

56. Andrew S. Erickson and David D. Yang, "Using the Land to Control the Sea?: Chinese Analysts Consider the Antiship Ballistic Missile," *Naval War College Review* 62, no. 4 (2009): 53-86.

57. Talmadge, "Would China Go Nuclear?" 87-90.

58. Ibid., 82-84.

59. John Hudson, Anne Gearan and Simon Denyer, "Abrupt end of summit may have exposed the limits of Trump's strategy on Kim," *The Washington Post,* February 28, 2019; Karen DeYoung and John Wagner, "Trump Kim declare summit a big success, but they diverge on the details," *The Washington Post,* June 13, 2018; Adam Taylor and Tim Meko, "What

made North Korea's weapons programs so much scarier in 2017," *The Washington Post,* December 21, 2017.

60. Kathleen J. McInnis et al., *The North Korean Nuclear Challenge: Military Options and Issues for Congress* (Washington, DC: Congressional Research Service, 2017).

61. Vipin Narang, "Nuclear Strategies of Emerging Nuclear Powers: North Korea and Iran," *Washington Quarterly* 38, no. 1 (Spring 2015): 73–91.

62. Michael J. Mazarr et al., "The Korean Peninsula: Three Dangerous Scenarios," *RAND Perspectives,* 2017.

63. Stephen Rademaker, "The North Korean nuclear threat is very real. Time to start treating it that way." *The Washington Post,* May 18, 2017.

64. Yochi Dreazen, "Here's What a War with North Korea Would Look Like," *Vox,* February 8, 2018, https://www.vox.com/world/2018/2/7/16974772/ north-korea-war-trump-kim-nuclear-weapon.

65. Beverly Banks, "Biological and chemical weapons: the other threats from North Korea," *Military Times,* March 7, 2019.

66. Forest E. Morgan et al., *Confronting Emergent Nuclear-Armed Regional Adversaries* (Santa Monica, CA: RAND Corporation, 2015); David Ochmanek and Lowell H. Schwartz, *The Challenge of Nuclear-Armed Regional Adversaries* (Santa Monica, CA: RAND Corporation, 2008); Dean Wilkening and Kenneth Watman, *Nuclear Deterrence in a Regional Context* (Santa Monica, CA: RAND Corporation, 1995).

67. Horowitz, "Coming next in military tech."

68. Martin C. Libicki, *Crisis and Escalation in Cyberspace* (Santa Monica, CA: RAND Corporation, 2012); Martin C. Libicki, *Cyberdeterrence and Cyberwar* (Santa Monica, CA: RAND Corporation, 2009).

69. Joseph S. Nye, Jr., "Deterrence and Dissuasion in Cyberspace," *International Security* 41, no. 3 (Winter 2016/17): 44-71; Rebecca Slayton, "What Is the Cyber Offense-Defense Balance? Conceptions, Causes, and Assessment," *International Security* 41, no. 3 (Winter 2016/2017): 72-109.

70. Joel F. Brenner, "Eyes wide shut: The growing threat of cyber-attacks on industrial control systems," *Bulletin of the Atomic Scientists* 69, no. 5 (2015): 15-20; Jeffrey Carr, "The misunderstood acronym: Why cyber weapons aren't WMD," *Bulletin of the Atomic Scientists* 69, no. 5 (2015): 32-37; Adam P. Liff, "Cyberwar A New 'Absolute Weapons?' The Proliferation of Cyberwarfare Capabilities and Interstate War," *Journal of Strategic Studies* 35, no. 2 (June 2012): 401-428; Andrew Krepinevich, *Cyberwarfare: A Nuclear Option?* (Washington, DC: Center for Strategic and Budgetary Assessments, 2012).

71. Jen Judson, "From Multi-Domain Battle to Multi-Domain Operations: Army Evolves its guiding concept," *Defense News*, October 9, 2019; David G. Perkins and James M. Holmes, "Multidomain Battle: Converging Concepts Toward a Joint Solution," *Joint Forces Quarterly* 88, no. 1 (2018): 55-57.

72. Christian Davenport, "Why the Pentagon fears the U.S. is losing the hypersonic arms race with Russia and China," *The Washington Post*, June 8, 2018.

73. Anton Troianovski and Paul Sonne, "Russia is poised to add a new hypersonic nuclear-capable glider to its arsenal," *The Washington Post*, December 26, 2018.

74. Amy F. Woolf, *Conventional Prompt Global Strike and Long-Range Ballistic Missiles: Background and Issues* (Washington, DC: Congressional Research Service, 2018).

75. On U.S. Department of Defense R&D investments, see David Ochmanek et al., *U.S. Military Capabilities and Forces for a Dangerous World: Rethinking the U.S. Approach to Force Planning* (Santa Monica, CA: RAND, 2017), Appendix A.

76. Amy L. Woolf, *U.S. Strategic Forces: Background, Developments, and Issues* (Washington, DC: Congressional Research Service, 2018).

77. *Approaches for Managing the Costs of U.S. Nuclear Forces, 2017 to 2046* (Washington, DC: Congressional Budget Office, 2017), 25-26.

78. Woolf, *U.S. Strategic Forces*, 21-24.

79. Austin Long and Brendan Rittenhouse Green, "Stalking the Secure Second Strike: Intelligence, Counterforce, and Nuclear Strategy," *Journal of Strategic Studies* 38, nos. 1–2 (2015): 38–73.

80. Forest E. Morgan, *Crisis Stability and Long-Range Strike: A Competitive Analysis of Fighters, Bombers, and Missiles* (Santa Monica, CA: RAND Corporation, 2013).

81. *Approaches for Managing the Costs of U.S. Nuclear Forces, 2017 to 2046*, 22-23.

82. Keith B. Payne and John S. Foster, Jr., *A New Nuclear Review for a New Age* (Washington, DC: National Institution Press, 2017).

83. Woolf, *U.S. Strategic Nuclear Forces*, 20-21.

84. Ibid., 27-31.

85. Ibid., 32-34.

86. Ibid., 35-39.

87. *Approaches for Managing the Costs of U.S. Nuclear Forces, 2017-2046* (Washington, DC: Congressional Budget Office, 2017).

88. *Nuclear Posture Review 2018* (Washington, DC: U.S. Department of Defense, 2018).

89. Susannah George, "Democrats rebuff GOP plans for low-yield nuclear weapons," *The Washington Post*, June 12, 2019.

90. On the Interoperable Warhead or "3 + 2" Plan see James E. Doyle, *Renewing America's Nuclear Arsenal: Options for the 21st Century* (New York: Routledge, 2017): 24-28.

91. *Fiscal Year 2019 Stockpile Stewardship and Management Plan – Biennial Plan Summary: Report to Congress* (Washington, DC: National Nuclear Security Administration, 2018)

92. *Nuclear Weapons: NNSA Has Taken Steps to Prepare to Restart a Program to Replace the W78 Warhead Capability* (Washington, DC: Government Accounting Office, 2018).

CHAPTER 3

NUCLEAR PRIMACY

The United States currently occupies a hegemonic leadership position in the world based upon a unipolar distribution of power across the international system, though that distribution may be slowly changing.[1] U.S. security interests are also expansive and global. In these circumstances, nuclear primacy is widely viewed as the logical corollary of this U.S. grand strategy.[2] Its intellectual lineage can be traced back to Cold War experts who advocated strongly for a policy of strategic superiority over the Soviet Union as the optimal means of deterring aggressive or provocative behavior.[3] Although the central objective of U.S. nuclear strategy is to deter attacks on the United States and its allies, damage limitation—should deterrence fail—is a closely related secondary objective. Maintaining a healthy skepticism about the effectiveness of deterrence against a revisionist adversary that was willing to assume significant costs to achieve its objectives, these experts viewed deterrence as difficult and the balance of terror as delicate. The most effective means of deterring the Soviet Union was thus to demonstrate the readiness to fight and win a nuclear war. Quantitatively expansive and qualitatively diverse strategic systems and a counterforce doctrine would provide escalation dominance and thus constituted the most reliable deterrent capability. Advocates of this position also tend to be highly skeptical of strategic arms control, preferring to avoid limitations on unilateral U.S. policy and the development and deployment of strategic capabilities. With regard to proliferation, they are less convinced of the need for or value of multilateral regimes and the influence of global norms, and they deny a linkage between U.S. strategic policy and the proliferation behavior of other states. Instead, they believe that the U.S. arsenal is likely to dissuade erstwhile proliferators from even attempting to acquire their own strategic capabilities. Should that dissuasion fail, harsh diplomatic sanctions backed by the threat of preventive conflict should raise the expected costs of proliferation to prohibitive levels.

ELEMENTS OF A STRATEGY OF NUCLEAR PRIMACY

The term *nuclear primacy* includes expansive offensive counterforce capabilities, offensive and defense damage limitation capabilities, and flexible and tailored limited nuclear options (LNOs) to deter adversaries at any level of conflict.[4] "Escalation dominance" in this context underscores the capacity to use a seamless continuum of nuclear capabilities that can address a variety of scenarios: a conventional scenario in which the adversary brandishes its nuclear forces, a limited strategic exchange in the tactical nuclear realm, and even an all-out, large-scale nuclear conflict. Because of the formidable technical challenges inherent to the development and deployment of large-scale missile defenses, offensive damage limitation requires the significant increase of quantitative strategic force levels to an imbalance that provides the United States with a credible ability to preemptively destroy or significantly degrade the offensive strategic forces of an adversary in a first strike. This is an extremely high bar to clear, particularly in the absence of even minimally effective area defenses.

Force Structure

To understand what this qualitative superiority might look like in practice, one can revisit the 2002 Nuclear Posture Review (NPR), which contains discussions of the proper role of nuclear weapons in a new and fundamentally different security environment.[5] Much of the discussion of a "Second Nuclear Age" captures this logic, even in a less than precise and coherent way.[6] The collapse of the Soviet Union removed the obvious need for large arsenals, but it did not remove the need for highly diversified, flexible, and adaptable nuclear capabilities.[7] The 2002 NPR conducted by the George W. Bush administration offered a serious examination of the requisites for a post-Cold War security environment where the central challenges confronting U.S. policy makers were regional powers with weapons of mass destruction (WMD) and access to ballistic missile technology.

> The NPR recommends new nuclear-targeting options and notes the utility of developing "credible," low-yield nuclear warhead. New nuclear capabilities are required to hold at risk a growing number or targets, particularly hardened and deeply buried targets (HDBTs) that can be used to protect WMD, C3 systems and other strategic assets. Active defenses could conceivably blunt a WMD "bolt-out-of-the-blue" or retaliatory strike against US forces and allies abroad, as well as provide strategic defenses against any spasm attack against North America.[8]

Strategic offensive counterforce capabilities, both nuclear and conventional, coupled with robust strategic defenses and a wide array of limited nuclear options, were viewed as necessary to deter the potentially irrational and highly risk-acceptant leaders of rogue regimes in the 1990s and 2000s, and more recently the revisionist great powers in the second decade of the twenty-first century.[9] The underlying logic of this approach can be traced back to the later Cold War period, when the Soviets had significantly expanded their strategic capabilities, achieved numerical parity with the United States, and appeared to be moving toward a position of quantitative advantage:

The public has not been told—and perhaps the defense community itself has not fully realized—that there are two distinct kinds of justification for development of what is called a war-fighting capability. First, there is widespread agreement that a perceived ability to wage a nuclear counterforce (including counter C3) war is probably critically important for the credibility of nuclear threats and hence for the stability of prewar deterrence. Second, a vigorous war-fighting capability may be justified on the ground that the nuclear deterrence system linking East and West is not foolproof or accident proof.[10]

A strategy of nuclear primacy would logically entail both quantitative and qualitative strategic superiority over any adversary, or perhaps a combination of adversaries. Even more important would be an expansion of the types of nuclear weapons that constitute the current U.S. arsenal. Beyond a highly robust and advanced strategic triad, advocates of nuclear primacy are also likely to seek to develop a new generation of diverse weapons systems that can offer a wide range of limited nuclear options and warheads with a variety of military effects. It is likely that smaller-yield, "clean" nuclear warheads will be particularly attractive precisely because of their ability to hold military targets at risk without the likelihood of severe collateral damage to civilians.[11] Beyond the relatively large strategic force levels and the expansion and diversification of nonstrategic nuclear forces, a renewed commitment to larger-scale strategic defenses can be expected.[12] Having argued for such capabilities for many years, advocates of nuclear primacy understand the value as well as the limitations of a reliance on offensive forces, even with extensive counterforce capacity, to provide a credible prediction of damage limitation in the absence of a strategic defense capability. Thus, as recent reports have indicated, the Trump administration has discussed a reconsideration of space-based assets, most likely a constellation of sensors that can track and discriminate between warhead and decoys.[13] Ultimately, a robust, multilayered ballistic (and cruise) missile defense is the objective of many of the advocates who embrace the tenets of nuclear primacy.[14]

Given the nuclear modernization program of record, it may be possible for the United States to achieve some level of quantitative superiority over Russia and maintain superiority over China if, for example, discussion on extending the New START Treaty collapsed and relations between the Washington and Moscow rapidly deteriorated. Three programs would significantly increase the number of deployed warheads beyond the current number of 1,550 and exploit the ongoing modernization program to maximize offensive counterforce capabilities, provided that the nuclear weapons complex can refurbish and/or build new warheads by the time these programs become operations.[15] A notional force structure is presented here:

Table 1. Nuclear Primacy: Notional Force Structure 2035.

System	Units	Max Upload	Warheads
GBSD	450	3 MIRV	1350
SSBN	12	16 SLBM x 8 MIRV	1536
B-21	30	16	480
Total Warheads			**3366**

First, as some advocates have argued, the Ground Based Strategic Deterrent (GBSD) program should be developed in ways that hedge against uncertainty.[16] The primary means of doing so is to develop the new intercontinental ballistic missile (ICBM) so that it can carry a variable payload. While it may initially carry a single warhead (as planned under the New START guidelines), it could be uploaded with additional warheads. Even with a return to the Minuteman III model, the capacity of the ICBM force could be tripled by expanding the force to 450, utilizing the maximum number of available silos, and uploading the GBSD to three multiple independently targetable reentry vehicles

(MIRVs) on each missile. The ICBM force would then account for almost four fifths of the deployed warheads allowed under New START. Given the nature of Russia's missile development and the reported capabilities of its new heavy missile, the RS-28 Sarmat, which may carry as many as ten MIRVs, the United States may recreate the conditions that precipitated the ICBM vulnerability controversy of the 1970s. Many analysts, however, agree that this controversy was somewhat overblown and that strategic defenses may provide a hedge against this threat. A more dramatic and costly way of expanding the contributions of the land-based ICBM force would be to move a portion of the new GBSD inventory to a road-mobile variant.[17] This change would provide greater counterforce capabilities without introducing the instabilities associated with fixed, silo-based missiles. The road-mobile missiles could be deployed with MIRVs, thus increasing the number of deliverable warheads in a more survivable mode.

Second, the United States could reverse course on its plans to decrease the size of the SSBN fleet and plans to decrease the number of missile tubes on each boat, which were devised to maintain the New START force levels. However, even at the programmed levels, a twelve-boat fleet of *Columbia* class nuclear-powered ballistic missile submarines (SSBNs) can account for 1,536 deployed warheads at maximum capacity.[18]

Finally, if the B-21 program is executed as unclassified accounts have portrayed it and if the Air Force is able to take delivery of up to 100 new long-range nuclear-capable bombers, Washington will have fairly wide discretion in the allocation of significant numbers of planes to the nuclear or conventional mission sets. With the Long-Range Standoff Ordinance (LRSO) and the B61-12, the nuclear-capable B-21 will be a formidable strategic asset capable of contributing in both highly contested and more permissive air defense environments. Given the New START counting rules and the somewhat questionable approach of counting each bomber as a single warhead, the United States could ostensibly commit a third of the B-21 force to nuclear missions and raise its de facto deployed warhead numbers significantly above what the current bomber force can provide today. If the B-21 has similar payload capacity as the B-2, it could carry up to sixteen gravity bombs.[19]

A decision by the United States to implement a strategy of nuclear primacy would likely entail additional—and very costly—commitments, including an expansion of strategic defense for damage limitation capabilities to complement offensive counterforce capabilities and an expansion of tactical or theater nuclear weapons systems to provide limited nuclear options to policymakers and achieve escalation dominance to deter risk-acceptant, revisionist adversaries. What should be apparent is that a strategic nuclear force consisting of the quantitative force levels, qualitative improvements, and complementary strategic defense and nonstrategic nuclear weapons capabilities described earlier would maximize the flexibility available to the national command authority. It would also prove most efficacious in fighting a protracted, large-scale nuclear war. The benefits may come at the cost of strategic stability and significantly increased program budgets, likely demanding a much larger percentage of the United States' defense budgets over the next three decades. Advocates argue, however, that nuclear primacy is worth the expense of maximizing U.S. national security in an era of renewed great power competition and conflict.[20]

Employment Policy

It is important to note that these advocates still maintain that their first objective is the effective deterrence of aggression against the United States or its allies. To enact this deterrence, however, the United States requires strategic and nonstrategic nuclear forces that adversaries believe the country may actually use. Thus, older legacy systems that would create disproportionate destruction and large-scale collateral damage may not be a credible threat in the context of a limited conflict in a key region. Precisely because the adversaries confronting the United States are not necessarily rational actors, threats based on society-wide punishment are not sufficient to deter them. A more effective approach is to threaten the military forces of such regimes, their leadership, and their strategic forces, causing risk-acceptant leaders to fear that they may not be able to achieve their objectives:

> Instead a credible deterrent should give U.S. leaders a range of retaliatory options, including the ability to respond to nuclear attacks with either conventional or nuclear strikes, to retaliate with strikes against an enemy's nuclear forces rather than its cities, and to minimize casualties. The foundation for the flexible deterrent exists. The current U.S. arsenal includes a mix of accurate high- and low-yield warheads, offering a wide range of retaliatory options—including the ability to launch precise, very low-casualty nuclear counterforce strikes. The United States must preserve that mix of capabilities—especially the low-yield weapons—as it cuts the size of its nuclear forces.[21]

As noted, strategic defenses play a critical role in this approach by preventing the adversary from escalating to threaten the United States homeland. Such an escalation may be the "trump card" in an adversary's theory of victory, particularly for a regional nuclear power like North Korea. Conversely, if the adversary believes it cannot possibly achieve its objectives through blackmail, demonstration, deliberate escalation, or all-out military conflict, it will have little incentive to initiate provocation.

At least theoretically, some of the advocates of nuclear primacy are less concerned about the size of the arsenal as a whole. All things being equal, they would prefer to have a larger arsenal than that of any adversary (or combination of adversaries). However, important recent statements seem to imply a shift of focus to the qualitative aspect of the U.S. strategic nuclear arsenal. The 2002 NPR developed the concept of a "new triad" that would combine the strategic nuclear arsenal with new conventional strategic offensive forces in one leg. Robust strategic defenses and an adaptable, highly effective network of intelligence would serve as the other two legs.[22] Assuming a newly cooperative relationship with Russia, the 2002 NPR focused squarely on rogue regional adversaries armed with nuclear weapons or other WMD. The potential for developing tailored nuclear weapons that could hold at risk hard and deeply buried targets (HDBTs) such as leadership, command and control, and WMD infrastructure stemmed from the strategic context, but also generated intense political controversy. Some initial discussions also proposed the development of a conventional prompt global strike program that might initially retrofit ICBMs or SLBMs with conventional payloads to hit time-sensitive, high-value targets anywhere in the world. Based on these developments, arms control advocates argued that the Bush administration was significantly "lowering the threshold" for nuclear use and making nuclear weapons "more usable":[23] "Whether the slight accuracy improvements come from GPS, next-generation inertial guidance, or other technologies, high accuracy delivery systems with low-yield weapons should form the backbone of the U.S. nuclear deterrent."[24] Given the nature of the adversaries who had driven the thinking behind the 2002 NPR, this argument was perhaps not surprising. However, the argument of opponents underscored a tension that has only become more prevalent over time: efforts to deter less capable but more risk-acceptant regional adversaries may undermine strategic stability with Russia. Moreover, as relations with China have become more difficult over the past decade, analysts have expressed concern that U.S. modernization efforts, especially continued investments in strategic defenses and conventional strategic strike systems, have driven Chinese planners to reassess their preference to maintain a limited, minimal deterrence posture capable of "assured retaliation." Instead, they are beginning to favor an expansion of their strategic arsenal.[25]

Shifting to address an environment that views great power conflict as a strategic priority, the Trump administration's 2018 NPR similarly received criticism for potentially "lowering the nuclear threshold" and introducing more usable nuclear weapons. Arms control advocates were already concerned about the strong likelihood that the B61 Model 12 nuclear gravity bomb would be endorsed by the Trump NPR, and they proved to be right. Two additional programs (or, more accurately, a new program and a redeployment) also caused consternation in the arms control community. The first was a nuclear-armed sea-launched cruise missile (SLCM) for use on U.S. Navy surface and subsurface vessels. The United States removed and retired the Tomahawk Land Attack Cruise Missile-Nuclear (TLAM-N) under the George H.W. Bush administration, and thus this procurement decision does seem to represent a "new" program, reversing the Obama administration's tendency to forego new nuclear capabilities and focus on modernizing existing capabilities. The second and more controversial program was the decision to download the MIRVs from a portion of the deployed Trident D5 SLBMs and replace them with a single, low-yield nuclear warhead. This was seen as a fairly direct countermeasure to the expansive Russian nonstrategic nuclear weapons (NSNW) arsenal and Moscow's perceived willingness to use its own low-yield tactical nuclear weapons under conflict conditions. Supporters of the program argue that it will enhance the U.S. ability to deter Russia from escalating to the nuclear threshold in the event of a crisis (in the Baltic region, for example) by providing the United States with an in-kind munition that can be delivered by a platform (SSBN) capable of operating in highly contested environments.[26] Once again, the "lowering of the nuclear threshold" is deemed necessary in response to the adversary's capabilities and perceived intentions (higher risk acceptance). This time, however, the threshold is being lowered as part of a great power conflict in Europe against a revisionist Russia, rather than in a conflict with a rogue regional nuclear power.

Declaratory Policy

A strategic policy of nuclear primacy, war-fighting, or damage limitation could widen the scope of nuclear weapons use and the threat of such use in United States foreign and national security policy. For the first time, the Trump administration's declaratory policy explicitly broached the potential use of nuclear weapons in response to a "non-nuclear strategic attack."[27] Although the policy did not specify exactly what such an attack might be, there appears to be a growing threat of a cyber or electromagnetic pulse (EMP) attack on the United States or an ally that would have the effects of a strategic nuclear or WMD attack. Considering today's rapid changes in technology, the Trump administration's effort to hedge against future threats seems prudent, though the arms control and nonproliferation communities expressed concern that the language in the Trump administration NPR was expanding the potential roles of nuclear weapons. Given the nature of such attacks and the levels of societal damage that they imply, these criticisms may be misguided. Although these communities may prefer a policy of calculated ambiguity in relation to non-nuclear strategic attacks, it is difficult to find fault with a strong and clear government response to a new or emerging threat to the United States and its key allies. It is more problematic to express a willingness to use nuclear weapons in conventional conflicts where the survival of an ally is at stake, and criticisms by the arms control and nonproliferation communities on this point seem more justified.

The potential roles of nuclear forces were delineated by the Trump administration in its 2018 NPR:

> The United States would only consider the employment of nuclear weapons in extreme circumstances to defend the vital interests of the United States, its allies and partners. Extreme circumstances could include significant non-nuclear strategic attacks. Significant non-nuclear strategic attacks include, but are not limited to, attacks on the U.S., allied or partner civilian population or infrastructure, and attacks on U.S. or allied nuclear forces, their command and control or warning and attack assessment capabilities.[28]

At the same time, the NPR states that "The United States will not use or threaten to use nuclear weapons against non-nuclear weapons states that are party to the NPT [Nonproliferation Treaty] and in compliance with their nuclear non-proliferation obligations."[29] It thus attempts to straddle the line between creating a perception of an increased reliance on nuclear weapons in U.S. national security strategy and supporting nonproliferation objectives. However, it is not clear whether this statement is enough for the policy's critics, and it seems clear that it emphasizes more direct challenges, including deterring adversaries, reassuring allies, maintaining the capacity to achieve U.S. strategic objectives should deterrence fail, and hedging against an uncertain geopolitical and technological future.

Alert Status

If the United States were to move toward the implementation of a policy of nuclear primacy, and if the ICBM force were not only modernized under the GBSD program but also expanded by placing MIRVs on the newly deployed missiles, the potential for vulnerability would grow, particularly in the face of Russia's deployment of heavy ICBMs. The United States' MIRVed ICBMs would be attractive targets, which could decrease crisis or first-strike stability. To rectify this situation, it might be necessary to return to some measure of Launch on Warning (LOW) or Launch Under Attack (LUA) postures that would be predicated on receiving clear and timely Early Warning alerts, underscoring the importance of the integration alert status with larger nuclear command, control and communications (NC3) and strategic command, control, communications, computers, intelligence, surveillance, and reconnaissance (C4ISR) systems and infrastructures. This could place a considerable burden on existing assets and capabilities, necessitating further investment.

NC3

To effectively implement a strategy of nuclear primacy and the offensive counterforce and damage limitation aspects of that strategy, extensive demands must be made on nuclear command, control, and communications. And to maintain robust command and control over a spectrum of nuclear operations, from tactical use to limited nuclear options to large-scale strikes under highly contested conditions, the resilience of NC3 networks and critical nodes is essential:

> The system is needed to ensure that the president and other national leaders receive accurate and timely information on threat warning and attack assessment, maintain the ability to support conferencing and decisionmaking, and are able to issue properly authorized orders to US nuclear forces. All of these capabilities

must be survivable and their functionality assured even in the most stressing conditions and without interference. Key elements of the existing nuclear command, control, and communications system (NC3) include early warning sensors such as launch detection satellites and fixed land based early warning radars; facilities to receive and analyze data from these and other sensors; mobile and fixed secure command and control centers and conferencing capabilities; and communications links between nuclear forces and national leaders.[30]

Although the Obama modernization program invested significant resources in refurbishing and enhancing nuclear command, control, and communication systems and infrastructure, it is not clear that those investments are sufficient for such an expansive counterforce and damage limitation strategy, and therefore further investment may be required.

Nuclear Enterprise

For a strategy of nuclear primacy that contains both offensive strategic counterforce capabilities and an emphasis on the nonstrategic nuclear weapons that will likely be required for escalation control against great power adversaries, it will be necessary to consolidate the existing warheads and to develop new warheads (and the plutonium pits necessary for such expanded capabilities): "Revitalizing infrastructure and maintaining a readiness capability to develop new weapons or replacements for existing nuclear weapons is fundamentally about providing resilience and reducing risk in the future."[31]

Some less enthusiastic observers have questioned the current plans for new pit production, arguing that they exceed what is necessary for the current forces, although others have questioned the reliability of the pits in their present state. However, the longer-term problems of an aging strategic arsenal and deployed warheads that are reaching the end of their service lives—in some cases after undergoing several life extension programs—seem to necessitate the expansion of pit production as a hedge against quantitative force level increases by Russia or China.

Moreover, new pits may be necessary for warheads on a new generation of cruise missiles, such as the LRSO and the SLCM envisioned by the Trump administration NPR.

In its pressing concern about responsive and flexible infrastructure, the Trump administration's NPR is similar to the Bush Administration's 2002 NPR:

> The new triad's emphasis on a responsive nuclear infrastructure is meant to forestall two potential problems that, according to the NPR, could result from the dilapidated nuclear-weapons production complex. On the one hand, the inability to build nuclear warheads, including such critical components as the plutonium pits, could pose a danger in the event that a serious problem is discovered in an existing warhead. The current reliance on the LEP, and its limited approach in maintaining the nuclear-explosive package of the warhead, means that the United States may simply be unable to cope with just such an eventuality. As such, the long term reliability of an increasingly ageing strategic arsenal, which was never intentionally designed to be maintained for decades after its original service life, could be questioned. On the other hand, the current approach towards maintaining the nuclear arsenal, at the expense of nuclear-weapons development and production, limits American options for dealing with future threat scenarios that might require new nuclear capabilities.[32]

Ultimately, the larger question associated with a renewed reliance on and expansion of nuclear forces is whether it will be necessary to test new weapons in the future.[33] The Trump NPR does not explicitly answer this question, perhaps because its authors anticipated the highly negative domestic and international political implications of such a policy. However, the expressed lack of willingness to consider ratifying the Comprehensive Test Ban Treaty indicates the possibility that renewed testing may be necessary and shows that the Trump administration is unwilling to foreclose this option.

Strategic Defenses

With a commitment to strategic superiority, the expansion and qualitative improvement of strategic defenses would be a logical extension of quantitative increases in force levels and of the diversification and qualitative enhancement of offensive forces at the strategic, theater, and tactical ranges.[34] For advocates of a nuclear war-fighting or damage limitation strategy, robust strategic defenses play an important role as complements to strategic offensive forces that could be used to disarm a smaller nuclear power like China or North Korea. The offensive forces could also preempt or significantly weaken a first strike by Russia, thereby decreasing the residual offensive forces to levels that could be effectively addressed by U.S. strategic defenses. The nature of the deployed strategic defenses, and specifically the scope and capabilities of such a system, has been an important focus of advocates of a war-fighting strategy since the mid-Cold War. Even with significant quantitative superiority, an inability to field effective strategic defenses is a well-understood and major vulnerability in a coherent strategic approach: "Any discussion of a potential new offensive force capability must at least note that it, and its complementary siblings in the triad, are burdened with the need to carry a deterrence story they cannot manage plausibly so long as they are hindered by the absence of U.S. homeland defenses."[35] Thus, after the George W. Bush administration decided in 2002 to withdraw from the 1972 Antiballistic Missile (ABM) Treaty and to order the implementation of a crash program to deploy interceptors in Alaska and California, the subsequent development and deployment of strategic defenses was predicated on responding to quantitatively smaller challenges rather than building the capacity necessary to defend against a peer nuclear power like Russia. Missile defense advocates describe the current state of strategic defenses as follows:

> One possible path would be to retain a bifurcated strategy and posture similar to that currently in force. This involves near-complete vulnerability of US territory and military forces to Russian and Chinese missiles, even of limited quantity, and reliance upon

offense-dominant posture to deter, while simultaneously working to outpace Iranian and North Korean threats with missile defense, and retaining an advantageous and relatively defense-dominant position relative to their short- and long-range missiles.[36]

Given the nature of the current U.S. system, such a strategic defense posture would likely require a significant expansion of the primary sites in Fort Greeley, Alaska and at Fort Vandenberg in California. It would also require the construction of a second, relatively expansive site on the East Coast. Preliminary discussions have taken place concerning the construction of an installation at Fort Drum in upstate New York, but continuing issues with the ground-based interceptor program have slowed decisions to break ground on an East Coast interceptor bed.

A crucial but underreported development was a decision made within the United States Congress to shift the objectives of the U.S. missile defense efforts. The 2017 National Defense Authorization Act (NDAA), which funds Pentagon spending, removed the term "limited" from national missile defense appropriations for the first time, ostensibly clearing a path for a major expansion of the national missile defense program.[37] Perhaps the most important decision will be whether the United States should move to develop and construct a space-based architecture for missile defenses.[38] Such an architecture would allow for a more ambitious approach: "Alternatively, the objects of US missile defense efforts could be revised to include protection against not only attacks from North Korea and Iran, but also selected missile threats from whatever sources, including Russia and China."[39] The Pentagon has recently signaled a willingness to explore these options, and the formal decision to create a "Space Force" as a new independent service also implies a greater emphasis on outer space operations and the potential for military conflict in space. The move to space competition will likely have significant ramifications for the Outer Space Treaty, and fears about the militarization of space could spur a new competition with Russia and China over the next decade.

Nonstrategic Nuclear Weapons

Should the United States seek to embrace a posture of strategic superiority vis-à-vis Russia and China, NSNWs may come to play a larger role in the United States' nuclear policy and its deterrent strategy in Europe and East Asia. Discussions concerning Russia's Intermediate Nuclear Forces (INF) Treaty violations prior to the October 2018 announcement that the United States would formally withdraw from the Treaty because of ongoing violations centered on the U.S. ability to develop systems that would respond "in kind" to Russia's perceived development of a Treaty-noncompliant system.[40] As noted, the 2018 NPR seemed to indirectly address the Russian deployment of a potentially nuclear-armed intermediate-range cruise missile with the announcement of a new program to reintroduce a nuclear-armed SLCM and the redeployment of a portion of submarine-launched ballistic missiles (SLBMs) with a lower-yield warhead.[41] Both of these programs seem to be responses to the perception that Russia possesses a much larger and more diverse stockpile of NSNWs than does the United States.

Although the Russian deployment of a proscribed ground-launched cruise missile (GLCM) system provides the United States with a formal rationale for withdrawal from the Treaty, concerns about the nature of China's decade-long military modernization program have led defense experts to consider the potential utility of a new conventional U.S. IRBM in the Western Pacific.[42] China's modernization has centered on the development of a robust missile force, consisting of short- and intermediate-range ballistic missiles and an intermediate-range cruise missile that can hold forward U.S. bases in the region and potentially U.S. aircraft carrier task forces that would be at risk in the event of a conflict over Taiwan or perhaps elsewhere in the region.[43] China has subsequently focused on improving its surface, subsurface, and air capabilities, but the threat posed by the missile forces serves as the foundation of its perceived A2/AD capability, which has influenced U.S. force planning in recent years. The deployment of a number of "Pershing III" missiles to Andersen Air Force Base on Guam could rectify this perceived imbalance in strike capabilities and enhance deterrence in the region. These would most likely be conventional weapons dedicated to holding Chinese targets, particularly fixed targets like airbases, at risk. But given China's ability to focus on this area of force development, U.S. defense planners see an "in kind response" as a potentially effective countermeasure.[44]

CONTRIBUTIONS OF STRATEGIC PRIMACY

Extended Deterrence/Reassurance

Advocates of nuclear primacy view deterrence as inherently difficult. Facing aggressive, highly risk-acceptant, and perhaps irrational revisionist actors, the United States and its allies must deploy the capabilities necessary to deter provocation at differing levels of intensity. During the late 1970s and 1980s, perceptions of a highly aggressive Soviet leadership that was ready and able to fight a protracted nuclear conflict drove advocates of strategic "war-fighting" doctrines to press for greater U.S. strategic offensive and defensive capabilities. Rejecting the logic of assured destruction and the notion that the Soviets shared a similar view of the strategic competition, these experts argued that the requisite capabilities for stable deterrence were much greater than those programmed and deployed in the post-Strategic Arms Limitation Talks (SALT) period. Today, advocates of nuclear primacy also argue that escalation dominance, or the ability to prevail over an adversary at any level of violence that adversary may choose, is necessary to effectively deter a highly aggressive, risk-acceptant enemy. Understanding what an adversary values most is critical. In the post-Cold War environment, advocates argued for the development of more usable nuclear weapons, such as those that could destroy hardened underground bunkers that provide protection for the leadership, command and control, and WMD production facilities of regional rogue states.[45] The perceived "usability" of nuclear weapons is thus critical to the deterrent value of those weapons. Thus, much of the legacy strategic nuclear weapons that make up the current U.S.

arsenal, with high-yield warheads and minimal flexibility, are viewed as making only a limited contribution to the United States' capacity to deter adversaries in the renewed era of great power competition. Weapons that will create disproportionate levels of destruction, particularly with predictably high levels of civilian collateral damage, are viewed with skepticism—they are seen as unlikely to deter a revisionist actor precisely because that actor does not believe that the United States would use such a weapon. Furthermore, such an actor may not be concerned about civilian casualties. Thus, the traditional threats of punishment are less useful and less credible:

> The new-triad posture, if fully realized, is seen to enable the US to hold at risk an adversary's deterrent more effectively and, with its combination of usable nuclear weapons and missile defense, to threaten the use of its strategic capabilities more credibly. This strategy is still firmly rooted in the notions of deterrence against its adversaries and the assurance (e.g. extended deterrence guarantees) of its allies.[46]

Advocates of nuclear primacy would prefer that the United States possess a wide range of nuclear options, from very low-yield "clean" warheads that would minimize collateral damage to other warheads that would provide special effects, such as those that can meet HDBT challenges of regional adversaries as well as respond to potential deliberate escalation by great power competitors today. The expansion and refinement of nonstrategic nuclear weapons would more effectively address the perceived threats.

Crisis Stability

Perhaps unsurprisingly, advocates of nuclear primacy are often dismissive of concerns about crisis stability. In their view, the best way to deter aggressive revisionist adversaries is to develop or acquire and deploy nuclear forces capable of providing the United States and its allies with escalation dominance vis-à-vis the opponent's forces. Incentives to use nuclear weapons early in a conflict or to threaten first use to achieve war aims should be negated because of the U.S. capacity to increase the expected costs in response to any level of nuclear usage. Rather than worrying about inadvertent escalation from a conventional clash of forces to a strategic exchange, these experts focus on the ability to purposefully and deliberately manage escalation to the advantage of the United States and its allies. By confronting the adversary with the reality that it cannot possibly succeed in achieving its objective at any level of violence, from irregular warfare to large-scale strategic exchanges, the United States will remove the adversary's incentive to consider the threat or use of nuclear strikes in the first place.

Therefore, if the adversary escalated to the use of nuclear weapons, whether at the tactical, theater, or even strategic level, the United States would possess the capabilities to address that escalation and counter with a proportional, in-kind response. It could even deliberately escalate to regain the initiative and press the adversary to relent. Clearly, this approach assumes that the United States would possess the requisite capabilities (both offensive and defensive) to prevent the adversary from achieving its objectives and that it would maintain the capacity to exact devastating punishment should the adversary fail to back down. With confidence in the underlying quantitative and qualitative superiority of U.S. nuclear forces, the concerns about an adversary's loss of control and the implications for U.S. security are less salient than the desire to achieve U.S. military objectives. However, the ultimate reliance on damage limitation, which may be premised on less-than-perfect strategic defenses, indicates a potential weakness of this approach:

> A third goal served by missile defense is damage limitation in the event that deterrence should fail. Escalation by means of missile attack could occur against forces or allies within a region or against the US homeland. Missile defense can simultaneously discourage an adversary from escalating a conflict and provide a degree of protection against such an attack.[47]

Arms Race Stability

With regard to arms race stability, proponents of nuclear primacy are also generally dismissive of the influence of U.S. acquisition and deployment policies on the behavior of potential adversaries. Embracing a traditional deterrence model view of the international system, these experts argue that only robust—and ideally superior—capabilities will effectively deter an adversary from engaging in unwanted behavior. If such a unilateral policy spurs action by other states to improve their own capabilities, then so be it. Ultimately, the confidence in America's capacity to provide the necessary quantitative increases in force levels and qualitative improvement in new weapons systems underlies the reliance on unilateral means to provide for U.S. security. This strategic policy position also relies heavily on faith in the United States' technological edge and ability to innovate when provided with sufficient budgetary resources and political and bureaucratic support to develop new solutions to complex challenges.

The potential for increased uncertainty in the system, including in the perceptions of U.S. intentions by adversaries and third parties, is considered an unfortunate but acceptable byproduct of maximizing the probability that the United States will confront national security threats from the best possible position. Most of these experts share a healthy skepticism of strategic arms control initiatives and prefer a situation in which the United States is not prevented from developing, fielding, and deploying the number and kinds of weapons that best suit its national security interests. In the event that an adversary moderates its behavior or engages in costly signaling to communicate more benign intentions, the United States may reciprocate in the form of negotiated mutual limitations on quantitative force levels or specific types of forces. These experts would argue, however, that Washington should do so only from a position of strength. Moreover, given the potential for rapid change, both geopolitical and technological, in the international system, strategic arms control or nonproliferation commitments that limit U.S. innovation may prevent the United States from implementing effective policies to hedge against future uncertainty and respond to new threats and opportunities.

Dissuasion

The concept of dissuasion has been used by advocates of larger and more diverse nuclear forces as an additional but related objective of nuclear strategy. They typically define dissuasion as confronting potential adversaries with a U.S. nuclear arsenal of such quantitative force levels and qualitatively advanced capabilities that they will not even consider attempting to improve their own capabilities or acquire nuclear weapons, if they do not already possess them. As an analysis of the 2002 NPR argued: "The dissuasion of potential adversaries from even pursuing threatening capabilities is now seen as a feasible possibility, while defeat of an adversary in the event of deterrence failure has now been embraced."[48] Although such an objective would not be relevant to a nuclear peer-competitor like Russia, the maintenance of a relatively large arsenal does have the effect of presenting China with a formidable task in the event that it seeks to achieve nuclear parity with the United States. Experts who view dissuasion as an important aspect of U.S. nuclear strategy and a benefit of larger, more diverse arsenals have opposed further reductions to the strategic arsenal, whether unilateral or in the context of formal negotiations with Moscow. For example, during the 2009 congressional hearings on the New START Treaty, skeptics and opponents expressed concerns that China would "sprint up" to achieve some measure of numerical parity that would create a multipolar nuclear system and would undermine or complicate the advancement of U.S. national security interests.

Many of these advocates also seem highly skeptical of the purported link between U.S. strategic force levels and global nuclear proliferation. They argue instead that the clear conventional military superiority possessed by the United States has pushed regional powers to seek nuclear weapons to deter or blackmail the United States and its allies. Maintaining a relatively large and diverse arsenal is a public good in and of itself because it contributes to advancing U.S. national security interests, deterring adversaries, underwriting the security of allies and partners, and preventing challengers from emerging in the first place. Given the potentially risk-acceptant or even irrational decision-making processes in revisionist states, the United States requires tailored, case-specific capabilities at sufficient levels to deny these actors' objectives and plausibly communicate that they will not achieve their goals.

Strategic Arms Control

If the United States were to embrace a policy of nuclear primacy, it is difficult to envision that strategic arms control would play a significant role in U.S. diplomacy. With the recent announcement of the Trump administration's intention to formally withdraw from the INF Treaty, a renewed emphasis on strategic arms control seems unlikely. The most pressing question in the wake of the INF Treaty withdrawal is whether the United States and Russia will work to extend the New START Treaty, which is due to expire in February 2021. If the Treaty is not extended, it is unclear whether the numerical limit of 1,550 deployed warheads would be maintained or whether the United States or Russia or both would move to increase force levels above the previously agreed-upon levels. Under the current nuclear modernization program, New START obligations are incorporated into planned acquisitions and deployments. Given the costs associated with the existing modernization program, it is uncertain whether Washington would be willing to dramatically expand the quantitative levels of strategic forces. Clearly, however, a post-New START environment would remove the formal constraints on moving toward some measure of quantitative superiority and a deterioration of relations with Russia and failure to extend the Treaty may provide political impetus to expand force levels beyond current programmed levels.

Nonproliferation

A decision to pursue strategic superiority would almost certainly undermine U.S. nonproliferation efforts and could create significant stress for the NPT regime. Given the recent passage of the Nuclear Ban Treaty, civil society nongovernmental organizations (NGOs) and sympathetic states have emphasized the failure of the United States and Russia to make further progress toward nuclear disarmament under Article VI of the NPT. Although the Trump administration has repeatedly questioned the linkage between progress on strategic arms control and the larger nonproliferation effort, it seems evident that a U.S. plan to significantly expand its nuclear arsenal in quantitative terms and a likely related reorientation of U.S. national security strategy to increase its reliance and expand its potential scenarios for use of nuclear weapons would create a negative backlash among these civil society elements and their allies. Moreover, such a move could place key U.S. allies, particularly in Western Europe and Japan, in the unenviable position of defending the behavior of their alliance partner, their place under the United States nuclear umbrella, and the implicit contribution of nuclear weapons to their own security in the face of mounting domestic political opposition.

The Costs of Nuclear Primacy

A significant expansion of the Obama administration's nuclear modernization program of record is likely to entail significant costs beyond the estimated $1.2 trillion. First, the development of the new sea-launched cruise missile, whose scope remains somewhat uncertain, would represent a significant program. If it is programmed for deployment on surface and subsurface vessels, it could be an extensive program. Early discussion, however, indicates that it may use the same warhead, the W80, which is planned for use with the LRSO, and the Navy may attempt to leverage existing cruise missile development programs to maximize efficiencies.

Second, a move to upload warheads on the GBSD program, which could be envisioned if Russia proves unwilling to consider negotiating a follow-on to New START or at least to extend the Treaty, would likely create a demand for additional warheads. As discussed earlier, given plans to use the existing Minuteman III silos and infrastructure, a three-MIRV ICBM replacement may be feasible, but it would also increase the estimated costs associated with modernizing the land-based leg of the triad. As noted, a decision to deploy a portion of the new GBSD force on mobile launchers would also be an expensive proposition.

Lastly, although it is not directly related to the planned modernization of strategic and nonstrategic offensive programs, a renewed emphasis on strategic defenses would likely demand significant defense dollars as well.

ASSESSING NUCLEAR PRIMACY

Advocates of nuclear primacy, and specifically the reorientation of U.S. strategic force structure and employment strategy toward a war-fighting, damage limitation posture, have also consistently criticized what they perceive as a prevailing view within the defense community that it is impossible to escape from mutual vulnerability. They criticize what they see as a dangerous and risky reliance on the precepts of mutual assured destruction (MAD) and strategic stability. These advocates call for not only quantitative superiority, but also the qualitative variety and flexibility that would give the national command authority options to use nuclear weapons across a spectrum of potential operational scenarios.

> The new triad represents a complex and potentially contradictory effort to reduce American self-deterrence by de-emphasizing the role of nuclear weapons through an expansion of non-nuclear components in US deterrence calculus, while simultaneously attempting to modify American nuclear forces to play a more tailored deterrent role against potential adversaries.[49]

During the Cold War, many of these experts were critical of the SALT process and the larger policy of détente with the Soviet Union. Takin a highly negative view of Soviet intentions, they worried as Soviet capabilities grew throughout the 1970s, fearing that Moscow could exploit a "window of opportunity" to make gains in the developing world and might even consider a disarming first strike against the United States. In the event of such an attack, it was thought that the Soviets would use their heavy MIRVed ICBMs to destroy the U.S. ICBM force. An American president would be left with the capacity to respond with devastating countervalue strikes against the Soviet Union, but these strikes were seen as less credible because the Soviets would still maintain enough strategic forces to devastate U.S. population centers. Thus, a U.S. president might be "self-deterred" from taking retaliatory action:

> The fundamental purpose of the strategic forces is to deter, or help deter, hostile actors against vital U.S. interests. The posture or doctrine outlined here should offer maximum discouragement to adventure and risk-taking on the Soviet part. However, deterrence is not sufficient for the mission of U.S. strategic forces. In addition to the negative task of dissuasion, those force have also laid on them by foreign policy a range of possible "compellence" duties.[50]

Skeptics argued that even a highly successful "limited" attack that destroyed much of the Minuteman force would nonetheless cause so many civilian casualties that the Kremlin could not possibly believe the United States would not strike back in retaliation. Given the nature of the existing U.S. submarine and bomber force, the Soviet Union would be highly vulnerable to a second strike, but the failure of the SALT II process to adequately address the Minuteman vulnerability issue remained a major concern. Although many U.S. defense experts were dismissive of this logic, the deterioration of relations between Washington and Moscow in the late 1970s seemed to validate the warnings of the more hawkish elements of the defense community. Highly critical of the Carter administration's handling of any number of issues, including strategic arms control negotiations and the Russian invasion of Afghanistan, many of these experts became supporters (and in some cases members) of the Reagan administration. Perhaps unsurprisingly, they advocated and supported the major military buildup that had begun in the last year of the Carter administration. Many had been vehemently opposed to the ABM Treaty and supported President Reagan's Strategic Defense Initiative (SDI, or "Star Wars"), favoring investments in the development of expansive strategic defense systems that could ultimately allow the

United States to escape the relationship of mutual vulnerability, which most of them found morally and strategically unacceptable:

> It is true that damage limitation entails making preparation for the conduct of nuclear war, which is hardly a novel activity; the Soviet and U.S. defense communities have been making such preparations for more than thirty-five years. A proponent of damage limiting strategy believes that the United States has no sensible choice other than to attempt to implement this idea in planning. In fact, this task is even worth doing badly.[51]

Today these advocates have reshaped their arguments, but the underlying logic remains similar to their Cold War views. Although they often accuse their opponents of "Cold War mentalities," these experts seem wedded to the view that nuclear weapons are an inherently useful tool of U.S. policy and a major advantage that the United States can and should wield over most other nations in the world.[52]

In general, advocates of nuclear primacy oppose most strategic arms control agreements, believing that they may limit the capacity of the United States to adapt to new threats. In terms of nonproliferation policy, most express skepticism with the NPT and deny that Article VI obliges the United States to make efforts to cut its nuclear (and eventually conventional) forces as part of a progression toward general disarmament. In this way, advocates of this strategy are the most open to charges of hypocrisy from arms control and nonproliferation advocates, but they also care the least. Their underlying view that U.S. national interests are always and everywhere aligned with the betterment of the world allows them to dismiss criticism. This is not to say, however, that they are not intently concerned about the proliferation of nuclear weapons and WMD. In fact, proliferation is one of their central concerns, and before the resurgence of Russia and the emergence of China, they saw it as the primary threat to U.S. national security. As Charles Krauthammer wrote in the early 2000s:

> The American hegemon has no great power enemies, an historical oddity of the first order. Yet it does face a serious threat to its dominance, indeed to its essential security. It comes from a source even more historically odd: an archipelago of rouge states (some connected with transnational terrorists) wielding weapons of mass destruction. This threat is not trivial. It is the single greatest danger to the United States because, for all of America's dominance, and for all of it recently demonstrated resilience, there is one thing it might not survive: decapitation. The detonation of a dozen nuclear weapons in major American cities, or the spreading of smallpox or anthrax throughout the general population, is an existential threat. It is perhaps the only realistic threat to America as a functioning hegemon, perhaps even to America as a functioning society.[53]

These advocates, however, typically prefer a unilateral response, eschewing international organizations or regimes that could limit United States' freedom to act to secure its interests. In terms of nuclear weapons and U.S. strategy, this logic was encapsulated in the 2002 NPR and has re-emerged in much of the discussion surrounding the 2018 Trump NPR. Whereas the latter is focused on the development of limited options to address the extended deterrence challenges created by the return of great power competition with Russia and China, it contains obvious echoes of the former and of arguments made for a strategic shift to a war-fighting doctrine during the Cold War.

It is important to note that many of the advocates of this strategic approach have been pressing for the same policy positions for over thirty years. Strategic offensive counterforce capabilities, coupled with robust strategic defenses and a wide array of limited nuclear options, were viewed as necessary for effectively deterring aggressive Soviet leaders in the 1970s and 1980s, the potentially irrational and highly risk-acceptant leaders of rogue regimes in the 1990s and 2000s, and the leaders of revisionist great powers in the second decade of the twenty-first century. In short, these positions are anything but new. To some degree, critics are correct when they assert that these prescriptions have merely been repackaged to meet the threat du jour.

Lowering the Threshold of Nuclear Use?

Critics of the 2002 NPR were quick to express concern about plans for relatively small, low-yield nuclear weapons to be used to target underground command bunkers or infrastructure related to WMD programs. Moreover, the coupling of nuclear and conventional strike programs worried some experts who viewed the NPR as officially "lowering the threshold" for nuclear use:

> But the current process of nuclear transformation goes beyond the dream of bunker busters, expanded targeting options, and other forms of nuclear counter-force modernization; it threatens to contribute to the notion that nuclear weapons can be equated with conventional weapons.[54]

The Bush Administration responded that these capabilities would enhance the deterrence of less "rational" rogue regimes, but the controversy ultimately prevented the implementation of many of the proposed initiatives. As noted earlier, the recently released Trump administration NPR announces plans to convert a small number of Trident SLBMs into single low-yield weapons and a program for a new nuclear-armed SLCM in response to the threat that Russia will use its NSNWs in a future conflict. These plans underscore the common ground among some of the experts who call for greater "usability" of nuclear weapons in the context of very different strategic rationales. They dismiss the criticism that their policies would lower the nuclear threshold, arguing that the possession of a diverse arsenal with a range of limited nuclear options and low-yield tactical and theater capabilities would actually raise the threshold. This disagreement is difficult to reconcile and verges on a semantic debate. What is clear, however, is that perceived usability is viewed as vital to the overall value of nuclear weapons, and the challenge of American "self-deterrence" is a recurring concern of these advocates.

Undermining Stability and Creating Challenges

Perhaps the greatest foreseeable impact of an attempt by the United States to achieve a positon of nuclear primacy, including quantitative and qualitative strategic superiority over great power competitors like Russia and China and an expansion of strategic defenses and nonstrategic nuclear weapons, is a significant erosion in strategic stability in the global system. Russia seems well positioned to engage in a competitive strategic armaments race in the short run, and given its current advantage in nonstrategic weapons, it may rely on them more heavily than its current doctrine indicates. Though the economic and industrial base of Russia's war-making capacity may be limited, Moscow has objectively excelled at the development of missile forces throughout the past six decades. Although China is starting at a much lower quantitative level, it has already proven adept at investing in offsetting military applications of new technologies, and in contrast to Russia, it seems to possess a sufficient industrial and technological base to compete with the United States over the longer term. This competition may differ from the relatively symmetric competition that defined the superpower strategic arms race. Given the current positon of the United States, it is not clear that a policy that will intensify a period of great power competition is its national interests.

The Question of Costs

In reality, it is unlikely that the United States could achieve such a quantitative force enhancement without a response from Moscow, and perhaps Beijing. An even more powerful practical constraint may be the resources necessary to approach such a capacity. Under the Obama administration's program of record, which has been mostly endorsed by the Trump administration, modernizing the strategic triad is expected to cost approximately $1.2 trillion over three decades. The prospect of additional spending would likely meet with domestic political opposition. This situation would place a new program like the nuclear-armed SLCM in almost immediate jeopardy. However, although quantitative superiority may be exceedingly difficult to achieve, and although the possibility of negative effects is recognized by even the most enthusiastic advocates, it may still prove attractive.

More importantly, any proposed expansion of the current strategic modernization program of record—even if it somehow succeeds in achieving the necessary legislative support—would almost certainly have significant implications for conventional force modernization and the ability of the United States to maintain its commitments to research that addresses the threats created by technological change. If a strategy of nuclear primacy were being proposed as a substitute for the conventional superiority that has served as the basis for U.S. global hegemony since the end of the Cold War, it might have seemed a more realistic prospect. A reliance on U.S. nuclear forces to deter aggression and provocation abroad —a revised "New Look" for the 2020s—could then have been debated. However, this approach is not being proposed by most advocates. Instead, nuclear primacy is discussed as a complement to conventional military primacy. When the probable needs for a reemphasis on strategic defenses are considered, it is difficult to see how such commitments could ever be funded. Thus, it is likely that an increased dedication of resources to expanded nuclear forces would preclude investment in conventional force modernization, readiness, and long-term research and development.

Finally, as discussed earlier, a secure, reliable, and effective strategic nuclear arsenal may prove useful as a hedge against not only geopolitical challenges and emerging threats, but also the potential for technological surprise. Although it is difficult to imagine a breakthrough technology that could fundamentally alter the current security environment, and nuclear weapons may be expected to provide the United States with a formidable hedge against yet unseen threats, the scope and magnitude of the strategic program envisioned by advocates of nuclear primacy far exceed what would be considered a prudent hedge. Indeed, such a commitment to nuclear forces is likely to make the United States less capable of addressing the new threats and challenges created by rapid technological change.

NOTES

1. Stephen G. Brooks and William C. Wohlforth, "The Rise and Fall of Great Powers in the Twenty-first Century: China's Rise and the Fate of America's Global Position," *International Security* 40, no. 3 (Winter 2015/16): 7-53.

2. Keir Lieber and Daryl Press, "The New Era of Counterforce: Technological Change and the Future of Deterrence," *International Security* 41, no. 4 (Spring 2017): 9–49; Keir A. Lieber and Daryl G. Press, "The New Era of Nuclear Weapons, Deterrence and Conflict," *Strategic Studies Quarterly* 7, no. 1 (Spring 2013): 3–14; Keir A. Lieber and Daryl G. Press, "The Nukes We Need: Preserving the American Deterrent," *Foreign Affairs* 88, no. 6 (November/December 2009): 39–51; Keir Lieber and Daryl G. Press, "The End of MAD? The Nuclear Dimension of U.S. Primacy," *International Security* 30, no. 4 (Spring 2006): 7-44; Matthew Kroenig, *The Logic of American Nuclear Strategy: Why Strategic Superiority Matters* (Oxford: Oxford University Press, 2018); Matthew Kroenig, "Nuclear Superiority and the Balance of Resolve: Explaining Nuclear Crisis Outcomes," *International Organization* 67, no. 1 (January 2013): 141–171.

3. Colin S. Gray, *Nuclear Strategy and National Style* (Lanham, MD: Hamilton Press, 1986); Keith B. Payne, *Nuclear Deterrence in U.S.-Soviet Relations* (Boulder, CO: Westview Press, 1982).

4. Lieber and Press set a particularly high bar, arguing for forces that "can destroy its adversary's retaliatory capabilities in a disarming strike. See Lieber and Press, "The End of Mad?" 8.

5. Keith B. Payne "The Nuclear Posture Review: Setting the Record Straight," *The Washington Quarterly* 28, no. 3 (Summer 2005): 135-151; Richard Sokolsky, "Demystifying the U.S. Nuclear Posture Review," *Survival* 44, no. 3 (Autumn 2002): 133-148.

6. Paul Bracken, *The Second Nuclear Age: Strategy, Danger, and the New Power Politics* (New York: St. Martin's Griffin, 2013); Colin S. Gray, *The Second Nuclear Age* (Boulder: Lynne Rienner, 1999).

7. Keith Payne, *Deterrence in the Second Nuclear Age* (Lexington: University Press of Kentucky, 1996).

8. David S. McDonough, "Nuclear Superiority: The 'New Triad' and the Evolution of Nuclear Strategy," *Adelphi Series* 46, no. 383 (2006/2007).

9. *Nuclear Posture Review 2018* (Washington, DC: U.S. Department of Defense, 2018).

10. Colin Gray, Nuclear Strategy and Strategic Planning (Philadelphia: Foreign Policy Research Institute, 1984): 7.

11. Lieber and Press, "The New Era of Counterforce," 27-32.

12. Thomas Karako (ed.), *Missile Defense and Defeat: Considerations for the New Policy Review* (Washington, DC: Center for Strategic and International Studies, 2017); David J. Trachtenberg, "Time to Reassess U.S. Missile Defense Policy," *National Institute for Public Policy Information Series*, no. 409 (July 2016).

13. Paul Sonne, "Pentagon seeks to expand scope and sophistication of U.S. missile defenses," *The Washington Post,* January 16, 2019; Paul Sonne, "Decades after 'Star Wars,' Pentagon looks back to the future on missile defense," *The Washington Post,* November 12, 2018.

14. *Missile Defense Review 2019* (Washington, DC: U.S. Department of Defense, 2019).

15. Amy F. Woolf, U.S. *Strategic Nuclear Forces: Background, Developments, and Issues* (Washington, DC: Congressional Research Service, 2017); Hans M. Kristensen and Robert S. Norris, "Nuclear Notebook: United States Nuclear Forces, 2018," *Bulletin of the Atomic Scientists* 74, no. 2 (2018): 120–131.

16. Keith B. Payne and John S. Foster (eds.), *A New Nuclear Review for a New Age* (Washington, DC: National Institute Press, 2017): 141-155.

17. Steven A. Pomeroy, *An Untaken Road: Strategy, Technology, and the Hidden History of America's Mobile ICBMs* (Annapolis: Naval Institute Press, 2016).

18. Payne and Foster (eds.), *A New Nuclear Review for a New Age,* 69-78.

19. Bombers were only counted as a single warhead under New START counting rules, but can carry up to 12 gravity bombs, Amy Wolf, *The New START Treaty: Central Limits and Key Provisions* (Washington, DC: Congressional Research Service, 2019).

20. *Nuclear Posture Review 2018,* 6-7.

21. Lieber and Press, "The Nukes We Need," 41.

22. Kurt Guthe, *The Nuclear Posture Review: How Is The "New Triad" New?* (Washington, DC: Center for Strategic and Budgetary Assessments, 2002).

23. McDonough, "Nuclear Superiority," 44.

24. Lieber and Press, "The Nukes We Need," 49.

25. Fiona S. Cunningham and M. Taylor Fravel, "Assuring Assured Retaliation: China's Nuclear Posture and U.S.-China Strategic Stability," *International Security* 40, no. 2 (Fall 2015): 7–50.

26. *Nuclear Posture Review 2018*, 52-55.

27. *Nuclear Posture Review 2018*, 21.

28. Ibid.

29. Ibid.

30. Ibid., 121-2.

31. Ibid., 119.

32. McDonough, "Nuclear Superiority," 57–58.

33. Payne and Foster (eds.), *A New Nuclear Review for a New Age*, 120-121.

34. Ibid., 141-155.

35. Colin Gray, *Nuclear Strategy and Strategic Planning* (Philadelphia: Foreign Policy Research Institute, 1984), 27.

36. Payne and Foster, *A New Nuclear Review for a New Age*, 146.

37. Thomas Karako, *Missile Defense and Defeat: Considerations for the New Policy Review* (Washington, DC: Center for Strategic and International Studies, 2017).

38. David J. Trachtenberg, "Time to Reassess U.S. Missile Defense Policy," *National Institute for Public Policy Information Series*, no. 409 (July 2016).

39. Payne and Foster, *A New Nuclear Review for a New Age*, 146.

40. Amy F. Woolf, "U.S. Withdrawal from the INF Treaty," *CRS Insight*, October 28, 2018.

41. Paul Sonne, "Mattis: Plans for new U.S. nuclear weapon could be bargaining chip with Russia," *The Washington Post*, February 2, 2018.

42. David W. Kearn, Jr., *Facing the Missile Challenge: U.S. Strategy and the Future of the INF Treaty* (Santa Monica, CA: RAND Corporation, 2012).

43. Adam Taylor, "How China plays into Trump's decision to pull out of INF Treaty with Russia," *The Washington Post*, October 23, 2018.

44. David W. Kearn, Jr., "The Future of US Deterrence in East Asia: Are Conventional Land-Based IRBMs a Silver Bullet?" *Strategic Studies Quarterly* 7, no. 4 (Winter 2013): 93–116.

45. Payne, "The Nuclear Posture Review."

46. McDonough, "Nuclear Superiority," 44.

47. Payne and Foster, *A New Nuclear Review for a New Age*, 149.

48. McDonough, "Nuclear Superiority," 44.

49. McDonough, "Nuclear Superiority," 11.

50. Gray, *Nuclear Strategy and Strategic Planning*, 79.

51. Ibid., 80.

52. For an alternative view, see: Charles L. Glaser and Steve Fetter, "Should the United States Reject MAD? Damage Limitation and U.S. Nuclear Strategy toward China," *International Security* 41, No. 1 (Summer 2016): 49-98, 85.

53. Charles Krauthammer, "The Unipolar Moment Revisited," *The National Interest* (Winter 2002/03): 8–9.

54. McDonough, "Nuclear Superiority," 7.

CHAPTER 4

ROBUST STRATEGIC DETERRENT

A robust deterrent strategy is presented here as the logical successor to the prevailing view that nuclear weapons played an critical role in keeping the Cold War "cold," but made a relatively limited contribution to the achievement of secondary foreign policy objectives.[1] This approach sees value in maintaining strategic stability with Russia and is skeptical of both the technical feasibility and the strategic desirability of strategic defense. It is ambivalent about the contributions of nonstrategic nuclear weapons, which are seen as primarily political tools that can enhance extended deterrent commitments but have limited military utility beyond this role.[2] This approach also supports prudent, verifiable arms control agreements. It strongly supports the Nonproliferation Treaty (NPT) and initiatives to strengthen the nonproliferation regime and prevent the spread of nuclear weapons programs to new actors.

ELEMENTS OF A ROBUST DETERRENT STRATEGY

The current U.S. force structure was arguably built to serve a strategy of robust strategic deterrence. Quantitative force reductions since the end of the Cold War have brought U.S. force levels down to 1,550 deployed warheads. The current modernization plan of record will rebuild all three legs of the strategic triad over a thirty-year period. Most of the currently deployed elements of the U.S. strategic arsenal were programmed, developed, and deployed during the last major buildup by the United States in the late 1970s and 1980s.[3] Advocates have argued that this comprehensive modernization is necessary, in large part because of Russian modernization and to a lesser degree because of the modernization and improvement of China's still-limited nuclear force.

Force Levels and Structure

In order to present the robust strategic deterrent approach as an ideal type distinct from the other alternative strategies and force structures considered in this study, the modernization of the strategic triad would be conducted as planned but both the B61-12 gravity bomb and long-range standoff ordinance (LRSO) would be curtailed and/or delayed, and conventional precision-guided munitions would be relied upon to carry out the mission of both programs. Thus, a refurbished strategic triad would constitute the nuclear force in the post-2035 period.

Table 2a. Robust Deterrent: Notional Force Structures 2035 – Current Modernization Program.

Current Modernization Program		
System	Units	Warheads
GBSD	400	400
12 SSBN	16 SLBMx 6 MIRV	1152
20 B-21	16	20 (320)
Total Deployed Warheads		**1572 (1872)**

Table 2b. Robust Deterrent: Notional Force Structures 2035 – Reconfigured Alternative.

Reconfigured Alternative

System	Units	Warheads
GBSD	300	300
10 SSBN	16 SLBM x 7 MIRV	1120
25 B-21	16	25(400)
Total Deployed Warheads		**1445 (1820)**

The two notional force structures represent the strategic component of the planned modernization program of record developed under the Obama administration and endorsed by the Trump administration and a slightly reconfigured alternative program that alters the force levels of each leg of the triad but maintains the warhead levels at roughly the New START levels. The reconfigured alternative was constructed by Lawrence Korb and Adam Mount, who argued that the *Columbia* class SSBN will need to spend less time out of service than the current *Ohio* class boat, and thus patrols can be maintained with ten, rather than twelve, new ballistic missile submarines.[4] Reducing the ICBM force by a third (rather than reducing it arbitrarily, e.g., by fifty missiles) is viewed as optimal from a cost-saving point of view. This approach envisions the elimination of an entire missile wing by the U.S. Air Force and a closing of the command center and support infrastructure along with the reassignment of personnel, thus maximizing the impact of the force reduction:

> To achieve significant savings, the Air Force will have to retire one of the three missile wings and close the base associated with it, which would save close to $500 million over the first five years plus the reduced cost of modernizing each of that wing's 150 missiles.[5]

These reductions could be made over time as the current forces are retired from service, minimizing any gap in the available deployed capabilities or disruptions. The core of the force structure, however, would remain an effective, responsive, and flexible strategic triad that can successfully execute the deterrent mission against great power competitors or new regional nuclear powers. As for the two more controversial procurement programs, for the purposes of this discussion, the B61-12 would be cancelled and the LRSO would be delayed. In reality, the B61-12 program will likely be deployed to provide NATO with a nuclear deterrent capability. In considering the LRSO, an effective cruise missile would enhance the overall air-breathing leg of the triad if the B-21 were found to be ineffective or incapable of executing its penetrating bomber mission because of the capabilities of deployed IADs. But the LRSO could be delayed, perhaps shifting the focus to a nuclear variant of the JASSM-ER that is under development. Given scarce budgetary resources, funds could then be spent on conventional munitions: "The national interest can be better served by investing funds in the conventional weapons systems most relevant to national defense —as well as America—itself in order to ensure that the United States remains competitive far into the future."[6]

Employment Policy

This refurbished strategic triad would seem more than sufficient to provide a robust deterrent strategy for the United States and its allies. At an estimated price of $1.2 trillion over roughly three decades, it has received significant criticism from the arms control community, which views it as beyond the needs of deterrence, and from budget hawks, who view the price tag as exorbitant, particularly when the overall defense budget has expanded in response to major conventional procurement and personnel needs but may face downward pressures. Moreover, the Obama administration was reportedly prepared to negotiate an additional one-third reduction of deployed warheads with Moscow during its second term. Such an agreement would have lowered the quantitative forces levels to approximately 1,000 deployed warheads. Although Russia proved unwilling to consider or discuss further reductions, the fact that the United States was prepared to accept these force levels as appropriate for a robust deterrent implies that the current force structure may be overly conservative. In any event, the Trump administration has not implied any desire to seek further reductions.[7]

As the 2013 Employment Strategy indicates, the primary role of U.S. strategic nuclear forces is to deter adversaries from direct nuclear attack on the United States or allies by holding at risk the vital elements of a potential adversary's state.[8] In practice, this role translates into a mix of counterforce and countervalue targeting, while deliberately attempting to avoid civilian population centers and excessive collateral damage. However, it is highly likely that critical infrastructure, industrial and war-making capacities, and, under some circumstances, command and control may be targeted as well.

The current force structure, which remains a legacy of the Cold War, provides a formidable capability to address a wide range of potential threats and operational scenarios. The strategic bomber force, currently comprised of B-52s armed with ALCMs and B-2s with B83-1 and B61-11 gravity bombs, can be placed on heightened alert levels or deployed to allied bases to enhance immediate deterrence under crisis conditions and provide a controlled response to provocation against allies. The SSBN force provides a guaranteed retaliatory capability and a secure nuclear strike capability in highly contested environments. These capabilities can enhance deployed conventional forces in the event that an adversary signals a willingness to escalate to the nuclear threshold or beyond. Finally, the ICBM force provides the national command authority with the capacity to deliver a prompt nuclear strike anywhere in the world. Even in the context of increased great power competition, this capacity is a source of U.S. advantage in any crisis that supports U.S. conventional capabilities and allied forces.

Declaratory Policy

Despite the controversy surrounding the 2018 Trump administration Nuclear Posture Review (NPR), its declaratory policy addresses key challenges and threats arising from geopolitical and technological trends.[9] As discussed in the previous chapter, the 2018 NPR limits the role of nuclear weapons to deterring nuclear attacks on the United States or its allies, along with non-nuclear strategic attacks, which may become more prevalent in the context of technological change.[10] In this way, the NPR effectively captures the increasingly important hedge mission that the U.S. strategic arsenal can play in a highly uncertain security environment. In contrast to the robust strategic deterrent considered here, the NPR overreaches in its endorsement of new nuclear-armed sea-launched cruise missiles (SLCMs), a program that will likely require significant budgetary resources without a clear rationale (depending on the missile that is developed), and in its program to retrofit a portion of the deployed D-5 Trident force with a single low-yield warhead, which may create discrimination problems if it is used during a crisis. Both of these programs seem redundant to existing capabilities and could be replaced with conventional weapon systems.

The 2010 NPR attempted to circumscribe the role of nuclear weapons in U.S. national security strategy.[11] Prioritizing nonproliferation and the prevention of nuclear terrorism, it did not engage in discussion of specific missions for U.S. nuclear forces, rather it stated: "The fundamental role of U.S. nuclear weapons, which will continue as long as nuclear weapons exist, is to deter nuclear attack on the United States, our allies and partners."[12] To support the NPT regime, the NPR asserted,

> the United States is now prepared to strengthen its long standing "negative security assurance" by declaring that the United States will not threaten or use nuclear weapons against non-nuclear weapons states that are party to the Nuclear Non-Proliferation Treaty (NPT) and in compliance with their nuclear non-proliferation obligations.[13]

Even in the case of an attack with chemical or biological weapons, the United States would threaten a "devastating conventional military response." [14] More generally, "The United States would only consider the use of nuclear weapons in extreme circumstances to defend the vital interests of the United States or its allies and partners."[15] This limiting of the role of nuclear weapons was prudent. However, moving further to embrace a No First Use policy, as was discussed at the end of the Obama administration, would have been short-sighted and could have complicated the extended deterrent commitment to key U.S. allies.[16]

Alert Status

Given the current security environment, the United States should continue to maintain current alert levels for all three legs of the strategic triad.[17] There is little apparent need to raise the existing levels, despite the challenge of great power competition. Where necessary, however, it should be considered a priority to implement new ISR and early warning capabilities based on emerging information and sensor technologies that enhance early warning capabilities and discrimination of potential targets to provide the maximum time for decision making by the national command authority.

NC3

As discussed in the introduction, planned investment in enhancing nuclear command control and communications is vitally important, particularly in the context of the growing sophistication of offensive cyber warfare capabilities among great power adversaries, regional actors, and even non-state actors. Nuclear command, control and communications (NC3) is often overlooked when strategic stability or crisis stability are discussed, but the ability to maintain control over nuclear forces during crisis and conflict conditions may be the only way to avoid a catastrophic outcome. With the growing threat of offensive cyber warfare capabilities and more advanced means of electronic warfare, it is possible that NC3 will be preemptively attacked during a crisis by adversaries seeking to exploit vulnerable networks or disrupt critical communications nodes to prevent U.S. strategic forces from executing operations effectively. James Steinbruner's analysis of the importance of NC3—and the counterintuitive implications concerning the relative vulnerability of the components of the strategic force structure—is even more appropriate today in an offensive cyber world:

> It is quite apparent, however, *that the preservation of a strong deterrent effect and the actual prevention of war are not the same thing.* Indeed the most serious threat of war under the current circumstances probably lies in the possibility that organizationally and technically complex military operations might override coherent policy decisions and produce a war that was not intended.[18]

Today the challenge may be even more severe, as the systems that military and political leaders depend upon could be targeted for debilitating attack at a time when they are most essential. Securing, hardening, and increasing the resilience of NC3 systems should be a central focus of the current modernization of U.S. strategic forces.[19] A robust strategic deterrent will only serve U.S. national security interests if the national command authority can trust the effectiveness and resilience of the NC3 system and infrastructure.

Nuclear Enterprise

Investment in the Department of Defense (DOD) and Department of Energy (DOE) nuclear weapons complex would seem to be a prudent commitment irrespective of the nuclear strategy that is implemented. Given the planned investment in the modernization of all three legs of the strategic triad, the proposed plans for the refurbishment and construction of new Interoperable Warheads should move forward.[20] This vitally important foundation of the nuclear weapons infrastructure suffered a prolonged period of neglect in the 1990s and early 2000s. Beyond the problems of the DOD nuclear enterprise that came to light in 2008 with a series of incidents and accidents involving the U.S. Air Force, the underlying infrastructure of labs and production facilities has more or less atrophied for almost two decades. President Obama attempted to prevent and reverse the erosion of the DOE's capacity to maintain a safe, secure, and reliable nuclear force, and the Trump administration has followed suit. Clearly, the recapitalization of the existing infrastructure is an important objective in almost any scenario in which nuclear weapons remain relevant to U.S. national security, but depending on the alternative nuclear strategy implemented, greater demands may be placed on the weapons complex over the next three decades.

In sum, a revitalized nuclear weapons infrastructure plays a vital role as a hedge against a potentially serious erosion of the international security environment, and the planned investment in recapitalizing the nuclear weapons complex and enhancing the workforce is a sensible policy objective for the United States.

Strategic Defenses

In the context of a robust deterrent strategy and force posture, the leadership of the United States may view continued investments in the existing limited missile defenses as prudent counters to the North Korean nuclear weapons program, and possibly a future Iranian program.[21] Thus far, technological limitations have made it impossible to achieve the capabilities desired by most ballistic missile defense advocates. However, it is now evident that the persistent U.S. commitment to developing and deploying strategic defenses has influenced both the Russian and the Chinese strategic modernization programs. As former Deputy Assistant Secretary of Defense Brad Roberts has argued, the United States has refused to accept a mutual vulnerability relationship with North Korea.[22] The relationship with China is less clear. The strategic relationship with Russia, in contrast, leaves little choice about what to do. By maintaining a robust but stable deterrent relationship, the United States would seek to avoid the potentially destabilizing aspects of what could be perceived as efforts to achieve an expansive, multilayered strategic defense capability. The implementation of grandiose plans for an extensive network of sensors and interceptors in outer space seems to be a threshold. Such efforts would likely spur a major effort (whether successful or not) by Moscow (and possibly Beijing) to develop space-based assets, creating a new realm for costly arms racing, or asymmetric countermeasures like further MIRV-ing (likely with decoys) of mobile ICBMs and SLBMs.

As mentioned earlier, a technological breakthrough (or a combination of smaller discrete advancements) that made strategic missile defenses viable would represent a truly dramatic and revolutionary transformation of the strategic security environment.[23] As experts have noted, it is highly unlikely that interceptors to offensive missiles or reentry vehicles would ever prove cost effective "at the margin" (the so-called Nitze criterion), and thus the grandiose vision of a ballistic missile "shield" seems unlikely and, more importantly, self-defeating. As the history of the late 1960s and early 1970s underscores, competition in strategic defenses is costly and ultimately fruitless. If Washington and Moscow can improve their relations and reconcile the violations that have driven the Trump administration to withdraw from the Intermediate Nuclear Forces (INF) Treaty—not a small task—they may be able to revisit the concept of a strategic defense treaty that would limit deployments and maintain some measure of mutual vulnerability. It may also be prudent to address accidental or unauthorized launches and smaller regional arsenals.

Nonstrategic Nuclear Weapons
As discussed earlier, an ideal type robust strategic deterrent strategy would curtail or delay investments in the LRSO and B61-12 programs. However, in practice, the B61-12 presents a difficult problem. Because of the planned deployment of the upgraded B61-12 gravity bomb to NATO with fifth-generation F-35 Joint Strike Fighters, the upgraded gravity bomb represents NATO's central deterrent. Thus, it is closely involved in the cohesion of the Alliance and its capacity to contribute to deterring Russian provocation and aggression in the future. In keeping with the deployment of tactical and theater nuclear weapons in Europe during the Cold War, the planned deployments are not projected to achieve a military capability that would be symmetric to Moscow's. Rather, the ability to move up the escalatory ladder prevents Russian planners from exploiting any gaps they perceive in Alliance capabilities. In the abstract,

these forces would be removed from Europe, and NATO's security would be based on forward-deployed conventional forces, British and French nuclear forces, and central U.S. deterrent forces. But because the decision to maintain a nuclear capability was made in Brussels, it would be difficult for the United States to reverse its policy. As two noted experts have recently argued, the deployment of the B61-12 may be a useful focus of NATO burden sharing, given the estimated costs of the program.[24]

CONTRIBUTIONS OF ROBUST DETERRENCE

Extended Deterrence/Reassurance

Advocates of a robust deterrent strategy view the requisites of assured destruction and guaranteed proportional retaliation as effective for deterring aggression by a great power competitor like Russia or China or a regional nuclear power like North Korea or Iran. The deterrence of nuclear strikes against the U.S. homeland is perceived as fairly straightforward. As long as the United States possesses a diverse, highly survivable strategic nuclear arsenal, an adversary contemplating an attack will be confronted with a mix of counterforce and countervalue retaliation that will effectively preclude its survival as a functioning state and undermine any of the possible benefits of aggression.

Extended deterrence may be more challenging, and the assurance of allies is a particularly difficult and painstaking task. The right combination of commitment and capabilities, however, can meet these challenges. The United States has over five decades of experience in managing this type of problem. By maintaining both a formidable level of diverse strategic forces and highly capable conventional military forces that can provide proportional and graduated responses to aggression, the United States can effectively deter its adversaries and assure its allies. The deployment of tactical nuclear weapons seems to be much more about reassurance than about actual deterrence in the current strategic context. The deployment of American forces to allied territory, even in a limited "tripwire" capacity, is a credible signal of commitment, as the United States exhibited during the Cold War. As two experts explained: "The long history of U.S. security commitments, and the sacrifices in blood and money that the American people have made in defense of these commitments, provide ample evidence that U.S. security guarantees are credible."[25]

In certain extreme cases, a reliance on tactical (or theater) nuclear weapons to control escalation may make sense, such as when the Soviets deployed the vaunted SS-20 IRBM in the mid-1970s and thereby shifted the "Euro-strategic" balance heavily in favor of the Soviet Union. The United States' subsequent deployment of a mix of Pershing-II intermediate-range ballistic missiles (IRBMs) and ground-launched cruise missiles (GLCMs) to several NATO members reaffirmed the U.S. commitment to the Alliance, re-established a rough balance of forces on the continent, and offset the perceived Soviet advantage. Today, when the roles of the United States and Russia are essentially reversed, the contribution of deployed tactical nuclear weapons to European security is less obvious.

Crisis Stability

Advocates of robust deterrence typically seek to develop and deploy military capabilities that strike an optimal balance between deterring provocation and aggression by adversaries, reassuring allies, and maintaining crisis stability. Although crisis stability may be less important than achieving credible deterrence against aggression and reassuring allies, the deployment of certain types of forces can decrease uncertainty, enhance transparency, and remove an adversary's incentives to engage in provocation or consider launching a first strike in the event of a diplomatic or political crisis.[26] During the Cold War, nuclear force structures based on a mix of highly survivable weapons systems were intended to minimize the probability that the Soviet Union would launch a first strike that could disarm the United States and thus leave Washington in the difficult position of launching retaliation while the Soviets still possessed residual forces capable of annihilating the homeland.[27]

Thus, much of the debate over the perceived vulnerability of the U.S. Minuteman III ICBM force during the late 1970s as the Soviet Union expanded its arsenal of large, MIRVed heavy ICBMs hinged upon crisis instability. If war seemed possible, Moscow might gamble and attempt to disarm the United States with a coordinated first strike. This view tended to downplay the existence of survivable SLBMs at sea on America's fleet of ballistic missile submarines, as well as its strategic bomber force, a large portion of which would have likely been in the air on patrol. The ICBM vulnerability debate highlights the logic of crisis instability and the dangers of a configuration of opposing forces that made it preferable to launch a first strike rather than absorb a first strike under intense crisis conditions. It is not always easy, however, to define which assets contribute to stability. Given the large numbers of warheads carried by the U.S. SSBN force and their ability to operate virtually undetected, the possibility of using the submarine leg to launch a devastating first strike on an adversary is not insignificant, particularly as multiple warhead technology improves over time and accuracy increases. Whereas strategic bombers are often viewed as contributing to crisis management and strategic stability, some experts argue that highly stealthy strategic platforms like the B-2 or its successor, the B-21, could create instability by serving as first strike weapons when deployed with stealthy cruise missiles like the LRSO.[28] But despite the persistent contribution of stealth technology, improvements in integrated air defenses and early warning sensors make this scenario unlikely and the ability to deploy an effective standoff platform with penetrating munition would offset a decreased ability to penetrate enemy air defense zones.[29]

Arms Race Stability

Advocates of robust deterrence acknowledge the importance of formidable strategic capabilities to deter adversaries from provocative or aggressive behavior against the United States or its allies. However, they also see the potential downsides of unrestrained unilateral strategic armament policies and are confident in the ability of deployed U.S. forces to deter unwanted behavior as long as those forces are sufficient in number and kind. Accepting the insights of both the security dilemma and spiral models of international relations, these experts recognize the potential negative effects of U.S. strategic policy and consider ways to mitigate them in relations with potential adversaries and third parties.[30] These policymakers and scholars view a secure, reliable, and diverse strategic nuclear force as central to U.S. national security against threats from other nuclear powers. They are relatively sanguine, however, about the ability of those forces to deter even risk-acceptant adversaries from taking unwanted actions against the United States or its allies. Thus, they believe that maintaining some level of numerical equivalence in strategic weapons and similarity of deployed forces, codified in a formal strategic arms control agreement, can decrease uncertainty, enhance transparency, and contribute to strategic stability.[31]

Dissuasion

A robust deterrent strategy would likely have some dissuasion value vis-à-vis China and other smaller nuclear powers, as long as some measure of rough parity with Russian strategic forces continues to serve as the benchmark for U.S. forces. However, the role of dissuasion, as a policy objective or unintended benefit of relatively large force levels, is much less pronounced in a robust deterrent strategy. Such a strategy would likely allow for additional negotiated reductions with Russia should the opportunity arise. The additional one-third cut in deployed warheads considered in the second term of the Obama administration would, in the view of robust deterrence advocates, likely provide the United States with sufficient forces to effectively deter a nuclear attack on the United States or its allies.[32] Further reductions would be assessed for their probable impact on the ability of the United States to deter nuclear attack rather than for their dissuasive effect on China or other relevant third parties. Advocates of a robust deterrent strategy tend to be ambivalent about the dissuasive impact of the strategic nuclear arsenal and skeptical of the political value of nuclear weapons beyond general deterrence and perhaps for the prevention of aggression under crisis conditions.

For advocates of a robust deterrent strategy (and the requisite deployment of relatively high force levels), any potential benefits of dissuading third parties and would-be adversaries are far less important than the two objectives of deterring aggression against the United States and its allies and maintaining strategic stability. The latter objective, in their view, can best be accomplished by avoiding competitive armament cycles and arms racing and preventing the development and deployment of capabilities that would create incentives for a first strike in a militarized crisis or in the early stages of a conventional conflict with a nuclear adversary.

Strategic Arms Control

Should the United States assume a robust deterrent posture that maintained the strategic triad, the role of arms control will be less than straightforward. For force planning purposes, the current ceiling of 1,550 deployed warheads under New START may be viewed as sufficient for a strong, credible deterrent in a period of renewed great power competition. The extension of New START may contribute to maintaining strategic stability in the context of U.S.-Russia relations by reducing the possibility of unconstrained building should the Treaty lapse.[33] Given the current cost projections associated with the modernization program of record, a follow-on strategic arms control agreement to New START could formally endorse the logic of modernization efforts, or perhaps even provide cost savings if further reductions can be negotiated. Another potential avenue to enhance strategic stability with Russia would involve negotiations to reduce Russia's large stocks of nonstrategic nuclear weapons. Such an approach would likely be predicated on the outstanding issue of the Russian INF Treaty violations.

Nonproliferation

Given the current nuclear modernization program of record, a robust deterrent strategy and force posture would likely maintain the status quo in the global nonproliferation regime. As reflected in the passage of the Nuclear Ban Treaty in 2017, consistent pressure from civil society groups and their allies has mobilized domestic political opposition within critical U.S. allies. The U.S. withdrawal from the INF Treaty and the uncertain future of New START after 2021 will be viewed as further evidence of Washington's lack of commitment to the goal of "global zero." Conversely, if Washington and Moscow agree to extend New START or perhaps to consider further limited mutual reductions in strategic forces, it is unlikely that supporters of the Nuclear Ban Treaty will embrace the developments with enthusiasm. Although any further reductions may be welcomed, they are more likely to be viewed as half-measures that do not go far enough in moving the United States and Soviet Union toward the elimination and abolition of nuclear weapons.[34]

The Costs of Maintaining a Robust Strategic Deterrent

As noted, the estimated cost of the current nuclear modernization program of record is approximately $1.2 trillion over the next three decades.[35] In the late 2020s, it will be particularly challenging to fully fund the program, because the procurement "bow wave" and the acquisition costs of all three major programs—the GBSD, the Ohio-replacement SSBN, and the B-21—will hit their respective peaks at roughly the same time. Unlike the other "ideal type" programs assessed in this study, the robust strategic deterrent strategy deliberately delays the LRSO program and cancels the tactical B62-12 gravity bomb and would not pursue the low-yield SLBM or new SLCM program. These programs are relatively small components in the grand scheme of the planned modernization program, and their removal would not significantly lower the topline modernization number. However, a cancellation of the LRSO and the B61-12 programs would produce over $50 billion in cost savings. As noted, a cancellation of the B61-12 would effectively end NATO nuclear sharing and therefore is highly unlikely, but for the purposes of the discussion, this ideal type would forego tactical nuclear weapons. A shift to Option 2, outlined earlier (moving to 10 Columbia Class SSBNs and 300 ICBMs), would save approximately $40 billion. Thus, a combination of the three, a "leaner" robust strategic deterrent approach, would allow for almost $100 billion in savings that could be directed to conventional force priorities.

ASSESSING ROBUST STRATEGIC DETERRENCE

In the current security environment, the maintenance of a robust strategic deterrent capability serves U.S. national security interests without creating the challenges associated with nuclear primacy and minimum deterrence. It provides a strong deterrent against attacks on the United States and its allies and allows for flexible options that can enhance the deterrent of forward-deployed conventional forces in key regions. It also contributes to both crisis and arms race stability with Russia by avoiding attempts to acquire quantitative or qualitative superiority.

The approach outlined in this chapter maintains a robust central strategic deterrent force that is credibly capable of deterring nuclear or other strategic-level attacks against the United States; deterring nuclear attack against allies; providing flexible, limited nuclear options should extended deterrence fail and an adversary cross the nuclear threshold; and hedges against geopolitical and technological changes to the security environment that might threaten U.S. national security interests. In foregoing investments in lower-yield tactical nuclear weapons, this approach also maximizes the resources available for conventional force modernization and readiness initiatives.

Too Inflexible?

One clear dividing line between the robust deterrent and nuclear primacy schools is their views on the importance of access to limited nuclear options. As discussed in the last chapter, advocates of nuclear primacy would prefer that the U.S. possess quantitative superiority and escalation dominance, which they view as the best method to deter highly risk-acceptant actors. To achieve this superiority and dominance in practice, the United States must possess an array of flexible, limited nuclear options that could be used with minimal collateral damage to remove a "theory of victory" from regional adversaries or from peer competitors like Russia that may seek to use their own limited nuclear options to pause or "de-escalate" a conventional conflict on their terms.[36] The existing technology and the conventional superiority of U.S. forces make limited nuclear use by adversaries more attractive:

> U.S. conventional superiority lowers the nuclear threshold, because it tempts conventionally weaker adversaries to early rather than last resort employment in order to avoid adverse results at the conventional level. By having a robust set of proportionate nuclear responses, the United States raises the nuclear threshold because it reduces the attractiveness of nuclear escalation. This may seem paradoxical, to be sure, but paradoxes seem to be endemic to any nuclear era.[37]

The potential for limited use may indeed be increasing, but it remains unclear why an in-kind response is the appropriate or optimal way to address such a scenario. For example, in considering how to respond to limited nuclear use by a regional power like North Korea, one prominent expert argued that a symmetric nuclear response would be a viable course of action, using a limited nuclear strike by the United States. However, he also argued persuasively for a conventional response:

> Others, however, are likely to argue that the United States should eschew a nuclear response and retaliate with precision guided munitions. The rationale, which assumes that conventional weapons are effective enough for a punitive response, would be that, in refraining from using nuclear weapons, the United States would help to delegitimize nuclear weapons. Additionally, relying on conventional weapons to retaliate would allow the United States to maintain the moral high ground.[38]

Conventional military technology may indeed provide capabilities that approach the destructiveness of nuclear weapons. But despite what some see as a blurring of the line between conventional and nuclear explosives, it is going too far to simply assume that the distinction is no longer relevant or important, particularly in the context of the larger U.S. diplomatic objectives.

This point leads to an important question that is often overlooked: why should the United States move away from its advantage in conventional precision-guided munitions and other advanced capabilities to compete with lesser military powers in a field where those powers have focused their energies, precisely because they cannot compete in other fields? The simple fact that Russia possesses a large stock of nonstrategic nuclear weapons does not necessarily mean that the United States requires a similar capability, particularly if it can rely on its conventional superiority and, if necessary, its strategic arsenal.

Advocates of the development of limited nuclear options point to the history of the Cold War to support their case:

> Despite the confidence that many outsiders had in the sufficiency of some combination of minimalist nuclear deterrence and conventional forces, the US government was never ready to rely on such a sanguine assessment of what deterrence against the Soviet Union required.[39]

This is a fair assessment. However, during the Cold War, the military situation in Europe was reversed: the United States was searching for tactical or theater nuclear options to address the Soviet conventional advantage, and U.S. policymakers were seeking the means to enhance pre-conflict and intraconflict deterrence without being left to rely on central strategic systems that would likely precipitate a large-scale exchange and a nuclear cataclysm. Even then, these options were much more about U.S. leaders being "self-deterred" than about their perceived contribution to influencing Soviet calculations. As Robert Jervis noted:

> The call for flexibility seeks to give the decisionmaker a lot of choices in a crisis but is not supported by analysis of what effect

the various options would have if they were implemented. Much of the explanation for this lack of analysis is that coherent answers are simply out of reach.[40]

The end of the Cold War and the removal of an existential competition with an ideologically driven peer competitor seem to have decreased the likelihood of large-scale nuclear exchange. A more limited use of nuclear weapons in the face of conventional inferiority, however, does not necessarily imply that the United States' best option is an in-kind, symmetric response. Support for a wider array of limited nuclear options in the current environment seems premised on a basic acceptance of a situation in which the willingness of the adversary to use nuclear weapons somehow trumps or forecloses the ability of the United States to respond in the way that is viewed as most advantageous for U.S. interests.

Upon limited nuclear use by an adversary in a conventional conflict, the United States might deliberately choose to respond with a limited but escalatory nuclear strike, perhaps from a central strategic U.S. asset like an SLBM. If the initial limited nuclear strike is constrained to a truly tactical or battlefield usage, the United States may be able to respond with a range of formidable conventional capabilities. But if the adversary's action is viewed as escalating beyond the battlefield, the use of a central strategic system would be logical and appropriate. It is simply not clear that a directly proportional response to a crossing of the nuclear threshold would be preferred or optimal. Ultimately, the argument for a wide and diverse array of limited nuclear options seems to be driven far more by concerns of "self-deterrence" and a fear that U.S. leaders would be unwilling to escalate when faced with an adversary that had crossed the nuclear threshold than with the dynamics of the conflict or with the stakes and political interests involved. An alternative approach would address any misperception that limited nuclear use would prove successful:

> The United States should reserve the option to respond to a tactical nuclear strike against in-theater conventional forces with the use of strategic nuclear weapons against tactical military targets,

such as command and control nodes, large troop formations, or military bases. U.S. policy should make clear that any step onto the nuclear escalation ladder would bring all of the dynamics of nuclear deterrence into play.[41]

In particular campaigns, the United States might still rely on conventional forces, but it could also deliberately escalate to a level of its choosing. It could carry out a similar tactical or operational strike, or it could threaten something more valuable to the adversary to signal its resolve in the face of the adversary's breach of the nuclear threshold. A final point is that in practical terms, the use of tactical nuclear weapons is likely to take place on Russian territory, introducing the potential for significant escalation. Perhaps more generally, if the United States' refurbishment of the nuclear stockpile and development of new warheads is naturally moving toward less powerful yields, which is described as a relatively straightforward process, it is prudent to question the need for niche programs to fill a gap that may not actually exist.

Requirements of Extended Deterrence

As noted earlier, the United States currently faces a very practical diplomatic challenge in the planned deployment of the B61-12 gravity bomb to Europe. A robust deterrent strategy would preferably forego the expense of such a program and rely on conventional forces and central strategic assets rather than limited tactical nuclear options. However, given the importance of the program to the NATO deterrent, and particularly in light of the erosion of relations with Russia, this is a difficult time to broach the idea of removing tactical weapons from NATO's deterrent posture. But it also important to note that these are effectively "political weapons," deployed more in service of alliance solidarity and cohesion than to address a threat from Russian conventional or nonstrategic nuclear forces. This situation, moreover, brings up a more basic issue regarding alliance management. Some experts, including many who sympathize with the nuclear primacy school, consistently seek new capabilities to assure (or reassure) allies. Capabilities may be important, but it can also be argued that the Cold War history shows the importance of perceptions of resolve, credibility, and commitment— meaning the intentions of leaders in Washington—in supporting or undermining alliance cohesion:

> Maintaining allies' confidence in U.S. commitments requires frequent consultations, political reassurances, high-level meetings, and cooperation in military planning. U.S. conventional forces also provide a global, visible, flexible, and credible means of reassuring allies—particularly if they are deployed on the ally's territory or conduct temporary deployments to exercise jointly with allied forces. Though nuclear guarantees are an important component of U.S. security commitments, allies doubt them more than they doubt conventional commitments because of the greater risk they pose to the U.S. homeland.[42]

Thus, whereas an ideal type robust strategic deterrent strategy would likely cancel the forward deployment of the B61-12 in Europe, reversing course now would create significant problems within NATO. As two experts have argued recently, however, this may be an area where the alliance's "burden sharing" (particularly in terms of program costs) could be reconsidered.[43]

High Prices for Insurance?

Arms control advocates and experts sympathetic to the minimum deterrence school and those favoring the abolition of nuclear weapons still view the U.S. strategic arsenal as too large and too expensive. If assured destruction and guaranteed second-strike capabilities are the measure of a robust deterrent force, then the current force structure, even without forward-deployed tactical weapons or a new, more advanced cruise missile, are more than enough for a deterrent mission. However, given the current security environment and the potential that geopolitical and technological trends will further challenge U.S. national security interests, a robust deterrent capability must achieve the fundamental objective of nuclear weapons in U.S. national security strategy, avoid creating unnecessary strategic instability, and guard against further erosion of the security environment. In maintaining a robust strategic force rather than a significantly reduced minimum deterrent posture, this approach should achieve an optimal balance of deterrence of adversaries and reassurance of allies. It should also support diplomatic and political-military efforts to sustain and improve alliance cohesion.

In maintaining and seeking to extend the New START force levels, this approach maintains a force structure and posture that could provide a basis for further strategic arms control cooperation with Russia if the opportunity arises, although multilateral efforts may be more relevant. A limitation on the scale of deployed strategic defenses to assuage Russian and Chinese concerns may stop the current spirals and enhance stability. Although advocates of this approach may not receive much credit from the nonproliferation community, their willingness to maintain the existing force levels in this challenging security environment and avoid investments in new programs like the B61-12 and the LRSO may be viewed somewhat favorably.

NOTES

1. Richard Betts, *Nuclear Blackmail and Nuclear Balance* (Washington, DC: Brookings Institution, 1987); Kenneth N. Waltz, "Nuclear Myths and Political Realities," *American Political Science Review* 84, no. 3 (September 1990): 731–744; Robert Jervis, "The Political Effects of Nuclear Weapons," *International Security* 13, no. 2 (Fall 1988), 80–90.

2. On strategic stability, see Brad Roberts, "Strategic Stability Under Obama and Trump," *Survival* 59, no. 4 (August–September 2017): 47–74; Dean A. Wilkening, "Strategic Stability Between the United States and Russia," in *Challenges in U.S. National Security Policy: A Festschrift Featuring Edward L. (Ted) Warner*, ed. David Ochmanek and Michael Sulmeyer (Santa Monica, CA: RAND Corporation, 2014), 123–141; Elbridge A. Colby and Michael S. Gerson (eds.), *Strategic Stability: Contending Interpretations* (Carlisle: U.S. Army War College Press, 2013).

3. Amy F. Woolf, *U.S. Strategic Nuclear Forces: Background, Developments, and Issues* (Washington, DC: Congressional Research Service, 2017).

4. Lawrence Korb and Adam Mount, *Setting Priorities for Nuclear Modernization* (Washington, DC: Center for American Progress, 2016).

5. Ibid., 27.

6. Ibid., 24.

7. James E. Doyle, *Renewing America's Nuclear Arsenal: Options for the 21st Century* (New York: Routledge, 2017). Doyle presents a number of alternative force structures that would maintain the warhead level of the New START Treaty (1,550).

8. *Report on Nuclear Employment Strategy of the United States* (Washington, DC: U.S. Department of Defense, 2013).

9. Frank A. Rose, *Policy Brief: Is The 2018 Nuclear Posture Review As Bad As the Critics Claim It Is?* (Washington: Brookings Institution, 2018).

10. *Nuclear Posture Review 2018* (Washington, DC: U.S. Department of Defense, 2018).

11. *Nuclear Posture Review Report* (Washington, DC: U.S. Department of Defense, 2010).

12. *Nuclear Posture Review Report*, 15.

13. Ibid.

14. Ibid., 16.

15. Ibid., 17.

16. Josh Rogin, "Obama plans major nuclear policy change in his final months," *The Washington Post,* July 10, 2016; Michael S. Gerson, "No First Use: The Next Step for U.S. Nuclear Policy," *International Security* 35, no. 2 (Fall 2010): 7–47.

17. Brad Roberts, *The Case for Nuclear Weapons in the 21st Century* (Stanford: Stanford University Press, 2016): 35.

18. John D. Steinbruner, "National Security and the Concept of Strategic Stability," *Journal of Conflict Resolution* 22, no. 3 (September 1978): 411-428.

19. Mark Fitzpatrick, "Artificial Intelligence and Nuclear Command and Control," *Survival* 61, no. 3 (June-July 2019): 81-92.

20. Amy F. Woolf and James D. Werner, *The U.S. Nuclear Weapons Complex: Overview of Department of Energy Sites* (Washington, DC: Congressional Research Service: 2018); Doyle, *Renewing America's Nuclear Arsenal,* 25–27.

21. James M. Lindsay and Michael O'Hanlon, *Defending America: The Case for a Limited National Missile Defense* (Washington, DC: Brooking Institution, 2001).

22. Roberts, "Strategic Stability Under Obama and Trump."

23. Kenneth N. Waltz, "Nuclear Myths and Political Realities"; Charles L. Glaser, *Analyzing Strategic Nuclear Policy* (Princeton, NJ: Princeton University Press, 1990).

24. Barry Blechman and Russell Rumbaugh, "Bombs Away: The Case for Phasing Out U.S. Tactical Nukes in Europe," *Foreign Affairs* (July/August 2014): 163–174.

25. Barry Blechman and Russell Rumbaugh, "Protecting U.S. Security by Minimizing the Role of Nuclear Weapons: A New U.S. Nuclear Policy," in *Project Atom: A Competitive Strategies Approach to Defining U.S. Nuclear Strategy and Posture for 2025–2050,* ed. Clark Murdock et al. (Washington, DC: Center for Strategic and International Studies, 2015), 35.

26. Roberts, "Strategic Stability Under Obama and Trump."

27. Paul Nitze, "Deterring Our Deterrent," *Foreign Policy* 25 (Winter 1976-77): 195-210.

28. William J. Perry and Andy Weber, "Mr. President, kill the new cruise missile," *The Washington Post,* October 15, 2015.

29. Mark Gunzinger, *Sustaining America's Advantage in Long-Range Strike* (Washington, DC: Center for Strategic and Budgetary Assessments, 2010).

30. Robert Jervis, "Deterrence and the Spiral Model," chapter 3 of *Perception and Misperception in World Politics* (Princeton, NJ: Princeton Univer-

sity Press, 1978), 58–113; Robert Jervis, "Cooperation under the Security Dilemma," *World Politics* 30, no. 2 (January 1978): 167–214; C. Glaser, "The Security Dilemma Revisited," *World Politics* (October 1997): 171–201.

31. Richard K. Betts, "The Lost Logic of Deterrence: What the Strategy That Won the Cold War Can--and Can't--Do Now," *Foreign Affairs* 92, no. 2 (March/April 2013: 87-99; Robert Jervis, "Why Nuclear Superiority Doesn't Matter," *Political Science Quarterly* 94, no. 4 (Winter 1979-80): 617-633.

32. Steven Pifer, "Obama's Faltering Nunclear Legacy: the 3 R's," *Washington Quarterly* 38:2 (Summer 2015) 101-118.

33. "Editorial: Trump want to negotiate nuclear deals. He should start with the one he already has." *The Washington Post*, May 8, 2019.

34. Robert, *The Case for Nuclear Weapons in the 21st Century*, 48-50.

35. *Approaches for Managing the Costs of U.S. Nuclear Forces, 2017–2046* (Washington, DC: Congressional Budget Office, 2017); Todd Harrison and Evan Braden Montgomery, *The Cost of U.S. Nuclear Forces: From BCA to Bow Wave and Beyond* (Washington, DC: Center for Strategic and Budgetary Assessments, 2015); Jon B. Wolfsthal, Jeffrey Lewis, and Marc Quint, *The Trillion Dollar Triad: US Strategic Nuclear Modernization Over the Next Thirty Years* (Monterey, CA: James Martin Center for Nonproliferation Studies, 2014).

36. Robert, *The Case for Nuclear Weapons in the 21st Century*, 62-69.

37. Clark Murdock et al., *Project Atom: A Competitive Strategies Approach to Defining U.S. Nuclear Strategy and Posture for 2025–2050* (Washington, DC: Center for Strategic and International Studies, 2015), 18.

38. Thomas G. Mahnken, "Future Scenarios of Limited Nuclear Conflict," in *On Limited Nuclear War in the 21st Century*, ed. Jeffrey A. Larsen and Kerry M. Kartchner (Stanford, CA: Stanford University Press, 2014), 136.

39. Elbridge A. Colby, "The United States and Discriminate Nuclear Options in the Cold War," in Larsen and Kartchner, *On Limited Nuclear War in the 21st Century*, 66.

40. Robert Jervis, *The Illogic of American Nuclear Strategy* (Ithaca, NY: Cornell University Press, 1984), 79.

41. Blechman and Rumbaugh, "Protecting U.S. Security by Minimizing the Role of Nuclear Weapons," 38.

42. Ibid., 35.

43. Blechman and Rumbaugh, "Bombs Away," 163–174.

CHAPTER 5

MINIMUM DETERRENT

A minimum (or "finite") deterrent strategy is predicated on the idea that the possession of a secure, highly survivable, and reliable strategic nuclear force, maintaining the capacity to retaliate for a nuclear attack on the United States with complete certainty, will deter even the most aggressive, reckless, and risk-acceptant states from engaging in nuclear strikes, provocation or aggression against allies, or other unwanted behavior.[1] By cutting the quantitative force levels and limiting the diversity of the deployed strategic retaliatory force, the United States could move away from what is perceived as its reliance on nuclear weapons, contemplating their use under only a very narrow and extreme set of circumstances. Such an approach is viewed as having political-military and diplomatic benefits because it underscores America's commitment to the Nonproliferation Treaty (NPT). It is also likely to bring significant cost savings relative to the alternative strategic approaches.

The concept of a minimum deterrent has existed since the mid-1960s when the prospect of a highly survivable submarine based deterrent force offered a potential path to avoid continued spending on vulnerable land-based systems.[2] It was consistently rejected by political and military leaders. Perhaps the closest this approach came to formal official consideration was during the 1992-1993 Nuclear Posture Review (NPR).[3] If the 2002 NPR explored a greater reliance on nuclear weapons in its "new strategic triad," the 1992-1993 NPR, which was undertaken in concert with the Clinton administration's Bottom-Up Review of the U.S. military for the post-Cold War world, explored more significant moves away from a reliance on nuclear weapons. While the process would ultimately result in the endorsement of a force structure that maintained the strategic triad at levels negotiated under START and START II, more dramatic options-- including major reductions or potentially the elimination of the inter- continental ballistic missile (ICBM) force--were reportedly considered. These explorations reportedly faced strong bureaucratic and military opposition within the Pentagon and political opposition outside, and in the turmoil that engulfed the Aspin Defense Department in the wake of the fiasco in Mogadishu, the Review endorsed a safe consensus in favor of maintaining the strategic triad.

Elements of a Minimum Deterrent Strategy

A minimum or finite deterrent force structure would, as the term implies, be much smaller than even the forces deployed today under New START. There is some diversity of opinion about "how little is enough," but important common themes can be found among advocates' views. Most of these advocates argue that the United States could unilaterally reduce its forces without negotiating mutual force reductions with Russia. Given the "absolute" nature of nuclear weapons and their influence on state behavior, a small force is sufficient to provide a strong deterrent against direct attack on the U.S. homeland. Thus, the mere presence of nuclear weapons is what drives the strategic calculus, decision making, and behavior of potential adversaries, rather than the quantitative force levels or the kinds of deployed delivery systems or warheads. According to this logic, the deterrence of strikes against the United States—also called general, direct, or central deterrence—is relatively easy. The threat to use nuclear weapons, even relatively large legacy weapons capable of causing extensive societal destruction and collateral damage, would be highly credible if made in the context of an attack against the continental United States in which American civilians were killed in large numbers. Even a highly risk-acceptant leader would have to be delusional to believe he could strike the United States with nuclear weapons and somehow escape devastating retaliation.

In practice, such an approach would still present challenges. Most importantly, in a minimum deterrent strategy, the survivability of strategic forces becomes absolutely vital. Thus, depending upon the nature of the deployed force structure, the ability to withstand a first strike and fully sustain operations is mandatory and therefore requires that deployed weapons, their support installations, and the nuclear command, control and communications (NC3) networks display maximum resilience and reliability.

Force Structure

Proponents of minimum deterrent strategies have differing views on the optimal strategic force structure. Given the survivability of nuclear-powered ballistic missile submarines (SSBNs), some have advocated a shift to an all-SSBN force and the elimination of vulnerable, silo-based ICBMs.[4] In addition, an SSBN force would provide greater operational flexibility to the national command authority than, for example, a force structure that relied heavily on ICBMs. However, critics express concern over the possibility that adversaries may achieve a breakthrough in antisubmarine warfare (ASW) capabilities.[5] In addition, the prevailing view that the SSBN force is primarily a retaliatory weapon has also changed over time.[6] Perhaps because of U.S. fears that Soviet submarine-launched ballistic missiles (SLBMs) could be used to attack the national command authority in the 1980s, and considering improvements in the accuracy and reliability of the multiple independently targetable reentry vehicles (MIRV) carried in the D-5 Trident SLBM, its contribution to an offensive first-strike mission would not be insignificant. Finally, the SSBN force is the most expensive to operate and maintain. The cost savings from moving away from the SSBN force would be considerable, and the funds could be used for other priorities.[7] If the other two legs of the triad were removed, however, those costs would be offset by savings in the retirement of land-based ICBMs and nuclear bombers.

Other advocates argue that for a minimum deterrent strategy to be credible, land-based ICBMs must be a central component of the force structure.[8] As Thomas Nichols explained, the deployment of these forces on U.S. soil, rather than at sea, is critically important to the deterrence mission:

> Whatever the decisions about submarines and bombers, land-based ICBMs must remain in the U.S. arsenal. Their location in the continental United States, rather than their number, is the source of their deterrent power, because there is no way to destroy them without violating the North American heartland and killing hundreds and thousands of Americans instantly. For an attacker, this endeavor is far more terrifying than playing a game of hide and seek on the high seas with U.S. submarines, or investing in the hope that American bombers can be stopped somewhere along the many hours of travel to their targets. As long as the U.S. deterrent includes land-based ICBMs, an enemy who is truly determined to escape retaliation will have no choice but to attack those missile fields and thus risk all-out war with the United States and its allies.[9]

As noted earlier, the United States is currently planning to replace the Minuteman III ICBM with the Ground Based Strategic Deterrent (GBSD) program. The planned deployment consists of 400 single-warhead missiles in 450 refurbished Minuteman silos, with approximately another 150 additional missiles for testing, replacement parts, and reserve usage. One key concern about shifting to a reliance on the land-based leg of the triad is the heightened necessity of hardened (or "super-hardened") underground silos and support and NC3 facilities. As the MX basing debate of the late 1970s illustrated, it is doubtful that mobility would be entertained or accepted by the American people, and mobility is incongruous with the tendency to move toward a lessened reliance on nuclear weapons in the post-Cold War environment.[10] Thus, it would be essential to make improvements in the survivability of the deployed missiles, their support infrastructure, and the means of command, control and communications, and linkage to the national command authority, but this effort would be a constant challenge in a world where warhead accuracy is constantly improving.

A sole reliance on the future ICBM force may be perceived as highly limiting and rigid. As presented, such a reliance would effectively constrain strategic nuclear capabilities to a completely retaliatory function and would preclude any ability to proactively influence crisis dynamics. Placing these missiles on alert would not necessarily be viewed by an adversary as a credible signal, because there is no real threat of losing them in an exchange. Moreover, the ICBMs' flight path from the current silo basing in the United States could be misinterpreted by Moscow as an attack on Russia if the U.S. targets were elsewhere, such as in North Korea or China. For these reasons, some advocates of a minimum deterrent believe that a fleet of strategic bombers would be a useful complement to the modernized ICBM force. Given the relative flexibility of bombers, their ability to signal resolve and enhance immediate deterrence through heightened alert levels or deployment to allied bases in a diplomatic crisis without undermining crisis stability, and their ability to contribute to conventional missions, an air-land strategic dyad or an air-sea dyad may thus be preferable to a monad. Bombers dedicated to the strategic mission would not have to maintain high alert status and could be deployed and operated without their nuclear payloads, which could be rapidly uploaded as warranted.[11]

Whereas some experts have argued that the total stock of deployed warheads could decrease to as low as 300, the minimum deterrent strategy under discussion would involve a strategic force level of approximately 500 deployed warheads.[12] As the two notional force structure options that follow reflect, this level can be achieved through different configurations of platforms and missiles, but a unilateral reduction to 500 would certainly represent a significant shift in U.S. nuclear strategy.

Table 3. Minimum Deterrent Posture: Notional Force Structure 2035.

Option 1: Sea Based Deterrent

System		Warheads
10 SSBNs	14 SLBMs x 4 MIRV	560

Option 2: Land-Air Dyad

System	Warheads
400 ICBM	400
25 B-21	100

Another option that is feasible, but not necessarily cost-effective, is the maintenance of a smaller strategic triad. [13]However, the complementarity of the respective modes of deployment and delivery would probably lose marginal utility as the warhead numbers significantly decreased. Similarly, as Option 1 (outlined earlier) indicates, reliance on an SSBN force is likely to be extremely cost-ineffective, given the operational and sustainment costs and the need to download warheads far below what a Trident D-5 SLBM can carry (typically four to five) and to leave open missile tubes (currently a maximum of sixteen per boat, with plans to reduce to fourteen). Fully equipped, the currently planned fleet of twelve Columbia-class SSBNs could carry almost the entire deployed warhead inventory (1,536) allowed under New START. Option 1 would cut the fleet down to ten boats, but it is not clear that this move would be viewed as cost-effective or desirable. Option 2 is a straightforward Land-Air Dyad, based on the programmed GBSD force with single warheads and the B-21s dedicated to the strategic mission equipped with four gravity bombs each, but likely to carry more. These numbers are also somewhat arbitrary and significantly downplay the typical START counting rules.

Employment Policy

A minimum deterrent strategy would hold at risk an adversary's high-value societal targets. For example, some advocates of this approach have argued for an employment strategy that targets the adversary's critical infrastructure rather than targeting population centers and civilians directly, an action that is viewed as both morally reprehensible and illegal under international law.[14] In reality, damage to population centers would likely be unavoidable, but cities would not be deliberately targeted. With a much smaller strategic force, more expansive counterforce employment policies would be impossible to implement, and most experts who advocate for a minimum deterrent strategy view such approaches as unnecessary and wasteful for the central mission of nuclear weapons: deterring nuclear attack on the United States or its allies. Thus, the concept of infrastructure targeting has been presented as follows:

> The targets are neither counterforce nor simply countervalue targets. A new targeting category and policy that we term infrastructure targeting would focus on a series of targets that are crucial to a nation's modern economy, for example electrical, oil, and energy nodes, transportation hubs.[15]

A joint study by the American Federation of Scientists and the Natural Resources Defense Council simulated the effects of such a retaliatory campaign against industrial and infrastructure targets in Russia, including twelve of the largest oil refineries, metal plants, and thermal power plants. Even with a deliberate choice of targets away from major urban areas, the casualties exceeded a million people, and the material damage to Russian infrastructure was significant, with the likelihood of long-lasting negative effects on reconstitution and recovery:

> So we must speculate on the stakes involved such that the incremental benefit to the Russians or Chinese of turning a conflict nuclear is worth destruction of their critical infrastructure and potentially millions of casualties. Given the complex interconnectedness of modern societies such as Russia and the United States and a rapidly changing China, we believe that the destruction of

key targets meeting our criteria would have profound effects upon the national infrastructure and economy and would negate any conceivable advantage an enemy might calculate it could gain by attacking the United States or its allies with nuclear weapons.[16]

The authors of the study cited a 1979 study by the Office of Technology Assessment titled *The Effects of Nuclear War* that simulated an attack on Soviet petroleum refineries and storage sites. Using just seventy-three warheads, the attack was estimated to have destroyed 73% of the refining capacity of the entire country and 16% of its storage capacity. The attack attempted to exclude cities where possible, but the total casualties approached 3–4 million people. More importantly, the destruction of refining capacity would precipitate an economic crisis that would reverse progress and lower the standard of living.[17] This underscores the destructive power of nuclear weapons and the devastation that even "limited" strikes could deliver to a modern society.

Declaratory Policy

Under a minimum deterrent strategy, declaratory policy would narrow the possible scenarios for nuclear use by the United States. Given that such scenarios would likely entail only direct nuclear attack on the United States or its allies, the formal endorsement of a No First Use policy would logically complement the highly restrictive usage of America's strategic arsenal.[18] Perhaps the most critical decision would be whether to extend this deterrent commitment to a nuclear attack on U.S. allies. Some advocates of a minimum deterrent policy underscore the difficulty of maintaining such a credible extended deterrent commitment, reflecting upon the troubled history of the Cold War and the challenges of maintaining NATO cohesion, particularly after the Soviet achievement of strategic parity. Thus, rather than attempt to extend a non-credible deterrent, it would be preferable for the United States to shift to a strictly conventional deterrent commitment to NATO and allies in East Asia. In the event of a conventional or chemical, biological, nuclear, or radiological (CBRN) attack on an ally, the United States would commit to executing a robust retaliatory campaign against the perpetrator, and perhaps also to treating regime change as the political aim of the military operation.[19]

An alternative declaratory policy would maintain the prospect of a U.S. retaliatory nuclear strike in response to a nuclear attack against its allies, but this policy might prove difficult to sustain in the absence of reciprocal cuts in Russia's deployed strategic forces and perhaps nonstrategic nuclear weapons.[20] However, if minimum deterrence were formally embraced in the context of significant further mutual reductions in offensive forces (and possibly limitations on strategic defensive forces) by the United States and Russia, codified within a formal arms control agreement and supported by a robust monitoring and verification regime, the security environment in Eastern Europe would likely be transformed. Such a watershed could, to a large extent, eliminate the perceived need for an extended nuclear deterrent commitment from the United States to its NATO allies, given the fundamental change in Russia's posture and apparent intentions vis-à-vis Europe. Although this scenario is highly unlikely in the near term, this type of situation would seem to betoken an end to great power competition in the region.

Under a minimum deterrent posture, the formally declared role of nuclear weapons would be highly circumscribed:

> Because of credibility and proliferation concerns, nuclear weapons are only legitimized as a deterrent against nuclear attacks. Only the latter endanger the survival of the state. The use of nuclear weapons against conventional, chemical or biological weapons attacks is explicitly denounced. Nuclear weapons will only be used as a very last resort and that should be announced as such.... Nuclear deterrence may only be extended to non-nuclear attacks that may threaten the survival in the case of small states that may easily be overrun by non-nuclear means.[21]

Such a development would certainly limit the scenarios in which the United States could threaten to use nuclear weapons. Interestingly, even this highly restrictive formulation of a future declaratory policy for the use of nuclear weapons does not explicitly embrace a No First Use doctrine, precisely because of the problem of extending deterrence to smaller allies who may confront regional adversaries with significant conventional military capabilities.

Warning and Alert Status

A major advantage of a minimum deterrent strategy is that it does not require nuclear forces to be maintained at high alert levels.[22] If they are housed within sufficiently hardened survivable installations, with robust and resilient access to the national command authority (something that should be achievable, particularly with a strategic retaliatory force that is primarily constructed around ICBMs and perhaps strategic bombers), there will be no incentive to use them hastily, even during an attack.[23] As long as the forces are capable of riding out the attack and the requisite hardened communications networks continue to function, the guaranteed devastating retaliation can come at a time and place of the president's choosing:

> A minimum nuclear deterrent policy and posture with infrastruc-
> ture targeting does not require nuclear forces to be on alert, to be
> configured for preemption, or to even retaliate quickly. Planning
> should shift from having nuclear forces in a ready-to-go OPLAN
> to a contingency war planning capability able to assemble an
> attack planning the event of an attack by another nuclear state, but
> focused on a new set of infrastructure targets. This new process
> would alleviate the pressures that current plans impose and lead
> to a relaxing of alert rates and reducing of nuclear weapons.[24]

In the post-Cold War environment, even with the erosion of U.S. relations with Russia, China's military modernization, and the growing threat of North Korea's developing nuclear missile capability, the nature of the strategic threat to the homeland has changed. At the extreme, under the worst of Cold War circumstances, the political and military leaders of the United States confronted the prospect of responding to a first strike by the Soviet Union that could involve thousands of warheads, with warning time that could be measured in minutes. Time and the ability to discern an attack were at a premium, placing a burden upon surveillance and early warning architecture that has persistently troubled experts.[25]

With the end of the Cold War, the collapse of the Soviet Union, and the subsequent reductions in strategic arsenals, the situation has become much different. Time is now a much less pressing concern. Proper identification, accurate discrimination, and the ability to deliver tracking and intercept information are essential, precisely because of the nature of nuclear weapons. As one prominent expert has written:

In summary, in the post-Cold War world, the emphasis on warning and attack assessment should change quite markedly. Timeliness and rapid response should be much less important and should be deemphasized. This is an idea that has been around for a while. Accurate identification of attackers and correct assessment of their motives could be much more difficult and should receive much more emphasis.[26]

NC3

The capacity to harden or disperse missile forces may be a difficult aspect of of moving toward a reliance upon a minimum deterrent strategy, but sufficiently enhancing the survivability and resilience of nuclear command and control has been a fundamental challenge since the advent of nuclear weapons and remains so.[27] Morton Halperin developed a comprehensive depiction of a minimum deterrent strategy for the United States in his book *Nuclear Fallacy*. One of the most critical elements of its implementation was hardening and enhancing the resilience of the NC3 assets and network: "[The U.S.] must develop survivable command centers with redundant capability to communicate with the strategic forces and with the president or his designated representative."[28] The capacity to maintain complete control over strategic nuclear forces even under the extreme conditions of a nuclear exchange is a necessary condition for the implementation of a minimum deterrent strategy. This, however, may be much more difficult in the current environment given improvements in warhead accuracy.[29]

Nuclear Enterprise

If the United States were to move toward a minimum deterrent posture, the rationale for the three planned Interoperable Warheads planned during the Obama administration would disappear. A reliance on a much smaller number of land-based ICBMs, SLBMs, gravity bombs, or some combination of the three would decrease the scope of the planned program as well as the need for new pits and could provide savings for the Nuclear Weapons Complex.[30]

Strategic Defenses

Should the United States move toward a minimum deterrent strategy, particularly in a context in which the United States and Russia formally agree to significant mutual reductions in strategic offensive forces, a logical diplomatic initiative will be the conclusion of a new treaty limiting the extent of deployed strategic defenses.[31] Although challenges from third-party countries may persist, limited ballistic missile defenses that are capable of addressing these threats will maintain domestic political support. However, it will be vitally important that such defenses do not credibly threaten the deterrent capacities of the United States and Russia without introducing significant instability into the relationship. As the numbers decline, this dynamic will likely become even more important. Even now, Moscow's expressed concern that European missile defenses are a component of a more comprehensive "multilayered" missile defense system is difficult to assuage. It is highly unlikely that Russian leaders will be assured by U.S. diplomatic initiatives in the absence of a new formal treaty that significantly constrains the size and scope of American strategic defenses. As will be discussed soon, an "ABM [Antiballistic Missile] 2.0 Treaty" may indeed be a logical and necessary companion to strategic offensive reductions that create the conditions for a minimum deterrent strategy and force posture for the United States, but for strategic and domestic political reasons, it is doubtful that such a treaty will be signed in the near to medium term.[32]

Nonstrategic Nuclear Weapons

Under a minimum deterrent strategy and force structure that significantly limited the scenarios within which the use of U.S. strategic nuclear weapons would be considered, the role of forward-deployed nonstrategic nuclear weapons would likely dissipate. A United States declaratory policy that limited the role of nuclear weapons to deterring (and retaliating in response to) nuclear attacks on the United States and its allies would seem to make tactical nuclear weapons unnecessary.[33] A shift to a solely conventional extended deterrent posture, which would require a revision of the current NATO policy, would remove the rationale for these deployments.[34]

THE CONTRIBUTION OF A MINIMAL DETERRENT STRATEGY

A minimum deterrent would have a number of advantages. A limited arsenal that would still credibly threaten unacceptable damage would present a formidable deterrent. Proponents of finite deterrence have argued for a policy of infrastructure targeting, which would avoid cities and civilians but "would seek to neutralize remaining Russian or Chinese military capability while inflicting grievous damage to industry, energy, transportation, and other key elements of enemy infrastructure."[35] This would still be a countervalue strategy, as opposed to a counterforce strategy targeting opposing nuclear forces or a more broadly counter-military strategy targeting conventional forces and support infrastructure, but it would avoid the deliberate (and immoral and illegal) targeting of cities and civilian populations:[36] "this strategy attempts to deter attack by promising that a U.S. response is not instant, but inevitable, and when it arrives, it will reduce the enemy—or what's left of it—to the status of a less-developed country."[37]

Both the United Kingdom and France have used a minimum deterrent strategy.[38] During the Cold War, neither European power sought capabilities beyond the strategic force levels that were thought to guarantee a punitive strike on the Soviet Union. As part of the unified NATO command structure, the United Kingdom worked closely with the United States even in the wake of the Skybolt and Multilateral Nuclear Force controversies, supporting the deployment of tactical and theater nuclear forces during the Cold War.[39] London also worked closely with Washington on nuclear weapons beginning in the immediate aftermath of World War II.

France, in contrast, took unilateral measures to develop its own nuclear deterrent force. As the Soviet Union moved toward parity and the capacity to strike the United States, President Charles de Gaulle doubted the extended deterrent commitment of the United States. As research has indicated, this decision had significant nonsecurity motivations as well, including perceptions of France's prestige and status as a great power.[40] Irrespective of these ulterior motivations, the structure of French forces and the nature of French nuclear strategy provide useful insights for considering a minimum deterrent.

Extended Deterrence/Reassurance

Proponents of minimum deterrent strategies view deterrence against nuclear strikes on the United States as relatively straightforward and easy. Some also view extended deterrence as similarly easy to achieve through a combination of declaratory policy, alliance and formal diplomatic commitments, and deployment of conventional U.S. forces. At the extreme, a minimal conventional force, forward deployed as a "trip wire," should signal to an adversary that the United States would react forcefully, potentially with nuclear weapons, in the event of an attack on allies and U.S. forces deployed on allied territory.[41] Assuming the adversary understands that even a conventional attack against a U.S. ally could escalate beyond the nuclear threshold, minimum deterrent advocates who take seriously the logic and implications of the nuclear revolution argue that an adversary would not risk nuclear retaliation to violate the sovereignty of a U.S. ally.

Some advocates of minimum deterrence are less sanguine about the ability to provide credible extended deterrent guarantees to allies, but argue that such an objective should be addressed with conventional force in any case. For example, Thomas Nichols has argued that U.S. extended deterrence capabilities should be shifted to strictly conventional forces.[42] This would be a major change from the current NATO policy, which continues to treat the alliance as a strategic one as long as nuclear weapons exist. The shift would also require a fundamental transformation of the underlying alliance compact. But whereas political and military leaders may express concern about a move away from America's nuclear umbrella, domestic political opposition to the persistence of deployed tactical nuclear weapons in Europe has increased. Before Russia's intervention in Georgia in 2008 and its continuing intervention in Ukraine and annexation of Crimea, several leading political figures in NATO member nations advocated the removal of nuclear weapons.[43]

The limited flexibility inherent in a reliance on a much lower number of strategic weapons would present practical difficulties for maintaining credible extended deterrence to Western Europe and East Asia. Perhaps one of the major implications of such a policy is the increased likelihood that U.S. allies would seek to develop and acquire their own nuclear deterrent forces. For example, without a U.S. commitment, Tokyo may view the acquisition of nuclear weapons as the best way to maintain a credible deterrent against Chinese aggression.

Crisis Stability

Minimum deterrence advocates view the diversification of nuclear weapons or the development of tailored, limited nuclear options to enhance extended deterrence as inherently destabilizing and self-defeating. Given the nature of nuclear weapons, even risk-acceptant adversaries would be extremely reluctant to engage in even conventional or irregular military aggression against an ally of the United States. The potential for a crisis or conventional military conflict to escalate to a strategic exchange that would precipitate an unacceptable level of societal damage is an effective and credible deterrent to aggression or provocation, confronting leaders with prohibitive costs that would outweigh any expected benefits of their actions. The mere possession of strategic nuclear weapons is perceived as enough to deter an adversary from running the risk that a conventional conflict could rapidly escalate to a nuclear one.

As discussed previously in the context of extended deterrence, a valid criticism of this approach emerges from the stability-instability paradox.[44] If the United States and an adversary like Russia both possess highly secure strategic nuclear forces capable of guaranteeing retaliation for a nuclear strike, does the credibility of extended deterrence decline? Would such a situation open the possibility of a strictly conventional limited conflict? This situation spurred the investigation of limited war during the early Cold War period and shaped the movement toward the development of Flexible Response under the Kennedy Administration. Some advocates of minimum deterrence recognize this inherent challenge and argue that under a minimum deterrent strategy, the United States would have to shift to a strictly conventional extended deterrent posture, effectively acknowledging the lack of credibility of extended deterrent commitments under such a strategic policy.[45]

Arms Race Stability

For experts who embrace a minimum deterrent strategy and force posture, nuclear revolution and the security dilemma and spiral models play a critical role in their worldview.[46] Given the absolute nature of nuclear weapons, they see little value in deploying strategic forces beyond levels that can guarantee unacceptable societal devastation in retaliation for an attack on the United States or its allies. They consider unilateral U.S. investments in forces beyond these levels to be wasteful, because they take up limited resources. Moreover, such investments undermine the security of the United States by spurring adversaries to improve their strategic forces and increasing uncertainty about U.S. intentions among adversaries, third parties, and perhaps even close allies. Thus, forces beyond those necessary to absorb a first strike and deliver guaranteed destruction to an adversary are unnecessary and may even be detrimental to the strategic environment.[47] The negotiation and conclusion of strategic arms control treaties may formalize the circumscribed role of nuclear weapons in relations between the United States and its adversaries, but such treaties are less important than advocates of robust deterrence may argue. The views of minimum deterrence advocates are relatively inelastic with regard to the qualitative and quantitative aspects of the strategic forces of adversaries, because the absolute nature of nuclear weapons makes them fundamentally different from conventional weapons. Beyond a survivable retaliatory force, they maintain, the United States has little need for weapons.[48]

With the formal implementation of a strategy of minimum deterrence and the deployment of a limited but highly survivable strategic force structure to support that strategy, advocates argue that adversaries would have little incentive to engage in competitive building beyond the levels of the United States. If adversaries do engage in such building, minimum deterrence advocates argue that their investments will prove futile, as greater quantitative force levels cannot be translated into political or diplomatic advantages. As long as the United States maintains the capacity to credibly retaliate for any nuclear attack on the United States or its allies, an imbalance in strategic forces in the adversary's favor will not enhance its security or undermine U.S. national security interests.

Dissuasion

Advocates of minimum or finite deterrence would prefer much smaller numbers of deployed warheads and delivery vehicles, limited to the singular mission of deterring a nuclear attack on the United States and (possibly) its allies. Given this highly circumscribed mission and the significantly reduced force structure associated with minimum deterrence, advocates do not generally view dissuasion as an important objective or benefit of U.S. nuclear weapons. Significantly reduced forces would support the United States' nonproliferation goals by underscoring Washington's commitment to its Article VI obligations to engage in serious disarmament efforts. In reenergizing the NPT regime, the United States would also strengthen global nonproliferation norms and reestablish its leadership in this realm. In their view, this diplomatic benefit would go a long way toward removing incentives for states to consider developing or obtaining nuclear weapons and would far outweigh the coercive approach to dissuading would-be nuclear states from pursuing their goals. In the absence of an attempt by China or other nuclear powers to expand their nuclear forces beyond the current quantitative force levels, a reversal of vertical proliferation—the quantitative expansion or qualitative improvement or diversification of nuclear arsenals—by the United States and Russia would likely be seen as having a positive impact on horizontal proliferation, or the overall spread of nuclear weapons capabilities to new states around the globe. Nonetheless, the use of a minimum deterrent strategy would provide the United States with the ability to respond to accusations of hypocrisy and cynicism in its dealing with the NPT regime and nuclear modernization.[49]

Strategic Arms Control

Strategic arms control would be a logical complement to a shift to a minimum deterrent strategy and force structure.[50] Although some advocates of minimum deterrence have argued that the United States could unilaterally reduce its overall quantitative levels of deployed warheads, including by retiring one or more legs of the strategic triad, it is difficult to envision a domestic political situation in the United States in which such a policy would receive the necessary support. A dramatic transformation of relations with Russia would also likely be a necessary condition for moving down a path toward minimum deterrence, though the formal codification of mutually agreed-upon offensive force levels, as well some agreement on strategic defenses, would likely be important for providing and sustaining strategic stability as force reductions were executed. The monitoring and verification of agreed-upon reductions and the deployment of remaining forces would likely be a vitally important component of the agreement, because both states would be concerned about potential breakout. A reliable, robust verification regime, likely including relatively intrusive inspections of nuclear weapons infrastructure in both the United States and Russia, would be essential.

Nonproliferation

A formal embrace of and concrete move toward a minimum deterrent capability, perhaps facilitated by a renewed engagement in strategic arms control negotiations with Moscow, would be welcomed by the global nonproliferation community and would send a powerful signal to the international community about the priority of nonproliferation in U.S. foreign policy.[51] Its impact would likely be greatest on the current non-nuclear weapons states who have, along with civil society groups, pushed for the nuclear weapons states to move further toward reductions on a path to the global abolition of nuclear weapons.[52] Skeptics would rightly argue that such a move by the United States would be unlikely to affect states outside the NPT, such as North Korea, but by reinforcing the normative and formal legal framework that has emerged around the NPT, it might push other states to accept the Additional Protocol of the NPT.

The likely ramifications of moving toward a declared minimum deterrent strategy and force posture for U.S. extended deterrent commitments would also contribute to a decrease in the perceived emphasis and practical reliance of the United States and its allies on nuclear weapons.[53] A shift to a strictly conventional deterrent (against conventional attack), or perhaps to a policy of nuclear response only in the event of a nuclear attack against allies, would significantly limit the number and variety of scenarios in which the use of U.S. strategic forces would be considered. Such a shift would address the stated concerns of nonproliferation advocates and signal a new U.S. willingness to take more concrete and tangible steps toward disarmament. It is important to underscore, however, that this approach seems extremely unlikely in the absence of a formally negotiated strategic arms control agreement with Moscow and perhaps with other nuclear weapons states.[54]

Similarly, the ratification of the CTBT would also send a strong signal of U.S. commitment to nonproliferation efforts.[55] If the United States moved toward a minimum deterrent posture, the demands on its nuclear weapons infrastructure, which is currently being expanded and refurbished, would be significantly reduced. A decision to embrace minimum deterrence would likely allow for a further consolidation of some warhead designs and a cancellation or retirement of others. During this process, the nuclear scientific community could conduct a review of the viability of the current warheads and their immediate replacements with the aim of determining whether testing could be safely avoided, thus setting the stage for a ratification of the CTBT by the United States. Even if the decision were made to maintain some redundancy and excess capacity within the DOE's warhead production infrastructure as a hedge against a reversal or breakout by Russia or an effort by Beijing to "sprint up" to the declining U.S. force levels, the signing of the CTBT in the context of a consolidation and downsizing of U.S. nuclear capacity under minimum deterrence would be a logical diplomatic initiative.

Costs of a Minimum Deterrent Force

Beyond its benefits for nonproliferation and ideally strategic arms control, a shift to a minimum deterrent strategy would bring significant cost savings that could be diverted into enhancing conventional force modernization and improved readiness programs that would likely be welcomed by the services. For example, Option A, the land-air dyad of GBSD missiles and B-21 bombers, would total approximately $904 billion, and Option B, the sea-based monad, based solely on a full force of twelve Columbia Class SSBNs, would total approximately $802 billion over a thirty-year period, according to Congressional Budget Office estimates. These costs may be somewhat high, as the fixed costs of nuclear activities (research, operation, and support activities), nuclear weapons labs and infrastructure, and nuclear command, control, and communications and early warning total approximately $489 billion. With less demand for warheads under these minimum deterrent options, these costs can be expected to decrease, though the "super" hardening of the ICBM force may add to the costs of Option A.[56]

ASSESSING A MINIMUM DETERRENT STRATEGY

The United States could certainly move toward a minimum deterrent, reversing its policy and embracing a strategy that was rejected throughout the Cold War. Advocates of reductions argue that a much smaller strategic force could meet America's deterrent needs, and the resources saved from strategic modernization programs could enhance critical conventional military capabilities and leverage the technological advantage traditionally enjoyed by the United States to address long-run challenges. Considering the two alternative minimum deterrent postures described earlier, it is clear that both would continue to allow the United States to visit catastrophic damage on any adversary in retaliation for a nuclear strike on the United States or its allies. Improvements in conventional forces may enhance the ability of the United States to maintain its role in the world and to dissuade or, perhaps more effectively, to respond to the challenges of key regional adversaries, including a higher-end conventional threat from China or Russia or a regional threat from North Korea and Iran. Beyond the freeing up of budgetary resources for the improvement and expansion of conventional forces, most advocates believe that the implementation of a minimum deterrent would have other critically important benefits for U.S. national security, such as restoring U.S. leadership in global nonproliferation efforts, reenergizing the NPT regime, and strengthening formal rules and norms against nuclear proliferation and technology transfer.

Clearly, a significantly reduced strategic nuclear force deployed under a minimum deterrent strategy could be criticized for lacking flexibility and the requisite capacity to execute a large-scale nuclear war against a peer nuclear power like Russia. However, advocates of this position would welcome these changes, arguing that the United States is unlikely to deliberately escalate to the nuclear threshold, particularly if robust conventional forces are available. The ability to fight a nuclear war is irrelevant because adversaries will be deterred by the highly survivable, if much smaller, strategic nuclear force deployed by the United States.[57] They also argue that given the nature of existing threats, reliance on conventional forces is more appropriate for maintaining extended deterrence commitments, and that the presence of forward-deployed U.S. troops serves as a highly credible signal of U.S. resolve.[58]

First, a formal minimum deterrent approach would strictly limit the use of U.S. nuclear forces in retaliation for a nuclear attack against the United States and its allies. Many experts argue that such retaliation is the only realistic and legitimate mission of these forces in the current security environment anyway, and that dispelling the notion that the United States would ever employ nuclear weapons in response to conventional attacks, or even biological or chemical weapons attacks, is unnecessary, and thus would do little to enhance deterrence.[59] Given the overwhelming U.S. conventional superiority in most foreseeable cases, there are far more appropriate and effective non-nuclear options to respond to these threats, and these options serve as a more credible deterrent.

Second, as noted above, if the United States unilaterally moved toward a minimum deterrent posture, it could regain its position as a leader among the current nuclear weapons states by minimizing the perceived utility of nuclear weapons, thus sending a potent and costly signal of America's commitment to the NPT regime.

Finally, a significant decrease in the size of the United States' nuclear arsenal would allow for a consolidation of deployed and reserve warheads, elimination of redundant capabilities and increased control over existing stock, contributing to greater safety and security and a decrease in the probability of accidents.[60]

The End of Extended Deterrence?

Opponents point out that such a policy would present serious difficulties for the future of U.S. extended deterrent commitments.[61] Some proponents of a minimum deterrent accept this criticism and argue that the United States should end these commitments.[62] Underscoring the traditional Cold War problem of whether to deploy capabilities and structure diplomatic commitments that would reflect a willingness to sacrifice "Chicago for Paris," a minimum deterrent would either have to rely on conventional deterrent guarantees or remain committed to what would effectively be a "massive retaliation" posture that would treat any nuclear use against an ally as an attack on the United States that warranted an objectively disproportionate response.

Enhancing Nonproliferation? Not Such a Clear Case

This point leads directly to the second potential problem with the American minimum deterrent: in the absence of a credible diplomatic guarantee to allies that had depended upon the nuclear umbrella for their security, and in the face of a nuclear-armed adversary, the prospect that allies will acquire their own strategic nuclear capabilities—their own "minimum deterrents"—becomes more likely. In other words, even as the United States' adoption of a minimum deterrent posture devalued nuclear weapons and contributed to global nonproliferation, a rush by its former allies to acquire their own deterrent forces could actually increase (perhaps significantly in number and speed) proliferation in key regions. This presents a serious conundrum for those who view nonproliferation as a policy priority and an underlying benefit of a shift to a minimum deterrent strategy.

Unrequited Cooperation: Undermining the U.S. Position?

Similarly, in terms of strategic arms control, the prescription for unilateral U.S. reductions and a move toward a minimum deterrent strategy implies an understandable frustration with the pace and progress of strategic arms control negotiations, but also implicitly acknowledges the difficulty of the challenge. Since the conclusion of New START, Russia has shown little willingness to engage in further cuts to its arsenal.[63] The Obama administration signaled a willingness for an additional round of cuts after New START, but Moscow did not reciprocate, and as discussed earlier, President Putin's return to power has only exacerbated the deterioration of relations with Russia's neighbors and the United States.[64] Perhaps more importantly, Russia has seemed to place greater emphasis on the importance of its nuclear forces (both strategic and nonstrategic) to its security. Taken in the context of Russia's military interventions in its "near abroad" and in Syria, and of its persistent (and dangerous) military provocations of NATO forces in the Baltic region, these are ominous signals that portend a larger crisis or confrontation.

What seems clear is that Russia has little appetite for further reductions. It has thus far been unwilling to broach discussions of its deployed nonstrategic nuclear weapons (NSNWs), which it views as a hedge against NATO conventional forces. It is highly unlikely that arms control initiatives will prove fruitful, but it is also highly improbable that unilateral reductions would be received positively in Moscow. In short, nuclear weapons are a critical aspect of Russia's power that maintains its relevance in the global system.[65] They are a hedge against further erosion of Russia's perceived power and influence and the guarantee of its security. It is difficult to see how, at the current time, unreciprocated American strategic reductions would enhance U.S. security, improve the security situation in Europe, or improve the U.S. diplomatic position.

Similarly, when considering China's strategic program, which has been often described as a minimum deterrent constructed to provide an "assured retaliation" capability, no progress has been made toward even minimal levels of transparency or confidence-building between Washington and Beijing. Given the small size of China's arsenal relative to those of the United States and Russia, this is perhaps not surprising. And considering the importance of secrecy and mobility to China's strategic systems, an unwillingness to respond to calls for transparency can be seen as a direct threat to its deterrent.[66] Nonetheless, given China's conventional military modernization and its increasingly assertive behavior toward its neighbors (including U.S. allies), the present time does not seem propitious for serious arms control dialogues.

NOTES

1. Thomas M. Nichols, *No Use: Nuclear Weapons and U.S. National Security* (Philadelphia: University of Pennsylvania Press, 2014); James M. Acton, *Deterrence During Disarmament: Deep Nuclear Reductions and International Security* (New York: Routledge, 2011); James Wood Forsyth, Jr., B. Chance Saltzman, and Gary Schaub, Jr., "Minimum Deterrence and Its Critics," *Strategic Studies Quarterly* (Winter 2010): 303–313; James Wood Forsyth, Jr., B. Chance Saltzman, and Gary Schaub, Jr., "Remembrance of Things Past: The Enduring Value of Nuclear Weapons," *Strategic Studies Quarterly* (Spring 2010): 74–89; Hans Kristensen, Robert S. Norris, and Ivan Olerich, *From Counterforce to Minimal Deterrence: A New Nuclear Policy on the Path Toward Eliminating Nuclear Weapons* (Washington, DC: Federation of American Scientists/Natural Resources Defense Council, 2009); Tom Saurer, "A Second Nuclear Revolution: From Nuclear Primacy to Post-Existential Deterrence," *Journal of Strategic Studies* 32, no. 5 (October 2009): 745–767; Morton H. Halperin, *Nuclear Fallacy: Dispelling the Myth of Nuclear Strategy* (Cambridge: Ballinger, 1987).
2. David Alan Rosenberg, "The Origins of Overkill: Nuclear Weapons and American Strategy, 1945-1960," *International Security* 7, no. 4 (Spring 1983): 3-71, 56-58.
3. Tom Saurer, *Nuclear Inertia: US Nuclear Weapons After The Cold War* (New York: Palgrave Macmillan, 2005); Janne E. Nolan, *An Elusive Consensus: Nuclear Weapons and America Security After the Cold War* (Washington, DC: Brookings Institution Press, 1999): 35-62.
4. William J. Perry and James E. Cartwright, "Spending less on nuclear weapons could actually make us safer," *The Washington Post*, November 16, 2017.
5. Richard L. Garwin, "Will Strategic Submarines be Vulnerable?" *International Security* 8, no. 2 (Fall 1983): 52–67.
6. Keir A. Lieber and Daryl G. Press, "The End of MAD? The Nuclear Dimension of U.S. Primacy," *International Security* 30, no. 4 (Spring 2006): 7–44; Desmond Ball, "The Counterforce Potential of American SLBM Systems," *Journal of Peace Research* 14, no. 1 (1977): 23–40.
7. Amy F. Woolf, *U.S. Strategic Nuclear Forces: Background, Developments, and Issues* (Washington, DC: Congressional Research Service, 2017).

8. Kristensen, Norris and Oelrich, *From Counterforce to Minimal Deterrence*, 43-44 3. Forsyth et al, *Remembrance of Things Past*, 385.

9. Nichols, *No Use*, 118.

10. Lauren H. Holland and Robert A. Hoover, *The MX Decision: A New Direction in U.S. Weapons Procurement Policy?* (Boulder, CO: Westview Press, 1985).

11. Kristensen, Norris, and Oelrich, *From Counterforce to Minimal Deterrence*, 41.

12. Ibid.; Forsyth, Jr., Saltzman, and Schaub, Jr., "Minimum Deterrence and its Critics."

13. Forsyth et al, *Remembrance of Things Past*, 385.

14. Keith B. Payne and James Schlesinger (eds.) *Minimum Deterrence: Examining the Evidence* (Washington, DC: National Institute Press, 2013), 17-18.

15. Kristensen, Norris, and Oelrich, *From Counterforce to Minimal Deterrence*, 31.

16. Ibid., 41.

17. Ibid., 34–35.

18. Michael S. Gerson, "No First Use: The Next Step for U.S. Nuclear Policy," *International Security* 35, no. 2 (Fall 2010): 7–47.

19. Nichols, *No Use*, 158.

20. Kristensen, Norris and Oelrich, *From Counterforce to Minimal Deterrence*, 21-22.

21. Saurer, *Nuclear Inertia*, 10.

22. Harold A. Feiveson (ed.) *The Nuclear Turning Point: A Blueprint for Deep Cuts and De-Alerting of Nuclear Weapons* (Washington, DC: Brookings Institution, 1999).

23. Kristensen, Norris, and Oelrich, *From Counterforce to Minimal Deterrence*, 33

24. John C. Toomay, "Warning and Assessment," in Ashton B. Carter, John D. Steinbruner, and Charles A. Zraket, *Managing Nuclear Operations* (Washington, DC: Brooking Institution, 1987): 282-321

25. Kristensen, Norris and Oelrich, *From Counterforce to Minimal Deterrence*, 21-22.

26. Glen C. Buchan, *U.S. Nuclear Strategy for the Post-Cold War Era* (Santa Monica, CA: RAND Corporation, 1994), 35.

27. Bruce G. Blair, *Strategic Command and Control: Redefining the Nuclear Threat* (Washington, DC: Brooking Institution, 1985).

28. Halperin, *Nuclear Fallacy*, 78.

29. Keir A. Lieber and Daryl G. Press, "The New Era of Counterforce: Technological Change and the Future of Deterrence," *International Security* 41, no. 4 (Spring 2017): 9-49.

30. James E. Doyle, *Renewing America's Nuclear Arsenal* (New York: Routledge, 2017): 24–27.

31. Nichols, *No Use*, 123–124.

32. Acton, "U.S. National Missile Defense Policy."

33. Nichols, *No Use*, 121.

34. Barry Blechman and Russell Rumbaugh, "Bombs Away: The Case for Phasing Out U.S. Tactical Nukes in Europe," *Foreign Affairs* (July/August 2014): 163–174.

35. Nichols, *No Use*, 112–113.

36. Robert Art, "To What Ends Military Power?" *International Security* 4, no. 4 (Spring 1980): 3–35.

37. Ibid., 113.

38. Avery Goldstein, *Deterrence and Security in the 21ˢᵗ Century: China, Britain, France and the Enduring Legacy of the Nuclear Revolution* (Stanford, CA: Stanford University Press, 2000); Vipin Narang, *Nuclear Strategy in the Modern Era: Regional Powers and International Conflict* (Princeton, NJ: Princeton University Press, 2014).

39. David N. Schwartz, *NATO's Nuclear Dilemmas* (Washington, DC: Brookings Institutions, 1983).

40. Scott Sagan, "Why Do States Build Nuclear Weapons? Three Models in Search of a Bomb," *International Security* 21, no. 3 (Winter 1996–1997): 54–86.

41. Nichols, *No Use*, 121.

42. Ibid.

43. Mark Landler, "U.S. To Resist NATO Push to Remove Tactical Arms," *International Herald Tribune*, April 23, 2010, p. 5.

44. Robert Jervis, *The Illogic of American Nuclear Strategy* (Ithaca, NY: Cornell University Press, 1984), 31–33.

45. Nichols, *No Use*, 121.

46. Robert Jervis, *Perception and Misperception in World Politics* (Princeton, NJ: Princeton University, 1976).

47. Robert Jervis, "Arms Control, Stability and Causes of War," *Political Science Quarterly* 108, no. 2 (Summer 1993): 248.

48. Nichols, *No Use*, 82-85.

49. Ibid., 157-58.

50. Acton, *Deterrence During Disarmament*, 64-65.

51. Paul Meyer and Tom Sauer, "The Nuclear Ban Treaty: A Sign of Global Impatience," *Survival* 60, no. 6 (April-May 2018): 61-72.

52. Nichols, *No Use*, 116.

53. Acton, *Deterrence During Disarmament*, 98-9.

54. Ibid., 157-158.

55. Christopher M. Jones and Kevin P. Marsh, "The Odyssey of the Comprehensive Nuclear-Test-Ban Treaty: Clinton, Obama, and the Politics of Treaty Ratification," *Nonproliferation Review* 21, no. 2 (2014): 207-227; David Hafemeister, "Assessing the Merits of the CTBT," *Nonproliferation Review* 16, no. 3 (2009): 473-482.

56. *Approaches for Managing the Costs of U.S. Nuclear Forces, 2017 to 2046* (Washington, DC: Congressional Budget Office, 2017).

57. Nichols, *No Use*, 85.

58. Ibid., 121.

59. Ibid. 158.

60. Ibid., 83.

61. Keith B. Payne and John S. Foster, Jr., *Nuclear Force Adaptability for Deterrence and Assurance: A Prudent Alternative to Minimum Deterrence* (Washington, DC: National Institute Press, 2014); Keith B. Payne and James Schlesinger, *Minimum Deterrence: Examining the Evidence* (Washington, DC: National Institute Press, 2013).

62. Jeffrey W. Hornung and Mike M. Mochizuki, "Japan: Still an Exceptional U.S. Ally," *The Washington Quarterly* 30, no. 1 (Spring 2016): 95-116; Emma Chanlett-Avery and Mary Beth Nitkin, *Japan's Nuclear Future: Policy Debate, Prospects, and U.S. Interests* (Washington, DC: Congressional Research Service, 2009); Tristan Volpe and Ulrich Kuhn, "Germany's Nuclear Education: Why a Few Elites Are Testing a Taboo," *The Washington Quarterly* 40, no 3 (Fall 2017): 7-27.

63. Nikolai Sokov, "Assessing Russian Attitudes Toward Phased, Deep Nuclear Reductions: Strategic and Regional Concerns," *Nonproliferation Review* 20, no. 2 (2013): 247-261.

64. Roberts, *The Case for Nuclear Weapons in the 21st Century*, 122-124.

65. Bruno Tertrais, "Russia's Nuclear Policy: Worrying for the Wrong Reasons," *Survival* 60, no. 2 (April-May 2018): 33-44; Alexey Arbartov, "Understanding the U.S.-Russia Nuclear Schism," *Survival* 59, no. 2 (April-May 2017): 33-66.

66. Christopher P. Twomey, "Nuclear Stability at Low Numbers: The Perspective from Beijing," *Nonproliferation Review* 20, no. 2 (2013): 289-303.

Conclusions

This book has presented a reassessment of the nuclear strategy of the United States. To develop an understanding of an optimal nuclear strategy for the United States, it examined three alternative ideal type nuclear strategies, taking into consideration the current geopolitical, technological, global proliferation, and fiscal and budgetary trends. Building upon the work of scholars and policy analysts, this study has constructed three major approaches to a U.S. nuclear strategy, associated force structure, and posture, as well as to key related issues such as strategic defenses, nonstrategic nuclear weapons (NSNWs), nuclear command, control and communications (NC3), and the underlying nuclear weapons enterprise. It has also considered the implications for several important factors: the deterrence of adversaries and the assurance of allies, strategic stability (which includes both crisis stability and arms race stability), strategic arms control, and nonproliferation efforts. It has assessed the relevance of each alternative strategy to the maintenance of robust conventional forces and the ability of the United States to address new threats arising from technological change.

The three ideal types examined in this study are nuclear primacy, constituted by a commitment to achieving quantitative strategic superiority, the fielding of extensive offensive counterforce capabilities, a variety of flexible nuclear capabilities, and expansive strategic defenses; a robust strategic deterrent, with a formidable offensive strategic nuclear force that would maintain a level of strategic stability with Russia, avoid incentivizing a major strategic buildup by China, and confront smaller nuclear powers with overwhelming deterrent capabilities; and a minimum deterrent strategy, defined by significant reductions in the current deployed forces and strategic modernization plans and a reliance on a smaller, highly secure and responsive nuclear force.

The study has presented each strategic approach on its own merits, wherever possible using the best cases made by advocates regarding important related issues and key implications for U.S. and international security. It also identified the key tradeoffs and/or potential problems of each approach, engaging both the academic and policy literatures and taking into account relevant history from the Cold War and the past two decades of attempts to restructure U.S. nuclear strategy. In doing so, the study has also made an earnest attempt to point out areas where the policy and academic communities speak past each other. The remainder of this chapter will briefly revisit the four major debates surrounding nuclear weapons discussed in the first chapter before revisiting the three alternative nuclear strategies the study has assessed. Given the nature of the security environment, as well as broader political-military and diplomatic interests and resource constrains, a robust deterrent strategy provides the optimal approach for the United States moving forward.

Revisiting the Major Debates on Nuclear Weapons

Given the nature of the security environment and the challenges created by geopolitical and technological change, the modernization of the strategic arsenal—including overdue investments in revitalizing the Nuclear Command, Control and Communications (NC3) system and the Department of Energy (DOE) nuclear weapons laboratories and support infrastructure—is warranted and a prudent investment of finite resources. However, considering the importance of extended deterrence commitments in Europe and Asia and ongoing missions in the Middle East, the modernization of U.S. strategic forces should be balanced against conventional force modernization and readiness needs. Moreover, given the rapid pace of technological change and the potentially decisive security implications of artificial intelligence, additive manufacturing, and synthetic biology, as well as pressing challenges of cyberwarfare and hypersonic weapons, the U.S. nuclear arsenal should maintain a formidable hedge against technological breakthroughs, but should not demand such resources as to preclude sufficient investment in research and development to sustain America's long-term technological edge.

Taking these considerations into account, the modernization of the strategic triad to maintain numerical equivalence with Russian strategic forces is a prudent approach to maintaining strategic stability without introducing new incentives for further quantitative expansion of forces (arms race instability) or considerations of first strikes even in the event of severe diplomatic crisis (crisis instability) between the United States and Moscow. Moreover it provides a formidable deterrent to a rising China and regional powers like North Korea and Iran.

The case for a wide and diverse stockpile of nuclear weapons beyond the strategic triad, particularly non-strategic nuclear weapons, is less compelling.[1] Proponents of fielding and deploying nuclear forces that provide the United States with a virtually seamless spectrum of capabilities to maintain escalation control at every foreseeable level of conflict downplay both the budgetary costs and potential diplomatic and political downsides of an overt, increased reliance on nuclear weapons. In the first place, new programs will only exacerbate the current fiscal challenges confronting the Department of Defense and undermines the ability to devote needed resources to conventional forces, modernization, readiness and long-term R&D. In the second place, such a shift in policy would likely weaken U.S. nonproliferation efforts and place allies with difficult domestic political constituencies in the position of defending their willingness to cooperate with the United States in the maintenance of extended deterrence objectives based more heavily on forward deployed nuclear weapons. Moreover, the perceived need for an expansion of U.S. nonstrategic nuclear weapons seems to ignore the existing conventional superiority enjoyed by the United States. In the event of an significant and dramatic erosion of U.S. conventional military capabilities, there may be a stronger case for a reliance on non-strategic nuclear weapons, but such a development would not resolve the conventional priorities challenges mentioned above and would likely require a more fundamental revision of alliance relations and commitments.

The perceived need for an expansive, highly diverse arsenal of nuclear weapons is not new. Its roots can be traced back to argument in favor of the development of a warfighting capability during the 1970s and 1980s.[2] Advocates are focused on the perceived need for capabilities that allow for deliberate escalation control and the effective prosecution of a protracted nuclear conflict and are skeptical that inadvertent escalation (or the fears of that escalation on the part of an adversary) would prevent limited nuclear use in the first place. Possession of lower-yield, tactical nuclear weapons would provide U.S. policymakers with a degree of escalation control, ideally keeping a limited nuclear war "limited" but providing a spectrum of gradual, proportional responses to nuclear use by an adversary. Such an approach enhances deterrence in the view of proponents. But as the limited war studies of the early Cold War period indicated, notions of escalation control and maintaining constraints on conflict is dubious, and strategic weapons are capable of providing limited, gradual responses.[3] Despite claims to the contrary, the major "firebreak" in military conflict remains that which exists between conventional and nuclear weapons, despite the increased capabilities of the former and potential scaled down, theater or operational value of the later.[4]

This view also is based upon an extreme concern with the perceived problem of self-deterrence. This thinking inspired the ICBM vulnerability debate in the 1970s and is particularly relevant to extended deterrence today.[5] Without a spectrum of limited, proportional nuclear strike options the political leadership of the United States may refrain from taking necessary action if an adversary escalates above the nuclear threshold but does not directly threatening the homeland but maintains the promise of further, unacceptable societal damage. This is a difficult proposition to reconcile with much of American history. However, it is also logically questionable that a president that feared to use nuclear weapons after Americans had been killed by an adversary's initial use would be more comfortable using lower-yield tactical nuclear weapons if likely escalation would lead to societal catastrophe.[6] Instead, reliance on a robust menu of conventional military options supported by limited and/ or deliberately escalatory strategic nuclear options would seemingly provide a preferable alternative approach. As discussed previously, the commitment to maintain a forward-based nuclear deterrent in Europe by providing B61-12 bombs for use with NATO dual capable aircraft is driven more by the political objective of maintaining alliance cohesion and reinforcing solidarity against a resurgent threat from Russia, than the actual military value of the planned forces.[7]

Finally, more expansive calls for a highly flexible nuclear force typically argue for the expansion of strategic ballistic missile defenses, which would play a complementary role in a war-fighting strategy against peer competitors. The Trump administration has seemed to move toward embracing such an expansion, including the consideration of spaced-based satellites and perhaps eventually the deployment of interceptors in outer space.[8] While limited defenses against regional threats based on forward-deployed theater missile defense systems and existing deployed homeland missile defenses may enhance deterrence by threatening to deny more risk-acceptant adversaries such as North Korea or Iran from contemplating an attack on the United States, moving significantly beyond such capabilities seems unwise. There is significant evidence that Russian and Chinese strategic modernization programs have been in large part driven by concerns about U.S. investment in strategic defenses and the implications for their respective deterrent capabilities, offsetting any perceived benefits that have been achieved since the Bush administration's withdrawal from the ABM Treaty in 2002.[9] Removal of constraints on future U.S. missile defense systems in recent Congressional defense authorizations are only likely to exacerbate these fears. Beyond these very important strategic concerns, the potential costs of these programs seems prohibitive by almost any objective measure.[10] The mission of limited strategic defenses should be targeted toward regional threats, while resources for the missiles defense enterprise should be focused primarily on R&D, thus avoiding the pattern of rushed deployment of untested and unreliable systems which has marked so much of the recent history of the program.

In considering the political influence of nuclear weapons, it clear that the strategic arsenal remains relevant to national security by deterring nuclear attacks against the United States and its allies. The U.S. nuclear arsenal also contributed to the deterrence of conventional attacks against key allies during the Cold War, and contributed to keeping that political conflict "cold" for almost five decades.[11] Scholars and policymakers may debate the extent of the contribution that nuclear weapons made to sustaining robust extended deterrence commitments to NATO and Japan, but where the Soviet Union or China could clearly understand the nature of the U.S. interests at stake, direct provocation became less probable over time. Certainly the experiences of early Cold War crises and the "close call" of the Cuban missile crisis presented leaders in Washington and Moscow with strong incentives to avoid direct confrontations in the future, and competition in the periphery would continue until the Cold War's end, but it is difficult to contend that the specter of nuclear weapons was not a critical factor in maintaining the peace between the superpowers.

Beyond this important contribution to U.S. security and international stability, however, the political influence of the U.S. nuclear arsenal is less clear.[12] Experts who advocated for numerical superiority both as the most effective means to confidently deter the Soviet Union during the Cold War and to provide maximum leverage in diplomatic crises face difficulty in reconciling their views with the empirical record. Efforts to develop and deploy expansive counterforce weapons, ostensibly to enhance the credibility of the U.S. deterrent, exacerbated Soviet fears of U.S. intentions in the early 1980s and increased the probability of war, culminating in the events of 1983.[13] This was a rough analog to the alarm created within the U.S. defense policy community over the growing vulnerability of the ICBM force created by the deployment of new Soviet capabilities in the mid-1970s. In the U.S.-Soviet relationship, efforts to significantly alter the strategic balance seemed to have the net result of decreasing stability, making crisis and conflict more likely.

As studies of Cold War crises reflect, the nature of the strategic balance generally did not play a decisive role in determining outcomes.[14] Moreover, a more persuasive case can be made for the presence of nuclear weapons as imposing restraint on leaders during crises irrespective of quantities of deployed forces.[15] This broad conclusion would seem to support the view of minimal or finite deterrence advocates that acknowledge the contribution of nuclear weapons to deterrence (particularly against the United States itself) but argue that much smaller forces would be sufficient for such a mission. However, this may overstate the power of nuclear weapons in the abstract and dismiss the influence of the size of the superpower arsenals dispelling any notions of pressing advantage or provoking military conflict when vital national interests were at stake. In considering the overseas commitments that the United States continues to maintain, dramatic negotiated reductions with Russia or unilateral cuts to the U.S. arsenal may significantly undermine extended deterrence commitments, even those predicated upon conventional forward defense.[16] In the case of unilateral cuts, such a policy may introduce dangerous strategic instability into the U.S.-Russia relationship as decreases in U.S. forces below certain levels may create first-strike incentives under intense crisis conditions. Significant resistance within the defense policy community as well as from the domestic political realm would be expected. The maintenance of current programmed strategic force levels based on the modernization of the triad would seem to be the most prudent way forward.[17]

Finally, arms control cooperation contributed to strategic stability during the Cold War and significantly aided in the conclusion of the superpower rivalry.[18] The Strategic Arms Limitation Talks (SALT) process produced two agreements. SALT I included the ABM Treaty, formally averting an arms race in strategic defenses, and an Interim Agreement to set limits on deployed offensive force. SALT II resulted in an agreement on force levels but proved incapable of addressing the concerns of skeptics over qualitative improvements in Soviet deployed forces, most notably the deployment of multiple independently targetable reentry vehicles (MIRV) on larger Russian missiles. SALT I was ratified by the United States Senate, and while SALT II was never ratified, both superpowers maintained the agreed limitation informally into the 1980s. The Intermediate Nuclear Forces (INF) Treaty eliminated theater missiles from the superpower arsenals and contributed to the transformation of the security environment in Europe and the Strategic Arms Reduction Treaty (START I) was the first in a series of negotiated reductions of strategic nuclear weapons from American and Soviet/Russian arsenals. Subsequent bilateral post-Cold War arms control negotiations including the "New START" Treaty have continued the trend toward reductions in strategic arsenals. It is unclear if the Trump administration will seek to extend the New START Treaty when it expires in 2021, and skeptics have argued against an extension because of Russia's provocative foreign policy and its violation of the INF Treaty, which the United States recently has announced its withdrawal from. However, given that the current modernization plan is structured to meet New START guidelines, it is unclear what benefit allowing the treaty to lapse would have for U.S. security interests.[19] Maintaining shared expectations concerning levels of deployed forces contributes to strategic stability by decreasing uncertainty. While other issues like the resolution of INF violations, Russia's large stockpile of tactical nuclear weapons, and new technologies like hypersonic propulsion may also be important, and while desires to bring other actors into a multilateral arms control regime (such as China, and perhaps India and Pakistan) are understandable, these concerns do not eliminate the potential benefit of an extension of New START and sustained bilateral transparency concerning strategic systems.

At the very least, an extension of New START may also send a signal, albeit one that will be received with little enthusiasm, that the United States and Russia continue to attempt to maintain their respective good faith efforts to work toward nuclear disarmament under Article IV of the Nonproliferation Treaty. As discussed earlier, the conclusion of the Nuclear Weapons Ban Treaty in the United Nations in 2017 was a reflection of frustration on the part of civil society and nonnuclear weapon states over the pace and scope of arms reduction efforts. These actors would favor the kinds of deep cuts or unilateral reductions proposed by finite deterrence advocates. Extending New START and maintaining proposed force levels would at least be a recognition of the importance of continued negotiations. Conversely, attempts to use the treaty's lapse to initiate a significant buildup of U.S. strategic forces beyond existing levels would likely have severe, negative consequences for the U.S. nonproliferation objectives. It seems that the Trump administration is generally less supportive of the multilateral nonproliferation regime but a dramatic break from the precedent of postwar reductions may severely undermine an already vulnerable regime, complicating the achievement of larger U.S. nonproliferation objectives.[20]

Having reconsidered these important debates on nuclear weapons, it is possible to draw some implications about the relative strengths and weaknesses of the alternative approaches to U.S. nuclear strategy considered in this study.

Nuclear Primacy: A Costly and Disproportionate Solution to Present Challenges

Although the advocates of nuclear primacy firmly believe that it is the best way to guarantee the United States' national security and maintain its extended deterrent commitments in the context of formidable geopolitical threats and rapid changes in military technology, this approach would introduce significant difficulties into efforts to achieve many U.S. policy objectives.[21] Perhaps the most straightforward difficulty is the estimated cost of attempting to achieve quantitative strategic superiority and a sufficient expansion of nonstrategic nuclear weapons to provide a variety of tailored, limited nuclear options and significantly enhanced strategic homeland and theater missile defenses. Although few advocates of this positon would support a large reduction of U.S. conventional forces, and thus a shift toward greater reliance upon these expansive nuclear capabilities, they implicitly dismiss concerns about budgetary pressures or constraints by suggesting that finding the funds is simply a matter of choice.[22] This attitude is neither new nor surprising, given that (as noted earlier) many of these same advocates vocally supported greatly expanded offensive counterforce capabilities and strategic defenses to provided damage limitation capabilities during the Cold War.[23] In the immediate post-Cold War period, they typically accepted the necessity of some quantitative force reductions but continued to advocate for a diverse array of limited nuclear options and strategic defenses.[24] With the return of great power competition, the policy prescription is remarkably similar, with the exception of calls for larger numbers of weapons (or at least opposition to further reductions). These advocates have consistently argued for enhanced capabilities precisely because of the difficulty of deterring leaders or regimes that may be more risk- and cost-acceptant than the rational actors assumed in much of the academic literature. They have made this argument in three distinct strategic contexts: while facing a highly aggressive Soviet leadership that was prepared to fight a protracted nuclear war in the 1970s; in the first two decades after the Cold War, facing regional actors with domestic political pathologies (pride and prestige) that inhibited their ability to rationally assess the costs and benefits of their regimes' survival and thus made them difficult to deter; and today, while confronting rising revisionist adversaries like Russia and China that may value expansion over the status quo and view nuclear weapons as providing a "theory of victory" against a conventionally superior United States.[25] Rejecting the insights of the nuclear revolution literature, the advocates of nuclear primacy view nuclear strategy as an extension of conventional military strategy and argue that the United States must be capable of fighting and winning a nuclear conflict across a spectrum of violence to prevent any perceived advantage that might allow for a deterrence failure.[26] While bristling at the "war-fighting" moniker, they maintain that deterrence is the fundamental objective, but that it is much harder to achieve than proponents of assured destruction or finite deterrence assume. They may display considerable consternation at the current state of the U.S. strategic arsenal and related forces, but the commitment of resources required to achieve the capabilities that nuclear primacists demand seems highly unrealistic in the context of conventional military modernization and readiness requirements. Such a commitment may similarly undermine the ability of the Defense Department to address the threats and vulnerabilities created by technological change. Unsurprisingly, the recommended nuclear forces would constitute far more than a hedge, and their demand for resources would likely undermine the capacity of the United States to exploit technological change and maintain an innovative edge in the medium to long term.

In addition, the implementation of a strategy of nuclear primacy, with the requisite offensive counterforce capabilities, expansion of nonstrategic limited nuclear options, and strategic defenses, is likely to have significant negative implications for U.S. security. First, it would undermine strategic stability with Russia and China. This is a price that most advocates are willing to pay, but a broad segment of the defense and foreign policy community is not. Although enhanced strategic and nonstrategic offensive modernization efforts and the expansion of strategic defenses are likely to prove costly from a fiscal perspective, they are also likely to increase the perception among Russian and Chinese leaders that the United States has malign intentions, which would require counters to prevent coercion and political blackmail by the United States. Some experts might welcome this development, arguing that the United States can simply out-build its competitors and force them to accept secondary status. With regard to Russia, whose economic base is in poor shape, this approach may be possible, but it is extremely costly and risky. Given China's economic modernization and potential power, the case is less clear; such a move could undermine the United States' economic and potential power. Moreover, beyond the foreseeable arms race instabilities that such a policy would create, there is no guarantee that a nation like China will not continue to size and shape its forces to maximize its advantages over the United States, preferring asymmetric responses that do not directly compete with the United States but may nonetheless undermine American interests and create vulnerabilities in other realms. Crisis instability may further be exacerbated if the actors that primacy advocates depict as less than rational become desperate under U.S. pressure, particularly in a crisis in which their interests are far more vital than those of United States. Perhaps the U.S. would be better prepared to prevail in such a conflict, but precipitating a crisis that escalates into a costly military great power conflict, whether it crosses the nuclear threshold or not, does not seem likely to serve U.S. national security interests or those of its allies.

Finally, and perhaps counterintuitively, advocates of nuclear primacy, in focusing on the difficulties of deterring an aggressive, risk-acceptant, and potentially irrational adversary, often downplay or overlook the concerns of the allies that the United States is attempting to protect and assure. In some cases, advocates of primacy believe that the adversaries are far more hostile, unreasonable, and willing to run extreme risks than they are perceived to be by the neighbors to which the United States is attempting to extend its deterrent commitment. This situation places their leaders in difficult domestic political situations that can undermine alliance cohesion, potentially weakening the U.S. position and creating a perception that the United States is willing to "decouple" its security from that of its allies. If the United States seeks to achieve what Chinese analysts have termed "absolute" security, defense officials in allied capitals may view the United States as willing to accept the potential for a localized nuclear conflict. The allies involved in such a conflict would pay a dear price, even if the U.S. was making an effort to defend them. Whereas proponents of nuclear primacy may continue to argue, in good faith, that the availability of more tailored, limited nuclear options to the United States may prevent a conflict in the first place, the increased "usability" of lower-yield, forward-deployed nuclear weapons could decrease crisis stability and precipitate a conflict involving nuclear weapons on allied territory. It is evident that allies are relatively comfortable with limited deployments of tactical nuclear weapons with dual capable aircraft (DCA) that provide a strong, visible presence of U.S. resolve to support its allies. However, the limited appetite for further expansive capabilities, particularly strike capabilities that could hit targets on Russia soil, would represent a qualitatively different threat and would return NATO to the domestic political turmoil of the Euromissile crisis of the late 1970s and 1980s.[27]

Minimum Deterrence: Too Far Too Fast

Conversely, advocates of finite deterrence argue that a relatively small, secure, survivable, and reliable strategic nuclear program can prevent a direct nuclear attack on the United States by adversaries.[28] Arguing that nuclear weapons have little relevance beyond deterring such an attack on the homeland, they believe that a significant reduction in U.S. strategic nuclear forces will provide a host of benefits that can enhance U.S. security. Perhaps most importantly, they argue that the United States can regain the leadership of the nonproliferation regime and the moral high ground among nuclear weapons states, aligning its policy more closely with the demands of non-nuclear weapons states and with the policies of key allies like the United Kingdom and France, which maintain limited or finite deterrent forces.[29] By reenergizing the international nonproliferation regime, the United States can work closely with its allies and other committed states to limit access to stocks of chemical, biological, radiological, or nuclear (CBRN) weapons, or WMD-related materials, thus improving U.S. security, strengthening global norms, and increasing the pressure on new nuclear powers to limit or even reverse their behavior.

Moreover, the freeing up of scarce resources would allow the U.S. Defense budget priorities to shift to modernizing the conventional forces, responding to new challenges like cyber and electronic warfare, and developing conventional military means of answering new threats from emerging technologies. The threats coming from Russia and China, small regional powers like North Korea and Iran, and global terrorism cannot be effectively addressed by nuclear weapons. However, as opponents point out and some advocates acknowledge, the very limited nature of the U.S. strategic arsenal under such a strategy would test the limits of extended deterrence. With a finite deterrent, the question of whether a U.S. president would sacrifice the nation to defend an ally against a nuclear-armed adversary takes on heightened salience. The hypothetical question of whether a United States president would be willing to "trade Chicago for Paris" was never answered to Paris's liking during the Cold War, leading France to decide to create its own deterrent force and withdraw from NATO's unified command structure.[30] Although the proponents of minimal deterrence argue that the mere presence of a secure retaliatory capability induces highly risk-averse, careful, and restrained behavior, the relatively dispersed and far-flung security commitments of the United States would put this assumption to the test. Recipients of the extended deterrent guarantee may feel vulnerable in the context of a formal U.S. shift to minimum deterrence, particularly in the absence of reciprocal reductions in adversary forces or the transformation of diplomatic relations in key regions. Thus, the erosion of the credibility of America's nuclear umbrella, particularly in Europe and Asia, may press some of these allies to seek out their own strategic nuclear deterrent, creating intense proliferation challenges and undermining the previously discussed nonproliferation benefits.

Some prominent scholars argue that the United States would be best served by a more restrained foreign policy with less engagement in regions like Europe and East Asia.[31] They argue that managed nuclear proliferation may actually provide a relatively cost-effective and easy way to establish stability in regions transitioning away from a U.S. security guarantee.[32] This view is not widely shared in the defense and foreign policy communities, which view the instability that would likely be precipitated by a transition away from extended deterrent guarantees as unnecessarily risky. The Trump administration's often harsh rhetoric toward Europe and persistent questioning of the value and relevance of alliances like NATO more broadly has reportedly created some interest in a reconsideration of the role of nuclear weapons among allies in a post-American extended deterrence world.[33]

Other scholars argue for a more basic reevaluation of alliance commitments and of extended deterrence guarantees. Acknowledging that it would be difficult to credibly extend finite strategic deterrence to allies, they assert that the United States should shift its relations with allies and recommit to a robust conventionally-based extended deterrent capability in the regions that are determined to be vital to U.S. national security interests. These scholars are confident that the forward positioning of U.S. troops who would be directly at risk in the event of a military conflict is a robust deterrent to an adversary that would also face a conventionally superior U.S. military backed up by the strategic capacity to respond to any nuclear escalation with a society-damaging nuclear strike. The role of forward-deployed nuclear weapons, therefore, would be redundant. The United States would continue to provide a robust international posture, formally articulated in a No First Use policy, but with decreasing reliance on its nuclear arsenal.[34]

Robust Strategic Deterrence: A Manageable Status Quo

Between the two extreme alternatives of nuclear primacy and minimum deterrence lies the option of a robust strategic deterrent. As discussed in chapter 4, the United States has already achieved such a deterrent. It should, moreover, be able to maintain this robust strategic deterrent over time, while also addressing some of the pressing needs confronting national security policymakers in the short and medium terms. The chapter has covered several means of achieving a measure of numerical equivalence with Russia and rebuilding the NC3 infrastructure to improve network effectiveness and resilience and maintain maximum warning and alert capabilities, which have reportedly been eroded by time and neglect. In light of the growing challenge of offensive cyber-capabilities, rebuilding this infrastructure should be a clear priority, not an afterthought. Similarly, the nuclear weapons infrastructure should also be recapitalized. The

Department of Energy network of laboratories and facilities should be adequately resourced and staffed with expert personnel. Given the reportedly troubled state of these two vital components of the nuclear enterprise, the long-term viability of the U.S. strategic deterrent and its contribution to U.S. national security will be challenged as long as the current conditions persist.[35]

A robust deterrent strategy would maintain some measure of strategic ambiguity with regard to declaratory policy to allow flexible responses to geopolitical and technological developments. Limiting the role of U.S. strategic nuclear weapons to deterring a nuclear strike on the United States or its allies or to responding to significant non-nuclear threats would continue the trend of limiting the United States' reliance on nuclear weapons, but would communicate to adversaries that retaliation would be swift, certain, and decisive. Moreover, maintaining elements of the strategic triad would allow for complementary elements of crisis management, which would increase survivability, promptness, and flexibility.

A practical challenge for this alternative would be the elimination of forward-positioned nuclear weapons in Europe, currently programmed to shift to the B61-12 nuclear gravity bomb to be deployed with F-35A Joint Strike Fighters or an alternative European platform. As discussed, the B61-12 program, even if it is largely a political signal of NATO cohesion and burden sharing, seems prudent if European NATO allies contribute to the resourcing of the program. Given Russia's provocative behavior, it would be difficult to reverse course on the planned B61-12 program, but an ideal type robust deterrent would move away from tactical nuclear weapons over time.

The case for the Long-Range Standoff Ordinance (LRSO) is less clear.[36] Because the B-21 Raider program is highly secret, it is difficult to estimate its future capabilities. Given the size and advertised per-unit costs of the B-21, it seems that it may attempt to exploit off-the-shelf technology to allow for a relatively rapid development program, but it is also expected to possess stealth and advanced electronic capabilities that would allow for a penetrating bomber role.[37] Still, concerns about the improvement, expansion, and diffusion of the advanced integrated air defense system call into question the capacity of the B-21 to perform a penetrating bomber role in highly contested environments over the longer term. Opponents of the LRSO believe it is costly and redundant and potentially destabilizing.[38] For proponents, it seems to be both a bridge for the remaining B-52H bombers devoted to the nuclear mission and a hedge for the B-21 should IADs advance beyond projected capabilities and thus erode the ability to execute the penetrating bomber mission. This issue is not trivial, but the penetrating strategic nuclear bomber should remain a component of the modernized nuclear triad. Given the B-1 bomber's projected lifetime and formidable capabilities, one wonders if there is now some regret in defense circles that it was removed from the strategic nuclear mission. With a limited capacity to perform the penetrating mission, particularly in advanced IAD environments, it would not serve as a "first strike" weapon, as some opponents have argued that a highly stealthy B-21 could when armed with a highly effective penetrating cruise missile. In fact, aside from the B-52, the B-1 could be the most stabilizing element of the strategic triad over the next two decades, providing a workhorse standoff platform with a highly effective cruise missile. Although it seems prudent to invest in a hedge against the potential failure of the B-21 to maintain a penetrating bomber capability over the long term, a more appropriate and cost-effective option would to be delay the acquisition and deployment of the LRSO until the B-21's ultimate capabilities are known and to focus instead on existing programs like the JASSM-ER and the development of a nuclear variant.[39]

The robust deterrent strategy would avoid many of the potential downsides of both the nuclear primacy and finite deterrence approaches by focusing on maintaining strategic stability with Russia and avoiding sparking an arms race with Beijing. This strategy would also allow the United States to sustain alliance partnerships while also remaining open to renewed negotiations on strategic arms control and further progress on the nonproliferation regime.

Ultimately, a robust strategic deterrent approach would provide the national command authority with a menu of options to deter nuclear use by an adversary. It is true that it would not provide a rung-by-rung capacity to control escalation from conventional warfare across the nuclear threshold. Such a capacity, however, is an extreme and extravagant requirement for a deterrent. A more reasonable assessment is that the combination of advanced conventional U.S. forces with a diverse, survivable, prompt, and versatile nuclear arsenal based on a modernized strategic triad would present a formidable, robust extended deterrent to the United States' adversaries, whether they are great powers or new regional nuclear powers.

Notes

1. Keith B. Payne and John S. Foster (eds.), *A New Nuclear Review for a New Age* (Washington, DC: National Institute Press, 2017).

2. Colin S. Gray, "War-Fighting for Deterrence," *Journal of Strategic Studies* 7, no. 1 (March 1984): 5-28.

3. Robert Jervis, *The Meaning of the Nuclear Revolution: Statecraft and the Prospect of Armageddon* (Ithaca: Cornell University Press, 1989): 19-22.

4. Barry Watts, *Nuclear-Conventional Firebreaks and the Nuclear Taboo* (Washington, DC: Center for Strategic and Budgetary Assessments, 2013).

5. Paul H. Nitze, "Deterring Our Deterrent," *Foreign Policy* 25 (Winter 1976-77), 195-210.

6. Robert Jervis, *The Illogic of American Nuclear Strategy* (Ithaca: Cornell University Press, 1984): 145-146; Kenneth N. Waltz, "Nuclear Myths and Political Realities," *American Political Science Review* Vol. 84, No. 3 (September 1990):731-745, 735.

7. Barry Blechman and Russell Rumbaugh, "Bombs Away: The Case for Phasing out U.S. Tactical Nukes in Europe," *Foreign Affairs* 93: 4 (July/August 2014): 163-174.

8. *Missile Defense Review 2019* (Washington, DC: U.S. Department of Defense, 2019): 36-37.

9. Alexey Arbatov, *Gambit or Endgame? The New State of Arms Control* (Washington, DC: Carnegie Endowment for International Peace, 2011); Lora Saalman, *China & The U.S. Nuclear Posture Review* (Washington, DC: Carnegie Endowment for International Peace, 2011).

10. Laura Grego, George N. Lewis, David Wright, Shielded from Oversight: The Disastrous US Approach to Strategic Missile Defense (Cambridge: Union of Concerned Scientists, 2016).

11. Jervis, *The Meaning of the Nuclear Revolution*, 29-38

12. Richard Ned Lebow and Janice Gross Stein, *We All Lost the Cold War* (Princeton: Princeton University Press, 1994).

13. Marc Ambinder, *The Brink: President Reagan and the Nuclear War Scare of 1983* (New York: Simon & Schuster, 2018); Fred Halliday, *The Making of the Second Cold War* (London: Verso: 1983).

14. Paul K. Huth, *Extended Deterrence and the Prevention of War* (New Haven: Yale University Press, 1988), Barry M. Blechman and Stephen S. Kaplan,

Force without War: U.S. Armed Forces as a Political Instrument (Washington, DC: Brookings Institution, 1978): 127-129.

15. Richard Ned Lebow and Janice Gross Stein, "Deterrence and the Cold War," *Political Science Quarterly* 110: 2 (Summer 1995), 157-181, 168-169.

16. Thomas M. Nichols, *No Use: Nuclear Weapons and U.S. National Security* (Philadelphia: University of Pennsylvania Press, 2014): 121.

17. *Nuclear Posture Review Report* (Washington, DC: U.S. Department of Defense, 2010).

18. Amy F. Woolf, Paul K. Kerr, and Mary Beth D. Nitkin, *Arms Control and Nonproliferation: A Catalog of Treaties and Agreements* (Washington, DC: Congressional Research Service, 2019).

19. 19. Amy F. Woolf, *The New START Treaty: Central Limits and Key Provisions* (Washington, DC: Congressional Research Service, 2019).

20. Steven Mufson, "Trump administration authorized nuclear energy companies to share technological information with Saudi Arabia," The Washington Post, February 21, 2019.

21. Keir A. Lieber and Daryl G. Press, "The End of MAD? The Nuclear Dimension of U.S. Primacy," *International Security* Vol. 30, no. 4 (Spring 2006): 7-44.

22. Colin S. Gray and Jeffrey C. Barlow, "Inexcusable Restraint: The Decline of American Military Power in the 1970s," *International Security* 10, no. 2 (Fall 1985): 27–69.

23. Colin S. Gray and Keith Payne, "Victory Is Possible," *Foreign Policy* 39 (1980): 14-27.

24. Paul Bracken, *The Second Nuclear Age: Strategy, Danger, and the New Power Politics* (New York: St. Martin's Press, 2012); Colin S. Gray, *The Second Nuclear Age* (Boulder, CO: Lynne Reinner Press, 1999); Keith B. Payne, *Deterrence in the Second Nuclear Age* (Lexington: University Press of Kentucky, 1996).

25. Colin S. Gray, Nuclear Strategy and National Style (Lanham, MD: Hamilton Press, 1986); Keith B. Payne, *Nuclear Deterrence in U.S.-Soviet Relations* (Boulder, CO: Westview Press, 1982).

26. Jervis, *The Meaning of the Nuclear Revolution;* Robert Jervis, *The Illogic of American Nuclear Strategy* (Ithaca, NY: Cornell University Press, 1984); Michael Mandelbaum, *The Nuclear Revolution: International Politics Before and After Hiroshima* (Cambridge: Cambridge University Press, 1980).

27. Leopoldo Nuti, Frederic Bozo, Marie-Pierre Rey, and Bernd Rother (eds.), *The Euromissile Crisis and the End of the Cold War* (Stanford, CA: Stanford University Press, 2017).

28. Tom Sauer, "A Second Nuclear Revolution: From Nuclear Primacy to Post-Existential Deterrence," *Journal of Strategic Studies*, Vol. 32, No. 5 (October 2009): 745-767.

29. Matthew Harries, "Britain and France as Nuclear Partners," *Survival* 54, no. 1 (February-March 2012): 7-30.

30. Avery Goldstein, *Deterrence and Security in the 21st Century: China, Britain, France, and the Enduring Legacy of the Nuclear Revolution* (Stanford: Stanford University Press, 2000): 181-216.

31. Barry R. Posen and Andrew L. Ross, "Competing Visions for U.S. Grand Strategy," *International Security* 21, no. 3 (Winter 1996/97): 5-53.

32. Kenneth Waltz, "The Spread of Nuclear Weapons: More May Be Better," Adephi Papers, No. 171 (September 1981); Scott D. Sagan and Kenneth N. Waltz, *The Spread of Nuclear Weapons: An Enduring Debate*, 3rd ed. (New York: W. W. Norton & Company, 2012).

33. Ulrich Kuhn and Tristan Volpe, "Keine Atombombe, Bitte: Why Germany Should Not Go Nuclear," *Foreign Affairs* 96, no. 4 (July/August 2017): 103–112.

34. Michael S. Gerson, "No First Use: The Next Step for U.S. Nuclear Policy," *International Security* 35, no. 2 (Fall 2010): 7-47.

35. Paul Sonne, "Energy Secretary Rick Perry Promises More Triggers for Nuclear Weapons," *The Washington Post*, March 22, 2018; Patrick Malone, "Safety Concerns Plague Key Sites Proposed for Nuclear Bomb Production," *USA Today*, May 2, 2018.

36. Kingston Reif, "This Debate Over A New Cruise Missile Had Gone Nuclear," *War On The Rocks*, April 5, 2016, https://warontherocks.com/2016/04/this-debate-over-a-new-cruise-missile-has-gone-nuclear/.

37. Mark Gunziger, *Sustaining America's Strategic Advantage in Long-Range Strike* (Washington, DC: Center for Strategic and Budgetary Assessments, 2010).

38. William J. Perry and Andy Weber, "Mr. President, kill the new cruise missile," The Washington Post, October 15, 2014.

39. Kyle Mizokami, "The Pentagon's New Strike Missile Just Saw Its First Combat," Popular Mechanics, April 17, 2018, https://www.popularmechanics.com/military/weapons/a19843076/syria-attack-jassmer-new-long-range-strike-missile/

INDEX

About The Author

David W. Kearn, Jr. is an Associate Professor in the Department of Government & Politics at St. John's University in Queens, New York. During the 2016–2017 academic year, he served as Strategic Advisor for Countering Weapons of Mass Destruction (CWMD) in the Office of the Secretary of Defense-Policy, with support from an International Affairs Fellowship (IAF) in Nuclear Security from the Council on Foreign Relations and the Frank Stanton Foundation. His research and teaching interests include international relations theory, U.S. foreign policy, military innovation, deterrence and nuclear strategy, and nonproliferation and arms control. His previous book *Great Power Security Cooperation: Arms Control and the Challenge of Technological Change* was published in 2014 by Lexington Books. His first book, *Facing the Missile Challenge: U.S. Strategy and the Future of the INF Treaty*, was published by the RAND Corporation in 2012 after he concluded a year-long Stanton Nuclear Security Fellowship in RAND's Washington, DC office. Dr. Kearn received his BA from Amherst College, a Master of Public Policy (MPP) from the John F. Kennedy School of Government at Harvard University, and a PhD in Foreign Affairs from the University of Virginia.

CAMBRIA RAPID COMMUNICATIONS IN CONFLICT AND SECURITY (RCCS) SERIES

General Editor: Geoffrey R. H. Burn

The aim of the RCCS series is to provide policy makers, practitioners, analysts, and academics with in-depth analysis of fast-moving topics that require urgent yet informed debate. Since its launch in October 2015, the RCCS series has the following book publications:

- *A New Strategy for Complex Warfare: Combined Effects in East Asia* by Thomas A. Drohan
- *US National Security: New Threats, Old Realities* by Paul Viotti
- *Security Forces in African States: Cases and Assessment* edited by Paul Shemella and Nicholas Tomb
- *Trust and Distrust in Sino-American Relations: Challenge and Opportunity* by Steve Chan
- *The Gathering Pacific Storm: Emerging US-China Strategic Competition in Defense Technological and Industrial Development* edited by Tai Ming Cheung and Thomas G. Mahnken
- *Military Strategy for the 21st Century: People, Connectivity, and Competitipauon* by Charles Cleveland, Benjamin Jensen, Susan Bryant, and Arnel David
- *Ensuring National Government Stability After US Counterinsurgency Operations: The Critical Measure of Success* by Dallas E. Shaw Jr.
- *Reassessing U.S. Nuclear Strategy* by David W. Kearn, Jr.
- *Deglobalization and International Security* by T. X. Hammes

For more information, visit www.cambriapress.com.